Henry G. Grey

Parliamentary Government Considered With Reference to Reform

Henry G. Grey

Parliamentary Government Considered With Reference to Reform

ISBN/EAN: 9783337297435

Printed in Europe, USA, Canada, Australia, Japan

Cover: Foto ©Suzi / pixelio.de

More available books at **www.hansebooks.com**

PARLIAMENTARY GOVERNMENT

CONSIDERED WITH REFERENCE TO

REFORM.

By EARL GREY.

A New Edition,

CONTAINING

SUGGESTIONS FOR THE IMPROVEMENT OF OUR
REPRESENTATIVE SYSTEM,

AND AN

EXAMINATION OF THE REFORM BILLS OF 1859 AND 1861.

LONDON:

JOHN MURRAY, ALBEMARLE STREET.

1864.

JOHN EDWARD TAYLOR, PRINTER,
LITTLE QUEEN STREET, LINCOLN'S INN FIELDS.

PREFACE.

In the first edition of my Essay on PARLIAMENTARY GOVERNMENT, I endeavoured to ascertain on what principles any new measure of Parliamentary Reform ought to be framed, and to what objects it ought to be directed; but I advisedly abstained from suggesting any means of carrying into effect the views I had stated. I venture now to offer to the Public a new edition of the Essay, for the purpose of supplying this intentional omission in the former one. I am induced to do so by my belief that the altered circumstances of the present time afford advantages which were previously wanting for discussing proposals for the improvement of our Representative system. The subject is no longer likely to give occasion for an immediate strife of political parties, since the House of Commons

JOHN EDWARD TAYLOR, PRINTER,
LITTLE QUEEN STREET, LINCOLN'S INN FIELDS.

PREFACE.

In the first edition of my Essay on PARLIAMENTARY GOVERNMENT, I endeavoured to ascertain on what principles any new measure of Parliamentary Reform ought to be framed, and to what objects it ought to be directed; but I advisedly abstained from suggesting any means of carrying into effect the views I had stated. I venture now to offer to the Public a new edition of the Essay, for the purpose of supplying this intentional omission in the former one. I am induced to do so by my belief that the altered circumstances of the present time afford advantages which were previously wanting for discussing proposals for the improvement of our Representative system. The subject is no longer likely to give occasion for an immediate strife of political parties, since the House of Commons

has equally rejected the Bills submitted to it
by the Administrations of Lord Derby and Lord
Palmerston; the first by a direct vote, the second by the less candid, but not less effectual,
process of delaying its progress by interminable
speeches, till it was withdrawn by its authors in
despair. In the debates on these Bills, the leading
Members of the House of Commons have stated
their views, not only on the measures before them,
but generally on the changes it would be proper
to make in our system of Representation. The
subject has also been discussed in many pamphlets,
reviews, and larger works, some of them written
with great ability and in a philosophic spirit, the
want of which, though perhaps unavoidable, is to be
remarked and regretted in the speeches of Parliamentary speakers. Much light has thus been thrown
on this difficult and important question, and many
of those who had given their assent to the expediency of attempting a Reform of the House of
Commons, have opened their eyes both to the tendency of such measures as have hitherto been proposed, to lead by steps more or less rapid to the
ascendancy of mere numbers in the government of
the country, and also to the danger of thus throwing a preponderance of political power into the
hands of the least educated classes of the commu-

nity. The wholesome dread of such an alteration in the character of our Constitution, has likewise been much increased by late events in America, and there is at present a manifest indisposition among a majority of the educated classes of all parties, to entertain projects of change having a Democratic tendency. Yet it would be a mistake to infer that this state of public opinion renders it unnecessary to consider the subject at all, or that it is either possible, or desirable, that the question of Parliamentary Reform should be indefinitely, or even very long, put aside. The defects in the constitution of the House of Commons are so real and so serious, that those who carefully consider them can hardly wish that all attempts to correct them should be finally abandoned; and if it were ever so much to be wished, it would be impossible that the present state of things should be permanently maintained unaltered.

Though I believe a large majority of the educated classes to be opposed to a Democratic Reform, we know that there is a numerous and active party bent upon carrying such a measure. In striving to attain their object this party possesses a great advantage, in the fact that the other considerable political parties in the Nation are irrevocably committed to the principle of Parliamen-

tary Reform; and though the current of opinion
is just now against Reform, we cannot expect that
it will always continue to be so. The prosperity
of the Nation, which has, on the whole, been so wonderfully maintained, notwithstanding the failure of
the supply of cotton, may be succeeded by general
distress, which would probably have its usual effect of producing political agitation. And even
without distress the cry for Reform may revive.
Even now we see that in elections for large towns
nearly every candidate finds it to be to his interest to declare himself ready to support at least an
extension of the Franchise, and the successful
candidates for the most part are those who have
pledged themselves to far more sweeping measures. No doubt these pledges are often given un-
willingly by men who would gladly, if they could,
defeat the measures they have promised to support. And sometimes the real opinion of the majority of the Constituents by whom they are exacted,
may not be favourable to such proposals, the imposition of these pledges on their Representatives
being the work of an active minority, skilled in the
manœuvres of elections.

But the state of parties, and the manner in
which elections are conducted, give an advantage
to those candidates who are most ready to meet

the demands of agitators; and whatever may be the opinions of Members of the House of Commons, their votes are almost always governed by the pledges they have been induced to give, in order to secure their return. Granting, therefore, that the desire for Reform in the great town Constituencies may be more apparent than real, it still produces its effect; and we must be blind to the signs of the times not to see that motions for carrying into effect the various schemes for increasing Democratic influence in the House of Commons will continue to be again and again brought forward, while it will become more and more difficult to oppose them with success, by a mere resistance to all change in the present constitution of Parliament. Hence we may expect that if this mode of opposition to the proposals of the Radical party should be adhered to, some of them will sooner or later be adopted. Probably it will be only some very slight change in a Democratic direction that will be carried in the first instance; but what we have to fear is, that when a first step has thus been made, a series of measures will be passed, which in the end, by their collective effect, will completely alter the character of our Constitution.

This is the more to be apprehended in consequence of the course taken in the House of Commons by the Ministers of the Crown. While they have refused to bring in any measures of Reform on their own responsibility, they have supported with the whole influence of the Government bills introduced by private Members of Parliament for extending the Franchise both in Counties and in Boroughs. The Chancellor of the Exchequer (without calling forth any public expression of dissent from his colleagues) has also rested his vote in favour of the second reading of the Borough Franchise Bill, on arguments which must make it difficult for him to find tenable grounds for resisting the widest extension of the right of voting ever asked for by the most extreme politicians. The present Parliament is likewise so rapidly approaching the legal term of its existence, that even if it should not be dissolved sooner than the law requires, a general election cannot be distant, and it is already certain that it will produce a greater change in the House of Commons than is usual on such occasions, from so many of its present members having signified their determination not to offer themselves for re-election. Among those who will retire are some of the most experienced and useful members of the present House, whose places, it is to be feared, will be but imperfectly supplied

by their successors, while there is reason to anticipate that in the new Parliament there will be an
increased proportion of members pledged to support what are called measures of Reform.

In these circumstances, the danger that changes
inconsistent with the principles of our present constitution may ultimately be carried, must be regarded
as very serious; nor do I see how it can be long
guarded against, except by effecting a reform which,
without being Democratic in its tendency, might
yet remove those defects in our Representative
System of which there is now just ground to complain.   I do not believe it to be at all impossible
that a Reform Bill answering this description should
be framed, but I am sure that one of such a character could not as yet be proposed with advantage
or with the slightest hope of success, because it is
clear that public opinion is not yet prepared for it.
For these reasons I think that the opportunity for
calm discussion afforded by the present political
lull, and the absence of serious agitation in favour
of Parliamentary Reform, ought not to be neglected; and this most difficult and important question
ought now to undergo such a thorough and searching examination, that when it shall become necessary to attempt its practical solution (as I am convinced it will at no very distant time), there may be

a better prospect of arriving at a satisfactory result
than there would be in the present state of opinion.
In the hope that I may contribute something, however little it may be, towards thus preparing the
way for the passing of a safe and useful measure of
Reform, I am desirous of laying before the Public
the conclusions to which I have been led as to the
nature of the changes it would be desirable to make
in the constitution of the House of Commons.
With this view I have added two Chapters to the
following Essay. In the one I have examined the
two schemes of Reform submitted to Parliament in
the years 1859 and 1860, and I have endeavoured to
show that neither of them would have been likely
to improve the character of the popular branch of
our Legislature, or to promote the good government of the country. In the other I have given
a general description of a measure which would,
in my opinion, be better calculated to effect these
objects. I have preferred stating my views as to
the kind of reform which is wanted in this shape,
rather than in a separate pamphlet, because I must
necessarily refer continually to arguments contained
in my Essay in explaining the suggestions I have to
offer, which are in fact merely an attempt to work
out in practice those principles which I had previously endeavoured to establish ; it is therefore

convenient that they should appear in the same volume with the explanation of the principles on which they rest.

The two Chapters I refer to are the sixth and seventh, and are substituted for the one entitled "Considerations as to a New Reform Bill," which was the sixth in the former edition of this Essay. They form the only part of the present edition, which is altogether new; but I have made considerable alterations in the other Chapters, which I have carefully revised, and I hope improved.

Howick, September, 1864.

CONTENTS.

————◆————

CHAPTER I.

ORIGIN AND RESULTS OF PARLIAMENTARY GOVERNMENT.

CHAPTER II.

ADVANTAGES OF PARLIAMENTARY GOVERNMENT.

CHAPTER III.

EVILS AND DANGERS OF PARLIAMENTARY GOVERNMENT.

Tendency of Parliamentary Government to encourage corruption.—Comparison with other free Governments.—Bribery of Members of Parliament. — Formerly common. — Gradually discontinued.—Systematic corruption not thereby got rid of.—Diminished by Reform of Parliament.—But favour still an instrument of Government.—How brought to bear on the House of Commons.—All Ad-

CHAPTER IV.

REASONS OF THE SUCCESS OF PARLIAMENTARY GOVERNMENT.

b

CHAPTER V.

EFFECTS OF PARLIAMENTARY REFORM.

CHAPTER VI.

THE REFORM BILLS OF 1859 AND 1860.

Proper object of Parliamentary Reform improved Government.—Experience to be taken as a guide.—A Reform Bill ought to afford the prospect of a durable settlement of the question.—Danger of frequent Constitutional changes.—Neither of the Bills of 1859 and 1860 fulfilled the conditions required for a good measure.—They were of the same character.—Principle adopted by both as to Franchise.—How applied in each.—Scheme as to Franchise most logical in first Bill.—Reasons in favour of it.—Objections to it.—Franchise proposed in 1860 more simple.—Less consistent.—Difference as to Householders in Counties and Boroughs.—Proposed extension of Borough Franchise not satisfactorily explained.—How it would have worked.—Provisions in both Bills as to re-distribution of seats.—No other important provision in either.—Faulty character of both measures.—Would not have tended to improve the House of Commons.—Calculated to become stepping-stones to further changes.—Involved recognition of the principles of the Radical Party.—Importance of this with regard to the re-distribution of Seats.—More alarm would have been created but for the predictions of evil in 1832.—But the policy of the recent measures the reverse of that of 1832.—Design of the Reform of 1832.—Opposite views adopted in 1859 and 1860.—Alleged moderation of these Bills a source of danger.—Complete Democracy generally established by degrees.—Danger of entering on course leading to it escaped for the present.—But likely to recur.—Effects of giving supreme power to the numerical majority.—Political power not an advantage to the People in itself, but to secure good government.—What constitutes good government.—Not secured by Democracy.—Opinion of ancient Political Philosophers.—Likeness of Democratic Governments in ancient and modern times.—Lesson afforded by United States.—Their Government before the Civil War.—Excluded the best men from Political power.—Character and conduct of Congress and State Legislatures.—The Executive Government.—Its arrogance towards other nations.—Its corruption.—Modes of corruption.——

CHAPTER VII.

SUGGESTIONS FOR A REFORM BILL.

CHAPTER VIII.

ON THE EXERCISE OF PATRONAGE UNDER PARLIA-
MENTARY GOVERNMENT.

CHAPTER IX.

PARLIAMENTARY GOVERNMENT IN THE BRITISH COLONIES.

PARLIAMENTARY GOVERNMENT

AND

REFORM OF PARLIAMENT.

CHAPTER I.

ORIGIN AND RESULTS OF PARLIAMENTARY GOVERNMENT.

OFTEN as the British Constitution has been described and discussed, it affords a subject for inquiry that is still far from being exhausted. The changes it has undergone, and the manner in which its working at the present day has been affected by these changes, do not appear to have been yet examined as closely as they deserve. And while it must always be interesting to study the Government under which we live, it is especially so at a time when alterations of extreme importance in its existing arrangements have lately been attempted,

B

and the renewal of that attempt is strongly urged by a party of no inconsiderable strength.

In speaking of that Government, Burke has admirably said, that " the machine of a free Constitution is no simple thing, but as intricate and as delicate as it is valuable." Concurring in this opinion, I believe that the whole construction of the machine requires to be very carefully examined before we can safely attempt to improve it, even in what may appear at first sight to be minor details; because parts of a machine which may seem to an ignorant or a careless observer very unimportant, may in reality be essential to its safe working. For this reason, I conceive that, as a first step towards arriving at a sound judgment with regard to the nature and extent of the reforms now required in our Constitution, it can hardly fail to be of use to inquire in what respects Parliamentary Government, as it now exists in this country, differs from other forms of Representative Government; what are its chief merits and faults ; whether any of the causes of its success among us can be traced ; how its working has been affected by the great constitutional change accomplished in 1832; what are the principal defects which experience has brought to light in our representative system, as it has been modified by the celebrated Acts passed in that year, "for the amendment of the Representation of the People in Parliament;" and what ought to be the character of the changes in the law by which the correction of these defects should be attempted.

Such are the questions which I propose to consider in the following pages; and although I am very sensible how little I can do justice to so difficult a subject, I would fain hope that my remarks may be found not altogether destitute of value, since they are the fruit of the observation of nearly forty years, during which time I have enjoyed no small opportunities of closely watching the working of our government. In discussing the questions I have undertaken to examine, I shall abstain from adverting further than may be necessary for the elucidation of my immediate subject, to the fundamental principles of our Constitution, and to the division of power between the different authorities of the State on which it is founded. These have been described and commented upon by writers of such eminence, that it would be worse than useless for me to go again over ground which they have fully occupied. Nor, in fact, have I any temptation to do so. The writers I allude to have considered the British Constitution with reference rather to the legal distribution of power among the several au-

thorities of the State, and to the manner in which
the power assigned to each was formerly exercised,
than to the practice of the present day; whereas
my object is to inquire into the nature and the
operation of the system of Parliamentary Government now established in this country.

In prosecuting this inquiry, I have in the first
place to remark, that, since the establishment of
Parliamentary Government, the common description of the British Constitution,* as one in which
the executive power belongs exclusively to the
Crown, while the power of legislation is vested
jointly in the Sovereign and the two Houses of
Parliament, has ceased to be correct, unless it is
understood as applying only to the legal and technical distribution of power. It is the distinguishing
characteristic of Parliamentary Government, that it
requires the powers belonging to the Crown to be
exercised through Ministers, who are held responsible for the manner in which they are used, who
are expected to be members of the two Houses of
Parliament, the proceedings of which they must
be able generally to guide, and who are considered
entitled to hold their offices only while they possess the confidence of Parliament, and more especially of the House of Commons.

* See Blackstone's 'Commentaries,' book i. ch. 2.

By this arrangement the Executive power and the power of Legislation are virtually united in the same hands, but both are limited,—the executive power by the law, and that of legislation by the necessity of obtaining the assent of Parliament to the measures brought forward, so that even the strongest administrations do not venture to propose the passing of laws to which public opinion is decidedly opposed. The exercise of this high authority is also placed under the check of a strict responsibility and control, and its possession is made to depend on the confidence placed by the Representatives of the People in the Ministers to whom it is committed. There is a further safeguard against abuse, in its being requisite that the Ministers of the Crown should obtain its direct sanction for all their most important measures. The Crown, it is true, seldom refuses to act upon the advice deliberately pressed upon it by its servants, nor could it do so frequently without creating great inconvenience. But the Sovereigns of this country nevertheless may, and generally have exercised much influence over the conduct of the Government; and in extreme cases the power of the Crown to refuse its consent to what is proposed by its servants, may be used with the greatest benefit to the Nation. A refusal on the part of the Sovereign to sanction measures which the Ministers persist in recommending as indispensable, is indeed a legitimate ground for their resignation: and if the question which leads to this is one on which they have the support of public opinion, they must in the end prevail.   But if this high power is exercised with wisdom, and is reserved for great emergencies, the Crown may generally calculate on the support of the Nation in refusing to sanction measures improperly pressed upon it by its Ministers, especially where the measures so urged involve an abuse of the royal authority for their own party objects.

Such a government as I have now described, has obviously but little resemblance to that under which our ancestors lived in the reigns of the Plantagenets, the Tudors, and even of the Stuarts.   The Sovereigns of these Houses took a far larger personal share in the government of the country than those of modern times.   Their Ministers, instead of being counsellors whose advice can seldom be rejected, and who cannot really be dismissed at pleasure, were, in the strictest sense of the words, the servants of the Crown, and the instruments for giving effect to its commands.   Parliament was then, as now, the guardian of the interests of the Nation ; but its mode of action was quite different from what it has since become.   It was seldom slow to interfere by remonstrance, by insisting on the removal and punishment of favourites and bad advisers, and even on great emergencies by the deposition of the King, when the abuse of the royal authority excited strong discontent in the Nation; but, except on such occasions, it meddled little with the conduct of the Executive Government. Its power, resting on its control over the public purse, was greatest when the demands for money were the most pressing; that is, practically, when there was most need for the exercise of its authority. When public affairs were ill-administered under weak and foolish princes, want of money almost invariably ensued, which compelled them to submit to the advice of their Parliaments. On the other hand, the ablest Sovereigns of those times exercised a larger measure of independent authority, by so managing their finances as generally to avoid the necessity of asking for extraordinary pecuniary aid, except when engaged in war, for which Englishmen have in all times been but too ready to give their money and their blood.

This comparatively simple form of government, which was well suited to the state of society and the circumstances of the country at the time, was very unlike (as I have already observed) our own far more complex system of Parliamentary Government. But, wide as is the difference between these two systems of Government, the one has grown naturally out of the other, by the gradual development of principles, which are to be recognized in the working of our Constitution almost from its earliest days. The change has been brought about partly by legislation, but far more by slow and silent alterations of practice and of usage, introduced to meet the new wants of an advancing society, and the new difficulties which from time to time arose in managing the more and more complicated affairs of a country continually increasing in wealth and population.

I will not attempt to trace the successive steps by which our present system of Parliamentary Government has been thus gradually created; it is sufficient for me to observe, that it may be considered to have begun, though at first in a very imperfect form, in the reign of William III.,* that it acquired more consistency and regularity in that of Anne, but can hardly be said to have been completely established until after the accession of the House of Hanover. So late as the beginning of the reign of George I., Lord Oxford pleaded the commands of the Sovereign as a justification of the acts of the Ministers, in the debate in the House of Lords on

* See Macaulay's ' History of England,' vol. iv. pp. 434–436.

his impeachment; on which Mr. Hallam remarks, that " the first instance where I can find the responsibility of some one for every act of the Crown strongly laid down, is in a speech of the Duke of Argyll, in 1739."* It is hardly necessary to observe that this rule is now regarded as one of the fundamental principles of our Constitution.†

* Hallam's 'Constitutional History of England,' vol. iii. p. 315.

† Arguments have sometimes been used, even of late years, which imply that the administration of the army ought to be an exception to this rule. It has been said more than once, and by very high authorities, that the administration of the army belongs solely to the Crown, and that any interference with it by the House of Commons ought to be carefully guarded against as unconstitutional. Any direct interference on the part of either House of Parliament with the management of the army, would undoubtedly be a violation of the principles of our Constitution; but the same observation applies to every branch of the executive authority. The Long Parliament, by its committees, assumed various executive functions; but its doing so is admitted to have been a usurpation, and since that time the rule has been recognized both in theory and in practice, that all such functions belong only to the Crown. This rule is quite consistent with another not less important, namely, that either House of Parliament is entitled to offer its advice to the Crown on the manner in which any of its powers are exercised, and that there can be nothing done by the royal authority for which some servant of the Crown must not be responsible to Parliament. There is no distinction in this respect between the exercise of the Royal authority over the army and over all other branches of the public service, and it certainly would not be for the true interests of the Sovereign that any such distinction should be drawn. If some servant of the Crown is not to be held responsible for every act done in the management of the army, that responsibility must of necessity fall on the Sovereign personally. But nothing could be more dangerous for the Sovereign

Even up to our own time, Parliamentary Government has continued to undergo important modifications, and to have its rules and practice more clearly defined and more firmly settled. From the first, these modifications have generally been effected through the establishment of some new practice for the sake of convenience, or the decision of undetermined constitutional questions by controversies which, arising accidentally from the events of the day, have produced permanent and sometimes very important results. Thus the highly beneficial custom of holding Cabinet Councils without the presence of the Sovereign arose from George the First's not knowing English; and the contest, which in the reign of George the Third ended in establishing the practice of publishing the debates of the two Houses of Parliament, made a change of transcen-

than to be subjected to such personal responsibility, by which the odium of having caused some great military disaster might be thrown upon the Crown instead of on its Ministers. Nor would the inconvenience be much less, if it were maintained that the Commander-in chief were to be singly responsible for all acts of military administration. The holder of that office would stand in a most unsafe position, if he could not depend upon the support of the Ministers of the Crown in case of his measures being questioned in Parliament; and they cannot be expected to give this support, unless the officer who trusts to it communicates with them in the performance of his duties, in such a manner as to enable them to guard against his taking, or omitting to take, any step for which they were not prepared to defend him.

dent importance in the working of the Constitution, without the passing of any new law.

Parliamentary Government having thus been more or less completely in operation among us for about a century and a half, we must judge of its merits by the state and progress of the Nation during that period, since the only real test of the advantages and disadvantages of different forms of government is that afforded by their results. Applying this test to our system of Parliamentary Government, and making due allowance for the imperfection of all human institutions, it must, I think, be admitted, that our judgment of it ought, on the whole, to be favourable. Our national annals since the Revolution of 1688 present, it is true, a sad picture of the selfishness, baseness, and corruption of the great majority of the actors on the political stage, and record too many lamentable follies and excesses into which the Nation has allowed itself to be misled by passion and prejudice. But this seems to be rather the fault of human nature than of our institutions; at least I am not aware that there is any country of which the history would not justify remarks equally severe on the conduct of its statesmen and of its people; while, on the other hand, we may safely assert that Great Britain stands distinguished among the nations of the earth* for the prosperity it has enjoyed, and for the social progress it has made during the time it has been under a Parliamentary Government.† Internal tranquillity has scarcely been interrupted during that whole period, except by the two brief rebellions of 1715 and 1745; and the security of persons and property has been almost uniformly maintained, together with a more than usual exemption from injurious restraints on the freedom of individual thought and action. The unfettered discussion on subjects of public interest, which has been encouraged both in and out of Parliament, has gradually dispelled many mischievous errors that

* I must acknowledge, with deep regret and shame for my country, that this would not be true if it were said of the whole United Kingdom, including Ireland; but Ireland has not been placed under the same government as Great Britain for much more than half a century, and it is not yet forty years since the Union of the two countries has been rendered complete by the repeal of the last of the penal laws against the Roman Catholics.

† M. de Rémusat, in his ' L'Angleterre au XVIIIme Siècle,' has well described the results of Parliamentary Government in this country during that century in the following passage :—" Qu'on recrie donc sur le mal, on le peut ; qu'on signale avec indignation les violences et les mensonges de l'esprit de parti, la vénalité effrontée, les excès de l'orgueil, de l'avidité et de la haine ; que l'on remarque même dans le passé de la société Anglaise une certaine rudesse d'égoïsme de l'ancienne Rome, il n'en reste pas moins vrai que nulle nation n'a été à la fois plus libre, plus heureuse et plus puissante, et que dans les temps modernes les vertus politiques n'ont brillé longtemps que chez elle. La race Anglo-Normande est restée digne de sa liberté." (Vol. i. p. 103.)

were formerly current, and the conclusions as to the true principles of legislation and government thus established in the minds of enlightened men, have gained more and more ascendancy in the practical conduct of affairs. In spite of occasional checks and delays, improvement has in this manner continued on the whole to go forward in our laws, and in our whole system of administration, which have become gradually better and more free from abuse. Fostered by these advantages, industry and commerce have flourished almost beyond example, and, in spite of the heavy drain on our national resources, occasioned by the wars in which we have been engaged, the population, wealth, and power of the country have been wonderfully increased. The material prosperity to which the Nation has risen while it has been under a Parliamentary Government is too well known to require to be further insisted upon ; but I must remark that this period is still more distinguished as one of great intellectual activity and moral improvement. The former has been evinced by the successful cultivation of literature and of science, and the application of science to all the useful arts. Abundant evidence of the moral improvement which has been going on may be found in the remarkable change for the better which has taken place in the habits of all classes of the people since the Revolution of 1688. Notwithstanding the vices and the political abuses and corruption which have undoubtedly prevailed, the standard of right and wrong to which opinion requires men to conform, both in public and private life, has been gradually raised, though it is still unfortunately much lower than it ought to be. This last point is one of paramount importance, and I think our form of government compares advantageously as regards its effect on the national character with the governments of other countries, whether we look to those which give a less amount of liberty to the people, or to those of a much more democratic character than our own, like that of the great kindred Republic of the United States of America.

I am far indeed from attributing all that is satisfactory in our condition to our form of government; but at all events the government to which this country has been subject has permitted its condition to become what we now see it. And perhaps little more can be expected from any government, than that it should allow a fair field for the exertions of individuals in working out the physical and moral welfare of the people, and that it should favour the growth of those habits and dispositions of mind which most contribute to that welfare. Parliamentary Government therefore, if judged by its fruits, may fairly be regarded as having proved successful in this country.

.But it is a remarkable circumstance that no other example can be found of a government of this kind having been able to maintain itself for any considerable time. There was no approach to this system of government among the various representative constitutions which prevailed in Europe during the Middle Ages, nor has the constitution of the United States at this day any resemblance to it. After the fall of Napoleon, a government modelled on our own was established in France; but two revolutions in little more than thirty years have shown that, hitherto at least, the scheme has failed. In some of the other States of Europe, and especially in the kingdoms of Belgium and Italy, governments of this kind have been adopted, but have been too short a time in operation to enable us as yet to assert with confidence that the experiment* has succeeded. The same remark applies to those British Colonies in which governments of a similar

---

* In Belgium, where Parliamentary Government has existed for above thirty years with great success, it has not yet stood the trial of a change of Sovereign, and it is difficult to decide how much of its success hitherto may have been due to the personal character of King Leopold, and to the skill and judgment with which he has played the part of a constitutional monarch.

kind have been introduced ; the definitive establishment of this system of government does not in any
of them date back so much as twenty years. Hence,
although the prospect of its succeeding is at least
in some cases encouraging, (in others I fear it is
the reverse,) it cannot yet be said to have stood
the test of experience.

Having thus taken a general view of the nature
and effects of Parliamentary Government in this
country, the succeeding Chapters of this Essay will
be devoted to a more particular examination of the
questions which it is my object to consider.

CHAPTER II.

ADVANTAGES OF PARLIAMENTARY GOVERNMENT.

ON comparing Parliamentary Government as it now exists in this country with other Representative Governments, the following seem to be the chief advantages belonging to the former.

First.—It enables the different powers of the State to work together with harmony and energy, and provides for the systematic direction of the measures of the Legislature to objects of public good, more perfectly than Representative Constitutions of a different kind. In the latter, the executive power and the power of legislation are lodged in separate and independent authorities, while under the system of Parliamentary Government they are virtually united, as I have already observed, since those to whom the executive authority is en-

c

trusted, have also the duty of recommending to the Legislature the measures it should adopt, and must retire if their advice is not generally followed.

To understand the full importance of this we must consider how difficult it has been found when there has been no bond of union between the Executive Government and a Representative Assembly, armed with the powers usually assigned to such a body, to prevent a conflict between them ; and also that the welfare of the state requires, not only that a struggle between these authorities should be guarded against, but also that their harmonious co-operation should be secured. In France, the many different Constitutions which have been established since 1789, on the principle of keeping the Legislative and Executive authorities as distinct and independent of each other as possible, have all had the same result, of leading to a struggle between the two, and at last to the violent overthrow of the arrangement that had been made.

In our own country, from the accession of the Stuarts (when the great power of the House of Commons may be said to have begun) till after the Revolution of 1688, the Crown and the House of Commons were in almost continual conflict; nor was their good understanding with each other secured till a bond of union between them was created by the

arrangement I have adverted to. Nor is this to
be wondered at, looking to the fact that in the
government of a great nation which has reached
an advanced stage of civilization, the Executive
and Legislative authorities have continual need of
each other. It is useless for the Legislature to
pass good laws if they are not properly enforced
by the Executive Government. On the other hand,
the Executive Government cannot perform its functions with vigour and effect if denied the active
support of the Legislature, to which it is continually compelled to apply for new powers, or new
laws to meet new exigencies that arise, and its action must be crippled if it cannot rely upon obtaining the assistance of this kind which it requires.

The harmonious co-operation of these different
powers in the State is especially necessary with respect to financial arrangements. The imposition
of taxes, and the appropriation of the revenue to
the public service, constitute one of the chief
duties of Representative Legislatures, as well as
the source of their power. In the performance
of this part of their duties, it is of the utmost importance that they should act in strict concert with
the Executive Government, or rather under its
direction. Without this there can be no security
for efficiency and economy in conducting the public

service. The Government cannot be responsible for the former, if it cannot command the grants of money it considers necessary for the different branches of the service ; while experience has demonstrated, that jobs and injudicious expenditure in some cases, are no less to be expected than equally injudicious parsimony in others, from entrusting the finances of a State to the uncontrolled management of a popular assembly. Under such a system there is no individual responsibility for errors and abuses that may be committed ; and the responsibility which is divided among all the members of a numerous body, is far too slight a restraint upon them to prevent these evils.

They have accordingly prevailed to a very great extent, both in the United States and in some of our own Colonies. Private and corrupt interests have had too much weight in deciding questions relating to the grant of money in their Legislatures, which have also not unfrequently been led into acts of real improvidence, by the reluctance of any individual member to incur the odium of proposing or supporting an unpopular outlay of money, or an increase of taxation, however urgently the one or the other might be called for by the true interests of the country. It is the nature of popular assemblies in a still higher degree than of men acting individually, to shrink from looking unpleasant truths in the face, and to listen with the greatest favour to those who tell them what they wish to believe, and who recommend the measures which will impose upon them the smallest immediate sacrifices. The effects of this disposition are not got rid of even by throwing on the Executive Government the duty of guiding the deliberations of the Legislature; for unhappily Ministers are too often tempted to propose rather what is agreeable at the moment, than what their judgment tells them would be best for the permanent interests of the Nation. Still, it may safely be asserted, that the responsibility which rests upon Ministers in this country for the financial measures which they propose to Parliament, or to which they assent, is a powerful, though by no means a perfect check upon the tendency to those errors in financial administration to which popular assemblies are most prone.

The same principle applies (though not with the same force) to legislation upon other subjects as well as upon finance. In order that such laws may be passed as are required for the welfare of the Nation, and for its social advancement, it is right that the Ministers should be held responsible both for preparing and carrying these measures, and also for opposing such as may be unwisely urged by others. This is a duty which has been imposed upon the advisers of the Crown only by degrees, and chiefly since the passing of the Reform Acts of 1832. Formerly Ministers took little charge of the proceedings of Parliament on matters not immediately connected with their executive duties. This led to much unwise legislation, and to the habitual neglect of all systematic endeavour to effect improvements in our laws as occasion for them arose. A different system has of late years grown up, and the Ministers of the Crown are now justly regarded as responsible for bringing forward such measures as are required, and for opposing any objectionable proposals from other quarters.

Secondly.—Closely connected with the advantage I have just described as belonging to Parliamentary Government, is that which it derives from the manner in which it brings the policy of the Executive Government under the review and control of the Legislature. Parliament does not interfere directly in carrying on the Executive Government; the supreme executive authority belongs to the Crown, nor do the measures adopted by its Ministers in the exercise of this authority require the previous sanction of Parliament. But all these measures are open to censure in either House, so that when there is just, or even plausible, ground for objecting to anything the Ministers have done, or omitted to do, they cannot escape being called upon to defend their conduct. By this arrangement the vigorous action of the Government is not impeded as it would be if Parliament were called upon to concur more directly in the conduct of affairs, and at the same time the large power thus entrusted to the servants of the Crown is guarded from being abused, both by their being made to feel that they must use this power in such a manner as to be prepared to meet the criticisms of opponents continually on the watch for any errors they may commit, and also by their being only allowed to retain their authority so long as they possess the confidence of Parliament. The Ministers of the Crown are bound to retire when that confidence is withdrawn from them, and to make way for others to whom it may be granted, so that the affairs of the country may always be conducted by men who, both in their internal administration and in their communications with foreign Powers, are able to act and speak with the authority which can only belong to the Executive Government while it is supported by the Legislature. A far more useful control over the policy of the Government is thus maintained by Parliament than it could exercise by attempting to take part directly in executive measures,—a function for which experience proves the unfitness of large deliberative assemblies.

These advantages are not equally secured by other forms of representative government. In the United States, for instance, the two Houses of Congress, and especially the Senate, have great power to thwart the measures of the President and of his Cabinet; but if they disagree with him as to the line of policy which ought to be pursued, they have no authority to enforce the adoption of that which they consider to be right, or to require him to change his Ministers; and the Constitution provides no means by which due concert between the executive and legislative authorities, in conducting either the domestic or the foreign policy of the Nation, can be restored, if it should be interrupted, during the term for which the President is elected.

Thirdly.—It is another great advantage which may, I think, justly be attributed to Parliamentary Government, that it renders the contests of men for power as little injurious as possible, and furnishes what seems on the whole the best solution hitherto discovered of the great problem, how to provide some safe mode of determining to what hands the principal direction of public affairs shall be entrusted. Ambition is so strong a passion of human nature, that in every age of the world, in every state of society, and under every different form of government, men have continually carried on, in some way or other, contests for political power. In the old despotisms of the East, the earliest Governments of which we have any historical record, open violence, murder, and treason seem to have played the principal part in these contests. We read of one despot thus wresting the sceptre from another ; or of ambitious Ministers snatching, by the destruction of their rivals, the power exercised in the name of their nominal masters. Among the semi-civilized nations and tribes of Asia, the same means are to this day employed for the same object, and bloody changes of rulers are of constant occurrence.

In other states of society, free Governments have not been exempt from evils of the same kind with those to which these despotisms have been liable, but have often been distracted, and sometimes ultimately overthrown, by sanguinary tumults and civil wars arising from contests for power among ambitious men. Society must be considered to have made a great step in advance, when violence and bloodshed can be excluded from these contests, but much evil may remain even when this has been accomplished. When force ceases to be employed, the struggle for power in despotic Governments usually assumes the form of a strife for the favour of the Sovereign. If he is a great and wise ruler, this favour is won by the ability and honesty of the servants he selects; but history teaches us, that even the best despots are apt to be deceived in this all-important matter, and that the favour of kings is not in general obtained by those qualities which render men most fit to be trusted with power. Too often, as in France before the Revolution, the surest road to power has been found in flattery, or in base compliances to mistresses and favourites. In a pure democracy, when the People at large directly choose their rulers, flattery and unworthy compliances seem equally to be the means resorted to for obtaining power, the arts used being much of the same character as under a despotism, with the single difference, that it is the People themselves whose passions and prejudices are encouraged and flattered, instead of the despot or his favourites. It is by no means clear that this difference renders the use of such arts less dangerous or less demoralizing to the Nation. The Presidential elections seem, from the accounts given to us by the best observers, to exercise a most pernicious influence on the national character in the United States; and the tone of the newspapers, and of the speeches made in favour of different parties, in these exciting contests, leads to the same conclusion.

In Parliamentary Government, as it now exists among us, the contest for power is still substantially a contest for the favour of the People. Public opinion determines, in the last resort, to what hands authority shall be entrusted; for though the Ministers are the servants of the Crown, and are appointed by the Sovereign, yet as the Sovereign must choose Ministers who can command the confidence of Parliament, it is practically the People who decide, through their Representatives, by whom the powers of Government shall be wielded. There is, however, a vast difference in the effect produced by giving to the People, instead of the power of nominating their rulers by direct election, only an indirect control, through their Representatives, over the selection of the Ministers by whose advice the powers of the Crown are exercised.

Parliament, and especially the House of Commons, is become, not only the authority which virtually decides the contest for power among the different candidates for it, but also the arena in which the contest is mainly carried on. Its debates are the means by which rival parties chiefly seek to recommend themselves both to the House itself and to the Public; and, though it is easy to perceive the imperfection of this method of determining by whom the affairs of the Nation are to be administered, and the very serious evils to which it gives rise, it may well be doubted whether any better method of deciding this great question has yet been discovered, and found to succeed in practice.

Experience has proved that the system of Parliamentary Government provides a safe mode of effecting changes, from time to time, in the persons to whom power is committed. It is impossible, while ambition continues to be one of the strongest passions of human nature, that such changes should not take place ; nor is ambition their only cause. Men seem to get tired of being very long subject to the same ruler, so that when the reigns of even the best and most popular Sovereigns who have kept power in their own hands, have been unusually protracted, the accession of unknown and perhaps very inferior successors has commonly been hailed with satisfaction by their subjects ; as when James the First was raised to the throne of England by the death of Queen Elizabeth. This feeling by no means arises from the mere capriciousness of human nature. The long possession of power has a tendency to unfit men for making the best use of it, and there can be no doubt of the great advantage which a nation derives from having the management of its affairs occasionally transferred to the hands of men who bring to the task fresh minds, and the knowledge and judgment acquired in private life. A change of rulers is also the only effectual means by which a Nation can obtain a change in the system of government, when this is called for by the state of its affairs or of public opinion. Thus the Emperor Paul* was murdered, in order to effect a change in the policy of Russia, which was considered necessary by its leading men. In this country a change of Ministers affords the means of accomplishing a transfer of power to new hands, without violence or disturbance of the public peace. The fall of Sir Robert Walpole, it has been said, probably averted a revolution,† since the intense desire of the Nation at that time for a transfer of power from the hands by which it had been so long held (and, it may be added, on the whole so wisely used) could hardly have failed to produce a change of dynasty if it had not been appeased by the overthrow of the Minister.

The practice of providing for occasional changes

* " Les institutions ont encore plus tort que les hommes. . . . A Pétersbourg on égorgeait un empereur pour amener un changement de politique ; à Londres, au contraire, sans catastrophe sanglante, la politique de la paix y succédait à la politique de la guerre, par la substitution de M. Addington à M. Pitt."—*Thiers, Histoire du Consulat et de l'Empire*, vol. ii. p. 437.

† See Lord J. Russell's 'Essay on the English Government,' p. 189.

in the persons to whom the administration of public affairs is entrusted, by changes of Ministry occurring at uncertain intervals, as the necessity for them arises, has also marked advantages over another system of government which, to a certain degree, meets the same object, by placing the supreme authority in the hands of a single individual, or of a council or more numerous body, elected for a fixed period. Under this last system, those who are chosen to exercise power can have it entrusted to them for only a very limited time, unless the risk is incurred of its being sometimes left in the hands of men whose policy has ceased to be in harmony with the feelings and opinions of the Nation. Though the President of the United States is elected for only four years, it is well known to have happened more than once, that those who have been called to that post by the votes of their countrymen, have lost the confidence of the public before the end of their term of office.

And if supreme power in the State is given to one or more persons for a fixed and short time, much inconvenience must arise from the frequent recurrence of the agitation and excitement produced in a Nation when it is called upon to choose its rulers, and also from the weakness and want of proper authority which those who hold power only for a limited term must necessarily experience when the expiration of that term approaches. Both these evils are strongly felt in the United States. All observers agree as to the mischievous consequences which arise from the almost unceasing excitement occasioned by the Presidential Elections, and by the preparations which, soon after one such contest is over, begin to be made for another. Scarcely less inconvenience arises from the want of proper authority in the President, which gradually becomes apparent as the time for his leaving power draws near.* A dying king is generally ill obeyed because men are looking to his heir, and in like manner the commands of the elected chief of a State can carry little weight, as soon as it becomes probable that he will not hold office long enough to punish disobedience or to reward zealous service; while it is by no means impossible that his subordinates may sometimes think, that to thwart his measures may be the surest mode of recommending themselves to his successor. The holders of a power which is about to expire must experience still greater difficulties in managing the relations of a State with foreign countries. But though the legitimate authority of the President becomes thus feeble

* See 'Démocratie en Amérique,' vol. ii. p. 154 (13th Edition).

towards the close of his term of office, this does
not prevent his being enabled during this period
to abuse the power still left in his hands. We
have been told, and I believe truly, that as soon as
it was ascertained that Mr. Buchanan would be
succeeded in the Presidency by Mr. Lincoln, and
that the party in power must in a few months
make it over to their bitter opponents, the President and his Ministers who were to go out, took
advantage of their last months of power to prepare
the way for the violent disruption of the Union by
sending as many arms and military stores as they
could to the South, and by making such a disposition of the naval and military forces of the Republic, as to render them as little available as possible to their successors.

Our system of Parliamentary Government, though
it must be admitted that it mitigates only, and does
not obviate, the evils arising from contests for
power, is at all events free from these inconveniences. The Nation is not kept in constant excitement by the progress or prospect of an election
of its chief magistrate; and when a change of Ministers becomes necessary, there is seldom an interval of more than a few days, or at most of a few
weeks, between the time when one Administration
loses its moral power, by its being ascertained that

it must retire, and the appointment of a new one. And during this short interval the Crown possesses ample power (which it is its duty to exercise) to prevent its retiring servants from abusing the authority they are about to surrender.

On the all-important point of providing for the selection of fit men to govern the Nation, experience seems also to be in favour of the system of Parliamentary Government. Taking the whole period, from the Revolution downwards, it can hardly be disputed, that the Statesmen by whom this Country has been governed, have generally shown themselves not wanting in ability, and need not fear a comparison, in this respect, with the successive rulers of any other Nation during an equal number of years. Greater men than perhaps even the greatest who have risen to eminence in Parliamentary contests, have been raised by other means to power in various countries, especially in times of political convulsion ; but the interest of a State requires, rather that its affairs should be managed by a succession of capable men, than that they should generally fall into inferior hands, with an occasional brilliant exception. It is also more for the interest of a Nation, that it should be governed even by the most ordinary men who may be brought into power without disturbance to its internal

D

peace, than that it should sacrifice the inestimable blessing of domestic tranquillity, to obtain a ruler of the highest genius. Mr. Carlyle, with all his contempt of mere talk, and all his admiration for his hero Oliver Cromwell, would hardly hold it to be desirable for a Nation to pass through the horrors of a civil war, in order to find out, and to raise to power, the unknown Cromwells who may be concealed among its inhabitants. I am not aware of any means of determining by whom a country is to be ruled, which experience will justify us in considering as more successful than our own system in bringing forward able men, and at the same time consistent with the maintenance of internal peace.

Success as a Parliamentary debater is indeed far from being a certain index of a man's fitness for the duties of a Minister, but it is, at least, no bad test of intellectual power, and of the knowledge which a Minister possesses of the affairs entrusted to his management. No prompting by subordinates, and no assistance which can be commanded, can prevent the ignorance of a Minister, when it exists, from being brought to light by the strict ordeal of Parliamentary discussion. Our system, therefore, affords a very tolerable security that the highest offices of the State shall, in general, be filled by

men not greatly wanting in the indispensable qualifications of capacity and knowledge. Nor is it true,
that the confidence of the House of Commons can
be gained merely by talents for debate. To win
and keep that confidence, other qualities are required; and these are undoubtedly of a far higher
kind, not only than those by which the Ministers
of a despotic Sovereign usually obtain the favour
of their master, but also than those by which, in
the United States, candidates for the Presidency
are often recommended to the Electors. A man
who has failed to establish, in the party he belongs
to, a character for judgment and for ability, can
hardly become, as the leader of the House of Commons, the most important member of a British
Ministry. But such a man may, as we know, not
only be elected President of the United States,
but may even owe his being raised to that high position to the fact of his not being distinguished by
the possession of eminent talents or any other great
qualities.

Fourthly.—It is another advantage of Parliamentary Government, that, by causing the inevitable
contests among men for power to assume the form
of debates on the policy by which the Nation is to
be governed, and on measures affecting its most
important interests, it has tended to raise these

contests above those of a mere selfish and personal
character. No doubt selfish and personal interests
have often really governed the conduct of Parliamentary leaders and their followers; but the motives publicly appealed to have been of a far higher
order; and though the practice of politicians has
fallen lamentably short of their theory, the habit
of Parliamentary debates, in which high principles
of right and wrong are recognized, and unworthy
conduct meets with severe reprobation, has tended
to raise by degrees the standard to which men are
expected to conform in public life, and to render
ambitious men less unscrupulous in their conduct
in this than in other countries. If we compare
our own political contests with those of other times
and of other nations, I think we may fairly take
credit to ourselves to this extent. At the same
time, we have little reason to boast; and we must
acknowledge and lament, that the improvement
made in our own political morality, during the last
century, is very small as compared to what it
ought to be. It is still common for improper
means, such as corruption and immoral compliances with the prejudices and passions of the day,
intrigue, or abuse of the great power of the Press,
to be employed for the purpose of securing victory
in Parliamentary contests, and of recommending

individuals and parties to the favour of the Nation and of its Representatives.

Fifthly.—The mode in which our Parliamentary contests have been carried on, has had the further and great advantage of contributing much to instruct the Nation at large on all the subjects most deeply concerning its interests, and to form and guide public opinion. If men's passions and feelings were not so much excited by political struggles, it is not likely they would read, as they do, the debates in Parliament in which these subjects are discussed, and in which, amidst all the trash and sophistry that disfigure them, the keen encounter of intellects seldom fails in the end to lead to the discovery of truth and to the triumph of sound reason over error. The value of Parliament as an instrument for the instruction of the Nation, and for enabling it to arrive at just and wise conclusions on matters affecting its welfare, is hardly less than that which belongs to it as the organ for expressing and enforcing the national will when it has been deliberately formed. The former function our Parliament discharges much more perfectly than the Congress of the United States,—probably, in part, because the debates in Congress are not read with the same interest, from their having no immediate effect on the tenure of power by those to whom the Executive Government is entrusted. The policy pursued by the Government in that important branch of public affairs which has reference to the relations of the State with foreign Powers, is likewise explained by the debates in Parliament, not only to the public at home, but to the civilized world, and the opinion of the world is thus brought to bear upon the Nation and on its rulers.

Such appear to be the chief advantages which belong to Parliamentary Government, as it now exists in this country. On the other hand, it has also its evils and its dangers, which I shall next proceed to consider.

CHAPTER III.

EVILS AND DANGERS OF PARLIAMENTARY GOVERNMENT.

AMONG the evils and dangers of our system of Parliamentary Government, the worst are probably those which arise from its tendency to encourage corruption,—including, under the general name of corruption, all the various methods which may be used to bias men from the right exercise of their political power, and the honest discharge of their political duties, by appeals to their selfish interests. A tendency to corruption in this sense of the word is the common evil of all free Governments. No such Government, of which we possess a trustworthy account, has been exempt from the taint, nor do I see any reason for believing that it has prevailed to a greater degree in this country than elsewhere.

Without going back to ancient times, if we turn

to the United States, which stand next to ourselves
in the list of nations possessing free Constitutions,
we shall find clear proofs (as I shall have occasion
more fully to show in a later chapter) of the existence of corruption not less extensive, and of a
worse kind, than here,* since in this country Parliament at least is not accessible to the direct
influence of money, nor would it be possible by
its means to secure the success of any legislative
measure.† But there is this peculiarity about Parliamentary Government, as compared with other
forms of free government, that in the latter, corruption is as it were an accident,—very probably

* See M. de Tocqueville's ' Démocratie en Amérique,' Tremenheere on the Constitution of the United States, etc.

† I fear this assertion only holds good with regard to our public
legislation. In the passing of private Bills, and especially of Railway Bills, it is believed that money or money's worth has had much
influence in both Houses of Parliament. I hope that the extent to
which this has been the case is exaggerated, but I am not prepared
to dispute the existence of some ground at least for the belief commonly entertained. It is however to be observed, that in private
legislation, the Members of both Houses are subject to much less
responsibility (as their conduct is less open to scrutiny) than they
are with regard to public Bills, and also that the Government in
general exercises a very slight control over the former. I must add
that the mode of conducting private legislation is perhaps the most
defective part of our Parliamentary system. A good deal has been
done towards correcting the abuses formerly complained of, but in
spite of the improvements made of late years in the practice of both
Houses, it can hardly be denied that much of the private business
of Parliament is still very badly done.

an accident which may always attend them, but still an evil, the entire extirpation of which, if it were possible, would have no tendency to derange their working; whereas Parliamentary Government derives its whole force and power of action from the exercise of an influence which is at least very much akin to corruption. The possession and exercise, by the Ministers of the Crown, of a large measure of authority in Parliament, is the foundation upon which our whole system of government rests; while this authority has from the first been maintained principally by means of the patronage of the Crown, and of the power vested in the Administration, of conferring favours of various kinds on its Parliamentary supporters. Sir Robert Walpole's Administration has become almost proverbial for its extreme corruption, and there is no doubt that he retained the command of his majority in the House of Commons mainly by corrupt means, among which were included the habitual use of direct money-bribes to Members of Parliament. But it seems pretty clear that, with respect to corruption, the chief difference between Sir Robert Walpole and the Ministers who preceded and followed him was, that he took less pains than others to conceal the methods he employed for obtaining Parliamentary support, and that the same methods continued long afterwards to be as largely and systematically used for the same purpose.

By degrees, corruption ceased to be practised in the coarse form of money bribes to Members of Parliament; but the same end was attained by jobs of all kinds, perpetrated for the benefit of those who had influence in returning Members of the House of Commons, and by the abuse of an enormous patronage, for their advantage. The arts by which this was accomplished, and by which votes in the House of Commons were obtained, in return for favours bestowed on Members themselves, their patrons, or constituents, were reduced to a regular system, and brought to a high pitch of perfection. This system continued in full force up to the time of passing the Reform Act, in 1832. By that measure, by the diffusion of education, and by the increasing power of opinion, a great improvement in political morality has been effected. No Minister would now dare to be guilty of the practices which were formerly common, and favour is become a far less potent instrument of government than it was. But it would be idle to deny that it still continues to be one of the chief sources of the moving force by which the action of the political machine is maintained. The power which the Ministry of the day possesses of conciliating

its Parliamentary supporters, by favours conferred
upon them, either directly, or indirectly, through
their friends and constituents, is one of the principal means by which the necessary authority of
the Government in both Houses of Parliament
is supported. Parliamentary Government is essentially a government by party, and one of the
bonds by which all parties are kept together is that
of the selfish interests of their adherents. Among
all classes of men who have any share of political
power, whether they are Peers, Members of the
House of Commons, or electors, there are too many
who allow considerations of their private advantage,
not those of the public good, to determine what
party they shall support. Electors, we know, are
influenced sometimes by actual bribes, or, what is
much the same, by money's worth, in the shape of
land or houses let to them below their value, sometimes by a wish to secure the favour of those persons in their town or county who are most able to
advance their interest. Others again, (often the
local leaders of parties,) are led to take an active
part in supporting this or that candidate for a seat
in the House of Commons, by the hope that, if
they are successful, and if the party they espouse
is also successful in Parliament, they may expect,
by the assistance of the Member to whose return

they have contributed, to enjoy a share in the patronage of the Government.

Corruption is the more apt to prevail in this form, because it is difficult in many cases to distinguish conduct which deserves to be branded with such a reproach, from that which is free from blame. No just objection can be taken to a man's seeking employment in the public service, for himself, his friends or relations, by honourable means; and he may fairly expect that his political as well as his personal friends will assist him in doing so. Nor can those to whom patronage is entrusted be reasonably censured for giving a preference to their own political friends, in the appointments they make, so long as they neither neglect any just claims to employment on the part of others, nor place it in unworthy hands. It is when men support measures or a party which their judgment condemns, for the sake of office, or when they make appointments, knowing them to be wrong, from favour, or to purchase political support, that their conduct is to be regarded as corrupt. The same actions therefore may be corrupt or not, according to the motives from which they spring; and thus men easily deceive themselves, not less than others, as to the true character of what they do.

This helps to account for the fact, of which I

fear there can be no doubt, that the abuse of patronage for the sake of influence is both very common and very injurious to the public interest; and
it is through their constituents that such influence
is brought with most power to bear upon Members
of the House of Commons. Owing to the love of
power and distinction natural to men, there is so
general a desire to have a seat in Parliament, and
the competition for seats is so keen, that few men
can obtain them, except as the adherents of some
considerable party; and the candidates who can
procure for their supporters the favours which the
Government has to confer, have a decided advantage over their rivals. Thus there is established a
chain of influence, from the elector to the Minister, which does not leave the latter at liberty to
use the patronage of the Crown with a single eye
to the public good, and which is apt to bias both
voters and their representatives in the exercise of
their respective political powers. The Minister
cannot dispense with Parliamentary support: to
secure it, he must keep those from whom he receives it in good humour; he cannot therefore resist their urgent applications for favours for their
constituents, when they come recommended to him
by the Parliamentary Secretary to the Treasury.
The Ministerial Member, in his turn, must press

upon that important functionary the clamorous
demands of those who have influence in the county
or borough he represents; and that his applications
may be favourably listened to, he must be ready to
answer the calls which the same functionary, in his
character of " Whip," makes for his vote on party
questions.

But though it is undoubtedly true, that there
never has been a Parliamentary Administration
which has not owed some part of its strength to
the exercise of an influence more or less corrupt in
its character, it is certain that in these days (and
probably it was true even in the worst times,) no
Minister can stand exclusively, or even principally,
by such means; nor has corruption so large a share
as some cynical writers would make us believe, in
carrying on the government of this country. All
Parliamentary parties have numbered in their ranks
many unscrupulous and self-interested adherents;
and if the motives of men's public conduct were
strictly scrutinized, they would seldom be found
altogether free from some taint of selfishness. But
admitting this to be true, it is not less true that a
love for their country, and a sincere desire to promote what they believe to be its interests, have generally a very large share (commonly, I hope, a principal share) in determining men's choice of a politi-

cal party. And when great occasions have arisen, a generous contempt of their own individual interest, in competition with their public duty, has been repeatedly shown by all ranks of our countrymen, from the leaders of parties, to the humblest voter in some petty borough. It is when no great public questions have been at issue, and when politics have degenerated into a scramble among individuals for the honours and emoluments of office, that corruption has chiefly prevailed. If we were to judge of Parliamentary Government by its character in such times, as, for instance, the earlier part of the reign of George III., it would be difficult to overcome the feeling of disgust created by the general prevalence of corruption, and the low and sordid motives by which the conduct of politicians seems to have been almost universally governed. But whenever great political questions have arisen, on which men's real opinions have been much divided, parties have been formed and bound together far more by agreement and sympathy on these subjects, than by the pursuit of selfish interests. Men have been found to adhere honourably to such parties, under circumstances of the greatest discouragement. I must be permitted to mention, that a conspicuous example of this is furnished by the conduct of the members of the Whig party in the first thirty years

of the present century. There can be no doubt
that during these years, which, with but slight exception, they passed in opposition, the leaders of
that party might have enjoyed no small share of
office and power if they had been content to fore-
go for that purpose the resolute assertion of their
conscientious opinions on the great questions of
the day, and especially on that of giving religious
liberty to Ireland. The people also on great occasions have shown themselves superior to all base
and mercenary motives, in the exercise of their
political rights. The general election in which
Mr. Pitt defeated the Coalition, and that of 1831,
which secured the passing of the Reform Act, may
be cited as cases in which this has happened.

A tendency to encourage corruption, and especially that kind of corruption which consists in the
misuse of patronage, must however be regarded as
inherent in the system of Parliamentary Government. Nor can it be denied that this system of
Government, even when most purely administered,
is unfavourable to the selection of men for the sub-
altern employments in the public service with a
single view to their fitness. Every Government
which depends for its existence upon the support
of a party, must necessarily be influenced more or
less by considerations of party interest, in making

its appointments, and cannot therefore enjoy the same facilities as Governments of another character for bringing only the fittest persons into the service of the State.

The practice of giving the patronage of the State chiefly to the party in power, has also a tendency to increase the bitterness of party contests, and to excite a spirit of faction in the Nation. This must be admitted to be a serious drawback from the advantages of Parliamentary Government; and it is an evil which springs so directly from the same sources as the advantages of the system, as hardly to admit of being separated from them. For Parliamentary Government is essentially a government by means of party, since the very condition of its existence is that the Ministers of the Crown should be able in general to guide the decisions of Parliament, and especially of the House of Commons; and all experience proves that no popular assembly can be made to act steadily under recognized leaders except by party organization.

In the above remarks, I have adverted to the exercise of patronage only so far as it relates to subordinate offices in the public service; I have already* endeavoured to show that the manner in which the distribution of the highest is provided

* See Chapter II.

E

for, under the system of Parliamentary Government, possesses great advantages. But it would be a mistake to suppose that its rules upon this subject do not, in some respects, lead to inconvenience. The difficulties arising from party connections, and the necessity of conferring these offices on men who belong to the same party and can act together, must generally prevent them from being all held, at any one time, by those most fit for them. A general change of Administration, even when most decidedly for the better on the whole, usually involves the transfer of some offices to worse hands; and the State has often lost services which could ill be spared in some department, because the person by whom it was well managed belonged to a Cabinet, of which the members, collectively, failed to satisfy Parliament and the Country. This is an inconvenience which obviously belongs to party government by its very nature; but the difficulty goes further. Even within the ranks of the same party, it has occasionally happened, that an important department cannot be entrusted to the person who, from his knowledge and experience, is the fittest to conduct it, because he does not agree in opinion, upon matters entirely unconnected with the business of that department, with those who would be his colleagues if he accepted office. Thus, the man most capable of carrying on the business of the Exchequer, or of the Admiralty, might be excluded from either of these departments, because he differed from the Prime Minister, or other Members of the Government, upon Church questions, or questions of foreign policy.

This has been regarded by some persons* as so serious an evil, that they have proposed to attempt its removal by a change of the rule which makes all the Members of the Cabinet answerable for the measures adopted in every department of the Government. Instead of this, it has been suggested that each Minister should only be held responsible for his own acts; by which arrangement, it has been argued, that far greater facilities than now exist would be afforded for obtaining the services of the ablest men in every branch of the Administration, with the further advantage of relieving those who conduct the great departments of the State from being embarrassed by the necessity of obtaining the assent to their measures of colleagues who must be less perfectly acquainted than themselves with the matters to which they relate. It is urged, that the affairs of this country are now so complicated and diversified, that it would be difficult to find even two men entertaining the same

* See Cox's 'British Commonwealth.'

views upon them in all points, and that it is absurd
to suppose that such an agreement is possible among
the larger number of persons composing a Cabinet.
Besides its increasing the difficulty of filling the
high offices of the Government in the best manner, the practice of making all the Members of
the Cabinet jointly responsible for each other's
acts, must therefore, it is said, have the effect of
compelling them to profess a concurrence of opinion with each other which cannot really exist, and
must at the same time expose each Minister to be
thwarted, in conducting his own department, by
the conflicting views of his colleagues.

No doubt this is a plausible objection to the
system of Parliamentary Government, and one
which is by no means entirely without foundation.
Under this system, as it now exists amongst us, it
is true that able men, who might each manage his
own department, under an absolute Sovereign, cannot always combine to carry on together a Government, for all the acts of which they must be jointly
responsible to Parliament; and that, when they do
so, they must be prepared to make considerable
concessions of their individual opinions to those of
their colleagues, without avowing the difference in
public. But the inconvenience arising from this
cause is not found in practice to be so serious as

might have been anticipated. A general concurrence of opinion among the Members of a Cabinet, as to the main objects to which the measures of the Government are to be directed, usually leads them to agree on the means by which these ends are to be pursued, so far as is necessary to enable them to act together. And, so long as no insurmountable differences arise on questions of importance to the welfare of the Nation, all those who have the honour of serving the Crown feel it to be their duty to waive some of their individual opinions, for the sake of rendering it possible for the Government to be carried on.

Nor ought the common responsibility of the whole Cabinet, for the measures taken by the several Ministers in their own departments, to interfere injuriously with the vigour and dispatch with which these departments are administered. It is only so far as regards the general line of policy pursued in each department, and as to important measures, that every Minister is to be considered liable to blame for what has been wrongly done by another. The amount of business to be transacted in the public offices of this Country is so great, that it is impossible its details should be submitted to the Cabinet; and it is clear that the Members of the Cabinet cannot be regarded as really answerable for measures taken without their concurrence, though it is very properly held that they are bound to support what has been done by a colleague, unless, on becoming aware of it, they have marked their disapproval by withdrawing from the Government. Among honourable men this can lead to no difficulty, since a Minister entitled to that character would never think of taking, without the knowledge of his colleagues, steps which he thinks they would disapprove; while they, on the other hand, feel that, in considering any question brought before them, much deference is due to the opinion of the Head of the Government, and to that of the Chief of the department to which it relates.

It is right, or rather it is absolutely necessary, that all the Members of a Ministry should be guided by this feeling, because, unless the measures adopted in any of the principal branches of the public service are allowed to take their main direction and colour from a single mind, they must necessarily become marked with that character of feebleness and uncertainty always attaching to any important course of action, the successive steps of which are decided upon by several persons entertaining views not perfectly identical. So long therefore as there is no such difference upon great questions of policy, as to make it necessary that the Members of a Cabinet should cease to act together, they best discharge their public duty by generally acquiescing in what may be recommended by each Minister in his own department, after he has fully heard the opinions of his colleagues. Every Minister presiding over a great department ought to derive much assistance from the advice of his colleagues, and his own views must often be modified by theirs; and yet it ought seldom to happen, that the difficulty of obtaining their assent should prevent him from following the final dictates of his own judgment, when he has a decided opinion on any important question he may bring before the Cabinet.

Injury to the public service is most apt to arise from the common responsibility of the Members of the Cabinet, when its Chief, or the Minister entrusted with any department, throws himself too much on the assistance of others, and does not recommend with sufficient decision what measures should be taken in pursuance of the policy he is charged with directing. The deliberations of a Cabinet seldom lead to a satisfactory result, when any question of difficulty is brought under its consideration by a Minister who is not prepared to lay before his colleagues some distinct opinion of his

own. The true cause of questions being submitted
to the Cabinet in this unsatisfactory manner, is
sometimes to be found in the fact, that a difference
of opinion on some great principle, or on some
vital point of policy, really exists among the Members of an Administration, though it is concealed
for a time by a reluctance on both sides to come
to a clear understanding on the subject. In such
cases both parties are generally wrong in seeking
to avoid, or to defer, a separation which ought, for
the public good, to take place at once. Of two
lines of policy, it often happens that either might
succeed if steadily pursued, while failure is certain,
if neither is consistently pursued ; and the conduct
of the Government is sure to be marked by a want
of consistency when the Members of an Administration, knowing that they could not agree, shrink
from coming to a clear decision as to the course
they are to adopt, and are content to determine
separately each step that has to be taken, so long
as it is possible to stave off a rupture by abstaining from any decided measure on the one side or
on the other. Were it not invidious, it would
be easy to point out some remarkable instances,
within the last thirty years, of the bad effects
which have been produced by the reluctance of
Cabinets to come to a clear understanding as to

what should be their policy on important subjects upon which their members have held conflicting opinions.

Upon the whole, I do not believe the inconvenience that results from holding all the Members of an Administration jointly answerable for its acts, to be so serious as is sometimes supposed; but were it greater than it really is, the existing practice could not be altered without altering the whole character of our Government. Party connection must cease to be the mainspring of its movements, if every Member of the Administration could no longer depend upon the support of his colleagues, and if they did not all continue to act in strict union. But further; those who have proposed that each Minister should be held responsible only for his own acts, seem to forget that the various departments of the Administration are but parts of a single machine, all the operations of which are directed to one common end, and that the various branches of the Government have a close connection and mutual dependence on each other. Questions of foreign policy, for instance, have constantly to be considered with reference to those affecting our domestic and colonial interests; and in the administration of the Army and Navy, the nature of the demands upon these services,

which are to be anticipated from the state of affairs
both at home and abroad, as well as the extent to
which it is proper to draw upon the resources of
the Nation, must be taken into account in coming
to every important decision. Instead of loosening
the bonds that unite the different branches of the
Government, it would rather be desirable to draw
them tighter. The fault of being too departmental
has been justly attributed to some Administrations,
of which the Chiefs have not held the reins with
firmness, and have failed to exercise the authority which properly belongs to their office, in order
to secure that harmonious co-operation among the
different departments on which the efficiency of
the Government so much depends. Perhaps it
would be for the advantage of the public service
if the hands of the Prime Minister were strengthened, and if a larger measure of authority were
entrusted to him, in order to render this less likely
to recur in future.

To return, however, to the point more immediately under consideration, I would remark, that
there is no form of Government in which evil
influences of some kind are not brought to bear
upon the choice of those who are to serve the
State, either in high or in subordinate offices.
These influences are different in each different

kind of Government; and while I admit their existence and their injurious effects under our own, I believe that no other can be shown to have suffered less from them in some of their many various shapes.

I have stated in the last Chapter, that one of the merits of this kind of government is, its tendency to make those contests for power which are inevitable amongst men, take the form of debates upon questions of policy, and upon the measures affecting the interests of the Nation which are brought before Parliament. These debates are thus rendered a valuable instrument for enlightening the public mind; but with this advantage is unfortunately united the great evil, that the same circumstance leads too often to questions deeply affecting the welfare of the People being decided, not on their merits, but according to their bearing on the interests of political parties. Measures are apt to be supported, or opposed, not because they are good or bad in themselves, but because they have been brought forward by this or that party; and nothing is more common than for a popular cry to be got up in favour of some mischievous scheme, or against some useful proposal, merely for the purpose of overturning or giving strength to a Ministry. Many examples are to be found in our history, of bad

measures having been carried, and of good ones
having been rejected or delayed, owing to this
cause.

So also there are drawbacks from the advantages
which I have stated in the last Chapter, to arise
from the practice of discussing questions of foreign
policy in Parliament. The debates upon such subjects, instead of serving, as they ought, to enlighten
the Nation with respect to its duties and its true
interests in its relations with foreign countries, have
sometimes become the means of encouraging the
most pernicious errors. Opponents of the Government, instead of condemning its errors, have occasionally been guilty of attacking it for having done
right, or for not having gone far enough in a wrong
policy, and in asserting unreasonable pretensions
against other Powers. Public men have not always
resisted the temptation of vying with each other in
courting the favour of the People, by flattering
their passions and prejudices, instead of enforcing
the principles of justice and a high standard of political morality.

An impartial consideration of the nature and
effects of Parliamentary Government, leads to a
recognition of the evils I have pointed out in this
Chapter, as detracting in no small degree from its
merits. At the same time, in admitting these faults,

it is to be observed that, for the most part, they belong to it in common with every other form of free Government, since they arise mainly from the tendency of political liberty to engender party spirit, and to tempt the People to abuse the power it places in their hands. And granting that there is this tendency in all free Governments, it by no means follows that we are wrong in preferring them to those of an opposite character. As in all the other concerns of men, so in their political institutions, we know that only comparative, not absolute, exemption from evil is to be hoped for ; and bad as may be the effects of faction and party spirit under free Governments, they are far less to be feared than the many evils inherent in despotism, and especially its deadening and corrupting influence both on the governed and on their rulers. Power must always be liable to abuse in whatever hands it may be placed, and flatterers, for their own purposes, will try to mislead those to whom it is entrusted, whether they are many or few ; but a long experience has proved, that the abuses prevailing in despotic Governments have been far greater, and far more injurious to the welfare of the People, than those to which political liberty gives rise under a well-regulated Constitution. If we compare what has been the condition of the People under free and under arbitrary Governments, in all ages of the world, we can have no hesitation, in spite of their faults, in giving a preference to the former; and among these, we may assert with confidence, that there is none in which evil has been found to be mixed up with good in a smaller proportion than in our own system of Parliamentary Government.*

* I cannot omit here referring to Mr. Mill's admirable vindication of the superiority of free Governments in the third Chapter of his 'Considerations on Representative Government.'

CHAPTER IV.

REASONS OF THE SUCCESS OF PARLIAMENTARY
GOVERNMENT.

I HAVE remarked in the first Chapter that our own
Country, since the Revolution of 1688, affords the
only example which is to be found, of a Parliamentary Government carried on with success for any
considerable number of years. In considering what
peculiar circumstances there may be to account for
the success of this kind of Government in this one
instance only, our attention cannot fail to be immediately arrested by the fact, that the British Parliament differs widely in its character from the Legislatures which have been elsewhere constituted
for the purpose of introducing a similar system of
government.

The House of Lords has always been recognized
as a body peculiar to this country, and one which

it is impossible to imitate by creating a Peerage, where such an institution has not grown up, so as to derive from long prescription the authority which nothing else could impart to it. And it has been held (I believe justly) by a majority of the best political writers, that whatever may be the theoretical objections to the constitution of the House of Lords, it has performed the important and difficult duties belonging to an Upper Chamber of the Legislature with greater success than any other body of the same kind which has hitherto been formed. It has been able to exercise a very substantial power, and to serve as a real check upon the popular branch of the Legislature, when it has been disposed to act with unwise precipitation, without pushing the exercise of this power so far as either to prevent the passing of measures on which public opinion has been finally made up, or yet to bring about a complete rupture with the House of Commons. Differences between the two Houses have more than once approached the point at which they must have brought the whole machine of Government to a stop, but happily the practical good sense which distinguishes our countrymen, has always hitherto brought about an accommodation or a compromise in time to avert the threatened evil. How it is that the House of Lords has been fitted thus successfully to fill its place in the Constitution would be an interesting subject of inquiry; it would, however, lead me too far from my object in this Essay, and I therefore forbear from entering upon it.

But the difference between the British Parliament and the Legislatures which have been established on the same general model in other countries, is by no means exclusively, nor perhaps even principally, due to the peculiar character of the Upper House. The House of Commons is also very unlike all the other Representative Bodies of which I have ever seen a description. It is distinguished from them mainly by the variety of the elements which enter into its composition, and by its having among its Members some returned by constituencies of a highly democratic character, with many others who owe their Seats to various kinds of influence, rather than to the free choice of large bodies of electors. Before the passing of the Reform Act, Members of the last description were so numerous, as to constitute a large majority of the whole House, and they still form no small proportion of it; since it was neither the design nor the effect of that measure to accomplish such a total change in the character of the House of Commons, as would have resulted from an attempt to make

F

it conform to the notion commonly entertained of a perfect Representation of the People.

The anomalies and irregularities of our Representative system are often, but I believe very incorrectly, regarded as mere abuses, the entire removal of which is indispensable for the purification of the British Constitution. Without denying the reality of the abuses which arose from the manner in which many Seats were obtained in the unreformed House of Commons, or even that these abuses still exist to a considerable extent, it seems to me that the evil has been by no means unmixed with good, and that reasons are not wanting for regarding the irregularities of our Representation as having constituted so important a part of the machine of our Government, that the purposes they have answered could not have been left unprovided for without putting a stop to its working. It is certain, at all events, that, from a much earlier date than the commencement of Parliamentary Government in this country, these irregularities have existed; and whether it be thought that cur Constitution would have been better or worse without them, there can be no doubt that it would have been very different from what it actually is.

Hence it can only be a matter of speculation, on which we have no experience to guide our judgement, how our system of government would have worked, with what is called a perfectly pure system of Representation. But in questions of government, the speculations of even the most enlightened reasoners are little to be trusted. We know that Constitutions drawn up on speculative principles, have almost invariably failed in practice ; consequently, nothing but experience can be considered to afford safe means of judging how any system of government will be found to work. I therefore hold, that the mere fact, that the history of the world affords, as yet, no example of the permanent success of Parliamentary Government with a Legislature formed on the strict principle of popular Representation, would alone be sufficient to create serious doubts whether it could be carried on under such conditions. But it is further to be observed, that we cannot examine with care the character and composition of the House of Commons, and the manner in which they have affected its conduct, without finding strong reasons for believing that the success with which it has been able to take so active a part in the government of the Country, and its peculiar excellencies, are to be attributed, quite as much as some of its faults, to what are regarded as defects and departures from principle in our Representative system.

In the first place. it is to be remarked, that it is
chiefly by means of these defects that the Ministers
of the Crown have been enabled to obtain the authority they have exercised in the House of Commons. Their possession of that authority is what
gives its peculiar character to Parliamentary, as
compared to other forms of Representative Government, and it is also what has enabled the House
of Commons to become distinguished from other
popular assemblies by the steadiness with which
it generally acts, and by its seldom allowing itself
to be led into rash and inconsistent decisions.   At
some periods the power of the Crown in Parliament
has doubtless been excessive, so as occasionally even
to threaten to deprive the Nation of the real enjoyment of political liberty ; but it is not the less certain that it is of the very essence of Parliamentary
Government, that the servants of the Crown should
possess some considerable power within the walls
of the House of Commons, and that hitherto they
have obtained this power through the irregularities
of its composition.   Had all its Members been returned by such constituencies as Westminster or
Yorkshire, it must be plain to the most careless
observer, that the working of the Government as it
has hitherto been carried on would have been impracticable.

A comparison of the House of Commons with other Representative Bodies elected under a more popular, and what is usually held to be a purer system, leads further to the conclusion, that the manner in which it has been chosen has been favourable to its character as a deliberative Assembly. Among such Bodies, that which may be regarded as coming next to it in importance, is the House of Representatives in the United States. That House exercises authority over a nation which stands in the very first rank among the nations of the world; it is chosen by a population which, taken altogether, cannot be regarded as inferior to our own in education and intelligence; indeed I fear that in these qualifications for the exercise of political power, the inhabitants of the British Empire are decidedly inferior to those of the Eastern States of the American Union, and are scarcely equal to the average of the whole Republic. If therefore the systems of election in the two countries were equally well calculated to secure the return of efficient legislative bodies, the House of Representatives in the United States ought to show no inferiority to the House of Commons; whereas the fact of its great inferiority is undoubted. So impartial and acute an observer as M. de Tocqueville* de-

* 'Démocratie en Amérique,' vol. i. p. 241. (13th Edition.)

scribes its deficiencies in the strongest terms, and
his testimony is confirmed by that of almost every
other traveller. Still more decisive evidence to the
same effect may be drawn from comparing the reports of the proceedings of the House of Representatives at Washington with those of the House of
Commons. No one can have been in the habit of
doing so, without being struck with the far higher
tone, both of intellectual power and of moral feeling, displayed in the debates of the latter. In the
decorum and dignity with which its business is
habitually conducted, the House of Commons has
a still greater advantage. Accordingly, the debates
of the British Parliament excite much more interest throughout the civilized world, and exercise
a much greater influence over opinion both at home
and abroad, than those of the American Congress.

This superiority of the House of Commons is, I
think, to be ascribed in a great measure to the circumstance of its Members not all owing their seats
to the choice of large bodies of constituents. Had
they all been thus returned, experience justifies the
inference, that they would have consisted almost
exclusively of men ready to adopt, and make themselves the organs of, the popular feeling of the day,
whatever it may be. The men of enlightened views
and independent character, but unfitted for encoun-

tering the storms of a popular election, who have hitherto been found in the House of Commons, would have been almost, if not altogether, excluded from it. But it is the mixture of men of this sort with others sympathizing more closely with the People, and expressing their passions and feelings, —the great variety, in short, of different elements entering into its composition,—which has given to the House of Commons its very peculiar character. To this we owe, more especially, its having answered so admirably the purpose of a public instructor. If there had not existed facilities for the entrance into the House of Commons of able men holding unpopular opinions, as well as of Members expressing the conflicting views of the various classes of society, and of the many different interests which exist in the Nation, its debates would have lost much of their interest, and still more of their value, as the means of enlightening the minds of the People, and gradually dispelling prevailing errors. I must add, that an examination of our Parliamentary records will prove, that a large majority of the chief ornaments of the House of Commons, from the Revolution to the present time, have been indebted for their first entrance within its walls to the existence of those irregularities in our system of Representation which have been so much complained of.

While the Reform Bill was under discussion, its opponents relied much on the argument that the rotten Boroughs had been the means of introducing into the House of Commons a large proportion of its most distinguished Members, nor was this assertion denied by the enlightened advocates of that measure. Without contesting the fact, that in this respect the then state of our Representation had been attended with advantage, they held, that it had become the source of evils outweighing any benefit derived from it, and that a state of things had grown up which rendered a change of the system, to the extent then proposed, necessary for the welfare of the country.

There is yet another consequence of the irregularities which have always existed, and still continue to exist, in our Representative system, that has contributed to the success of Parliamentary Government. It has been remarked by Blackstone, that "in all tyrannical governments, the supreme magistracy, or the right of both making and enforcing the laws, is vested in one and the same man, or in one and the same body of men; and whenever these two powers are united together, there can be no public liberty. The magistrate may enact tyrannical laws, and execute them in a tyrannical manner, since he is possessed, in his quality of dispenser of justice, with all the power he, as legislator, thinks proper to give himself."* The House of Commons, under the system of Parliamentary Government, unites with its legislative authority a complete control over the Executive Government, through the Ministers of the Crown, who hold their offices only while they retain its confidence. There would thus seem to be some danger that our Constitution might produce that concentration of power in the same hands, which Blackstone, in the foregoing passage, has justly described as constituting a tyranny. We have however escaped this danger, and may congratulate ourselves upon enjoying a larger measure of public liberty (meaning by that phrase a state of things in which all men enjoy security for their persons and property, together with an absence of any undue restrictions on the freedom of individual thought and action), than any other nation on the earth.

For this great happiness, I believe that we are indebted to the peculiar character of our system of Representation, which has admitted the democratic element into the House of Commons without allowing it to become predominant. The powers already enjoyed by that House are so large,

* Blackstone's Commentaries, Book I. chap. ii.

that, if it were to abuse them, and to be supported in doing so by the Nation, it might easily
engross all those which properly belong to the
other constituted authorities of the State, and thus
establish a complete tyranny. That this should
not have happened, notwithstanding the general
tendency to encroachment which belongs to all
rulers and ruling bodies, is, I think, to be accounted for only by the circumstance that our system of Representation has always given an ascendancy in the House of Commons to the upper classes
of society, who have felt that they could not hope
to retain the great power thus placed in their hands,
unless they exercised it in a spirit of moderation
and of respect for the rights of others. If the
House of Commons had been so constituted as
to render it the mere organ of the popular will,
this motive to moderation in the exercise of its
powers would have been wanting, and these powers
would at the same time have been enormously increased, because there would have existed no appeal against any abuse of power by the House of
Commons, to the opinion of a larger public than
that by which it is elected. Various examples
might be quoted from our history, showing how
useful a check has been exercised on the House of
Commons by opinion out of doors. I will, how-

ever, only refer to the famous case of Wilkes, and
to the questions which have more than once arisen
between the House and the other authorities of
the State, as to the extent of its privileges.

This check would be almost entirely destroyed,
if the House of Commons were chosen in such a
manner as to make it directly reflect the wishes,
and express the feelings and passions of the numerical majority of the population. To estimate
the importance of such a change, we must bear
in mind that the House of Commons so constituted would wield a larger power than has ever, I
believe, been exercised by any Legislative Body
elected upon the principles of extreme democracy,
except perhaps the Assemblies which ruled over
France in the earlier days of the first French
Revolution. The House of Representatives in the
United States of America is a purely democratic
body, but it possesses neither executive power, nor
the means of imposing its orders on those to whom
that power is committed. The American Union
was so constituted that, while its operation was not
disturbed by violence, the division of authority
between the Central and State Governments, and
in the Central Government between the Senate,
the House of Representatives, and the President
(who is in a great degree independent of Congress),

together with the control given to the Supreme
Court, effectually prevented the concentration of
all power in the hands of one man or of one set
of men. But in this country, the machinery of the
Government places in the hands of the House of
Commons such means of overruling all the other
authorities of the State, that, if it were elected
under a purely democratic system, it could hardly
fail, in times of popular excitement, to become an
irresistible engine for carrying into effect any measure, however violent, which the passions of the
People might dictate. Unrestrained by any of the
checks upon abuse created in the United States
by the division of authority, such a House of Commons would find, in the extreme use of its acknowledged powers, easy means of compelling the
Crown, the House of Lords, and even the Courts
of Law, to become the mere instruments of its will.

Among the circumstances which have produced
a marked effect upon the character of the House
of Commons, that of its being elected for a period
of seven years, unless sooner dissolved by the authority of the Crown, must not be lost sight of.
Although it was formerly, and is still to a certain
extent, a popular doctrine, that the duration of
Parliament ought to be abridged, and that the
Septennial Act was an unfortunate and improper

measure, I see no ground whatever for this opinion. On the contrary, I concur in the opinion entertained by some of the highest authorities of our own times, and which is said also to have been held by Speaker Onslow,* that the beginning of a great improvement in the character, and a corresponding increase in the influence, of the House of Commons, may be dated from the passing of the Septennial Act. From not being too frequently renewed, the Members of that House have become, as a body, more experienced in the transaction of business, and there has been a greater consistency and steadiness in its conduct than when the duration of Parliaments was limited to three years. Above all, the extension of the term for which the House has been elected, has been favourable to its maintaining its proper character, as a deliberative assembly, instead of becoming an assembly of delegates, not exercising their own judgment on the various questions submitted to them, but merely expressing the wishes of the several bodies of constituents by whom they are returned. The extreme importance of not lowering the Members of the House of Commons into mere delegates, has been admirably explained by Burke, in

* See Lord John Russell's 'Essay on the English Government,' p. 214.

his well-known speech at Bristol; and very little
observation of the proceedings of Parliament, and
of popular elections is necessary, in order to perceive how difficult it would be for Members of the
House of Commons to preserve the power of acting at all on their own independent judgment, if
they were compelled too frequently to submit to
the ordeal of a new election. Even as it is, I fear
that Members are far too much disposed to vote
against their own opinions and their own knowledge of what is right, in deference to popular
clamour excited by ignorance or passion, and that
their tendency to do so is increasing. It is an
alarming system of deterioration in the character
of public men and of the House of Commons, that
it has more than once happened of late years,
that motions have been carried, so decidedly against
the opinion of a large proportion of those who
have voted for them, that they have not scrupled
in private to express their regret at finding themselves in a majority.

Some of the objections which might otherwise
be urged against having the House of Commons
elected for so long a term as seven years, are also
obviated by the power of dissolution possessed by
the Crown. By the exercise of this power the Sovereign is enabled to appeal to the Nation when-

ever there is reason to believe that the House of Commons does not correctly represent its opinions and wishes. At the time of the celebrated struggle between Pitt and the leaders of the Coalition, it was strenuously urged by the latter that the Crown was guilty of an abuse of its prerogative by resorting to what was called a penal dissolution. But since that time it has been completely established as the rule of the Constitution, that when the House of Commons refuses its confidence to the Ministers of the Crown, the question whether in doing so it has correctly expressed the opinion of the country, may properly be tested by a dissolution, and that the House of Commons cannot attempt to resist this exercise of the Prerogative by withholding the grants of money necessary for carrying on the public service till a new Parliament can be assembled, without incurring the reproach of faction. Of late years some persons have tried to push this principle still further, and to maintain that the Crown is not only entitled to appeal to the Nation when the House of Commons has come to a vote hostile to its Ministers, but is under a sort of obligation to them to allow them to dissolve the Parliament which has condemned them. This I hold to be an error, and to be entirely inconsistent with the view of

the powers and the duties belonging to the Sovereign, which has hitherto been adopted by all the
highest authorities. As I have already remarked,*
the Sovereign ought by no means to be a passive
instrument in the hands of his Ministers; it is not
merely his right, but his duty, to exercise his judgment in the advice they may tender to him. And
though by refusing to act upon that advice he
incurs a serious responsibility, if they should in
the end prove to be supported by public opinion,
there is perhaps no case in which this responsibility may be more safely and more usefully incurred than when the Ministers ask to be allowed
to appeal to the People from a decision pronounced against them by the House of Commons.
From a reckless desire to prolong, at all hazards,
their tenure of power, though it may be only for
a few weeks, the servants of the Crown might ask
to be allowed to dissolve a Parliament which had
come to a vote against them, when there would
be no probability of its decision being reversed by
the Nation, and when the measure would be injurious to the public interest. In such cases the Sovereign ought clearly to refuse to allow a dissolution to take place, and as a general rule I doubt
whether a defeated Minister should ever be per-

* See p. 5.

mitted to make such an appeal to the country, unless he can show good grounds for expecting that
it will prove successful.

Before I quit the subject of the character of
the House of Commons, I must notice one objection
that is frequently made, to its being composed in
such a manner as to include men of such various
opinions, and to place a preponderating influence
in the hands of those who do not represent the
wishes of the numerical majority of the Nation.
It is said that, owing to this, great delay arises
in effecting the various reforms that are required,
and in carrying all useful legislation; and it is a
common complaint, that there is so much talking
and so little done in Parliament. No doubt this
is, to some extent, an evil; but I believe it to
be one much exaggerated, and for which there is
ample compensation in advantages which would
be lost if attempts were made, unless with extreme
caution, to render the action of Parliament more
prompt and easy. The facilities which the existing constitution of Parliament affords, for resistance to changes in our legislation, by those who
conceive their interests to be threatened by them,
are not so great as ever to prevent the ultimate
passing of measures called for by the voice of the
Nation. At present, the fault of the House of

G

Commons is, not that the power it gives to popular opinion, or clamour (for they are not always easily distinguished), is too small, but rather that it is perhaps too great. From this cause it sometimes happens that measures, for which there is a momentary cry, are rashly granted, contrary to the true interests of the Nation, and to the opinion of the majority of enlightened men; while various other measures, which such men would generally concur in recommending as wise, are not even proposed, from a fear of offending the prejudices of the day.

Certainly it cannot be said, with any colour of reason, that public opinion is too weak, since, when it is finally and clearly formed upon any question, it invariably triumphs. The difficulty which it has to surmount in doing so, is not more than is necessary in order to secure the due consideration of objections to measures for which there is a popular cry, and to afford means for testing by discussion the soundness or fallacy of conflicting arguments. A few years, though much in the life of an individual, are little in the life of a Nation; and some delay in passing useful measures may well be submitted to, as cheaply purchasing the advantages we obtain in return for it. Among these advantages, the intellectual and moral training which the

Nation derives from the discussion of changes in the law which encounter serious resistance, is not perhaps one of the smallest; but what is most important is, that such changes can seldom be carried until after they have received such ample deliberation, and till public opinion is so completely settled with regard to them, that, when once passed, they are almost invariably permanent, and more completely effective than they could become if adopted in a different manner. If we look back at the history of our legislation for many years past, we shall find that it has been steadily progressive; and that, although some of the greatest improvements in our laws have not been achieved without years of arduous struggle, yet, when once accomplished, they have been secure against all attempts to repeal them, and have commanded the complete obedience of the Nation.

Experience proves that these advantages are not equally enjoyed in countries the institutions of which present greater facilities for prompt legislation. Good laws, passed prematurely, before the minds and habits of the People are prepared for them, are seldom properly obeyed; nor would it be difficult to point out cases in which measures, wise in themselves, adopted by despotic rulers more enlightened than their subjects, have, from this cause, failed to produce the benefit which might have been reasonably expected from them. So also in those popular governments where no obstacle exists to the immediate accomplishment of every change in the law which is demanded by the majority of the People, it is found that that majority is disposed to act under the influence of sudden impulse rather than of deliberate conviction, and that the instability of the law too often detracts from its usefulness. M. de Tocqueville informs us that this is strikingly the case in the United States, where he describes it as common for laws to be made and again repealed, with a lightness amounting to caprice, and leading to serious inconvenience.* Though the progress of legislative improvement in this country may seem too slow to men of eager and impatient tempers, if we consider fairly what has been done since the meeting of the first reformed Parliament, we shall find no just grounds for complaining of the rate of our advance, when we remember how safely and surely that progress has been made.

* He quotes the opinions expressed by Hamilton, Madison, and Jefferson, as to the magnitude of the evil arising from the instability of legislation in the United States. The first of these distinguished men speaks of it as "the greatest blemish in the character and genius of our government;" and Jefferson thought the inconvenience so great as to require the adoption of very severe restrictions on the power of the Legislature.—*Démocratie en Amérique*, vol. i. p. 243.

At the same time, I am far from denying that there is a constant tendency in Parliament, or rather in the House of Commons, unduly to retard its proper work, by undertaking business for which it is unfit, and by indulging in discussions of unnecessary length. The inconvenience of excessively protracted debates has already attracted public attention, which of itself will probably go far to diminish the evil. Members will learn moderation in the exercise of their right of speaking and of bringing forward motions, when they find that by failing in this discretion they incur the disapproval of the House and of the Country. The tendency of the House of Commons to deprive itself of sufficient time for the due discharge of its most important functions, by undertaking unnecessary business, is more to be feared, because it is encouraged both by the public and by persons of high influence. Injudicious changes in this direction are usually received with general applause.

Striking examples of this may be found in the recent Acts of Parliament, by which various permanent charges have been removed from the Consolidated Fund, and by which it is required that the gross instead of the net revenue should in future be paid into the Exchequer, leaving the expense of collecting the revenue to be voted by the House of Commons in Committee of Supply, instead of being paid, as heretofore, by the authority of the Crown. These measures, and especially the abolition of the power of the Crown to provide for the cost of collecting the revenue by deductions from the gross receipts, have been exceedingly applauded; yet it may be safely asserted, that their effect has been to encumber the House of Commons with a considerable amount of additional business, with which there was not the slightest occasion that it should be burdened, and which it is impossible that it can perform properly. There was no reason for the House thus to increase the demands upon its time and attention, because it already possessed a complete control over the expense incurred by the Government in the collection of the revenue, and in the management of services provided for by permanent charges on the Consolidated Fund. Full accounts of this expenditure were habitually laid before Parliament, and if more ample information upon particular points was asked for, it was never withheld. Members of the House of Commons could therefore call its attention, when they thought fit, to any objectionable expenses. Such expenses, instead of being safer from detection and reproof, from having been incurred on the responsibility of the Ministers, without the previous sanction of Parliament, were, on the contrary, only the more exposed to censure. A vote of the House of Commons may afford convenient cover for a job, and perhaps the worst jobs of recent years have been those perpetrated by means of votes in Committee of Supply.

The House also nominally assumed a duty which it was utterly impossible for it really to perform. To regulate the various establishments for the collection of the revenue, in such a manner as at once to avoid unnecessary expense, and to ensure the efficient performance of this important branch of the public service, is a task requiring great experience, and great knowledge of minute details. When an estimate is presented to the House of Commons, to provide for the charge of a certain number of officers of different ranks, and receiving different rates of pay, in the various Revenue departments, the Members who discuss the estimate in Committee of Supply have no means whatever of forming a sound judgment on the details of the establishment submitted for their approval. To those who know how business is done in a Committee of Supply, it can hardly be necessary to point out how impossible it is that such details should there be usefully discussed. All that the House of Commons can really do is, to compare

the revenue with the amount spent in collecting
it, and if the cost of collection should appear to
exceed a reasonable percentage on the income rea-
lized, to call upon the Government to take care
that it is reduced, imposing upon the servants of
the Crown the responsibility which properly belongs to them of enforcing strict economy. Without any change in the ancient practice of paying
only the net revenue into the Exchequer, the
House of Commons had many years ago succeeded
in putting an end to the old abuses of making
improper payments out of the gross revenue, and
in providing for the collection of the revenue at a
singularly moderate cost. In determining to go
further, and to take upon itself the duty of voting
annually the charges for the collection of the revenue, the House of Commons has, in my opinion,
altogether mistaken its proper function in this
matter. That function is, to exercise a watchful,
but general, control over the Executive Government, not to attempt to scrutinize details, upon
which it may waste precious hours required for far
more important purposes.

In like manner, the removal from the Consolidated Fund of many charges formerly borne on it,
for the purpose of voting them in the estimates, involves a worse than useless addition to the labours

of the House, and to its opportunities for indulging in unnecessary discussion. With scarcely an exception, these charges are to provide for services of a permanent character, and it is a part of true economy that the means allotted for such services should not vary from year to year, but should continue unaltered so long as the circumstances remain the same. When there was any change of circumstances calling for a change in these appropriations, their being provided for from the Consolidated Fund opposed no obstacle to its being effected ; the only effect of their being so charged was to avoid giving opportunities for debates that lead to nothing.

Even in the discussion of those estimates which must be voted annually, in consequence of their varying amount, and the nature of the services for which they are intended to provide, few experienced Members of the House of Commons would deny that the sort of nibbling at details which is sometimes practised, is a mere waste of time. There has been some improvement in this respect in the last few Sessions, but before that the House had carried this waste of time to a pass that was almost ludicrous, and showed an extraordinary misconception of its proper functions, by entering into details with which it is impossible for any large assembly to deal with success, and which ought to be left to the Executive Government. Complaints were even made that the forms of the House did not afford an opportunity of pushing still further this ill-advised scrutiny of the petty items of expenditure; and a Select Committee has advised that these forms should be altered. The necessary consequence of this error is, that when time has been so wasted, the most important legislative business must afterwards be neglected, or most imperfectly done. Thus in the year 1857, even the clauses of the Divorce Bill could only be considered in a most unsatisfactory manner, in the month of August, by a House jaded with fatigue, and deprived of the services of a large proportion of its Members, because days, and even weeks, had been previously thrown away in unprofitable and wearisome talking in the Committee of Supply.

There is, also, no greater error, than to suppose that the mere fact of certain charges being annually voted by the House of Commons, is the slightest security for economy in providing for them. Extravagant charges are at least as apt to escape detection in estimates of proposed expenditure, as in accounts laid before Parliament of that already incurred, while the Government is sheltered from responsibility by votes in supply. If the publicity necessary to prevent jobs is maintained, and corrupt extravagance is thus guarded against, the Ministers of the Crown have every motive, both of duty and of interest, to induce them to enforce economy in the public service. They usually do this far more effectually, and above all far more steadily, than the House of Commons, which, like all popular bodies, is apt to be led sometimes into extravagance, sometimes into injudicious parsimony.

A curious example of the changes of temper to which the House of Commons is liable on questions of economy, and of the inconsistencies into which it is apt to fall when it refuses to follow its accustomed leaders, is afforded by its conduct with respect to the Civil Service Bill in the same Session of 1857.* The object of this Bill was to relieve the permanent civil servants of the Crown from deductions made from their salaries under an Act of Parliament, for the purpose of raising a fund for superannuations,—a relief which would be equivalent to augmenting their salaries by an amount varying from two and a half to five per

* It deserves to be noticed that this Session, which was remarkable, beyond any other of late years, for the great waste of time by the House of Commons in laborious trifling, was the first Session of a new Parliament, after a dissolution which had deprived many old and experienced Members of their seats.

cent. The second reading of this Bill was carried against the Government by a large majority, though only nine or ten years before the Ministers of that day had had the greatest difficulty in resisting a proposal precisely the reverse of that since adopted, namely, to diminish all salaries by ten per cent. This proposal, for cutting down salaries generally, was supported, at the time when the economical fit was strong upon the House of Commons, by many of the very Members whose votes have since swelled the majority for augmenting them. The Superannuation Act, the chief clauses of which this Bill was intended to repeal, was itself passed, in deference to the feeling of the House, in one of its fits of economy. The defeat of the Government upon this question also illustrates the power now exercised by means of an artificial and organized agitation. This machinery (an invention of the last few years), skilfully worked by those interested in the measure, had led so many Members of the new Parliament to pledge themselves in favour of the Bill, as to ensure its success.

I have dwelt at greater length than I should otherwise have done on the error I conceive the House of Commons to have committed in undertaking duties that do not properly belong to it, because there appears to be a strong disposition on the part of the public to encourage the House in a mistake which, if persisted in, may detract materially from its usefulness. If, however, either from this or from any other cause, the proper business of Parliament should suffer such delay as to create serious inconvenience, we may trust that the practical good sense of the Nation will lead to the adoption of some mode of correcting the evil. Hitherto (as I have said) I think we have had no real reason to complain of the slowness with which the work of legislative improvement has been carried on.

CHAPTER V.

EFFECTS OF PARLIAMENTARY REFORM.

HAVING, in the preceding Chapters, considered the nature of our system of Parliamentary Government, its merits and its faults, I propose now to inquire in what manner the working of this system has been affected by the Reform of the Representation which was carried in 1832, and to offer some remarks on the character and consequences of that celebrated measure.

The three Acts for the Amendment of the Representation of the People in Parliament, in England, Scotland, and Ireland, must be regarded as forming together a single measure, having for its object the transfer of a large amount of political power to the People, from the hands of a comparatively small number of persons, who were previously enabled to command a majority of the Seats in the House of Commons. So great a change in the distribution of political power has, probably, seldom or never been accomplished in any country without violence or convulsion; it amounted, in fact, (as was justly said at the time,) to a revolution, though a peaceful and, I believe, a most beneficial revolution. Still, large as it was, the measure did not profess to sweep away all the anomalies and irregularities of our system of Representation, in order to create a new one more in accordance with what is considered by some persons to be the true theory of Representation. On the contrary, the design was to correct evils which had been practically felt, but to make no further changes than were indispensable for this purpose, in a Constitution of which, in spite of some imperfections, the general excellence was recognized Experience had proved that, in the House of Commons as then constituted, public opinion was so weak, and influence of another kind so powerful, that the conduct, both of Parliament and of the Executive Government, was habitually biassed in a manner detrimental to the general welfare of the Nation. Clear evidence of this was to be found in the manner in which the Country had for many years been governed, and especially in the heavy burden of taxation imposed upon the people. There

could be little doubt that some branches of the
public expenditure had been constantly maintained
upon a scale beyond what was required by the real
interest of the Nation, with the view of securing
the support of those who had a commanding influence in the election of the House of Commons.
But while this was an evil urgently requiring to be
remedied, it was believed that it was neither necessary for that purpose, nor safe, to make the total
change in the character of the House of Commons,
which would ensue were all its Members to be returned by large popular Constituencies.

The Reform Acts for the three divisions of the
United Kingdom, which received the sanction of
Parliament in 1832, were framed in conformity
with these views. By the preservation of many of
the smaller Boroughs, and by regulating the County
Representation in a manner which left much influence to the great landed proprietors, the former mixture of classes and interests in the House of Commons was to a great extent preserved ; and, though
the strength of the democratic element in its composition was greatly augmented, it was neither the in-
tention nor the effect of the measure to render that
element all-powerful. What was aimed at, and accomplished more successfully than could well have
been anticipated, was, to redress the balance of the

Constitution, not to make it incline as much on one side as it had previously done on the other.

The wisdom with which this great change in the Constitution was designed, is shown by its results. It has now been above thirty years in operation, and it is impossible to compare the spirit of our legislation and government during that period with that of former times, without perceiving how much it has been altered for the better. No doubt, during this period, many mistakes have been made, both by Parliament and by the different Administrations which, under its control, have exercised the powers of the Executive Government. But it may be safely asserted, that these mistakes have been only such as are to be accounted for by errors of judgment in the Nation itself, and as may be looked for under the best of human institutions. The measures of Parliament and of the Government have been directed by a sincere desire to promote the general welfare, and upon the whole, it must be admitted, with success, if we consider the number of important reforms in every branch of Administration which have been effected in a comparatively short time. Lastly, this great stimulus has been given to improvement with no social disturbance, beyond the temporary agitation of the struggle by which the Reform Bill was carried, and without

H

giving that shake to the power and authority of the Government, either at home or abroad, which is so often the consequence of political changes, and is the source, when it occurs, of so much danger.

But though the measure of Parliamentary Reform which was passed in 1832 has been thus successful, and is, I think, conclusively proved by its results to have been, upon the whole, a wise and good one, it was by no means perfect. It had, on the contrary, serious faults, which were so easily to be discerned, even while it was under discussion, that it is impossible to suppose they could have escaped the observation of its authors, though it was not in their power to avoid them. The strength of the opposition to be overcome before the Bills could pass, and the excitement under the influence of which they were carried, were such, as not only to account for the errors to be found in the plan, but to make it marvellous that they were not far greater.

On considering the whole scheme of the Parliamentary Reform of 1832, with the light thrown upon it by the experience we have had of the working of our amended system of Representation during more than thirty years, the following appear to be the chief defects of the measure. First: I consider it to have been a very great fault that it failed to provide adequately against the danger that the

removal of abuses might incidentally diminish too
much the power of the Government in Parliament.
It has often been said, and with truth, that, under
our present Constitution, the worst Administration
we can have is a weak one. A weak Ministry has
not the power of acting rightly; it must bring forward in Parliament, not the measures it knows to
be best for the interests of the Country, but those
it can hope to carry; it cannot venture to conduct
the Executive Government according to the dictates
of its own judgment; and in the exercise of the authority and patronage of the Crown, it is compelled
to yield to every popular cry and to the unreasonable claims of its adherents; it is under a constant
temptation unduly to court popularity, and to ex-
aggerate the faults of party Government, by striving, in all its measures, to promote the interests
of its Party rather than those of the Nation. Such
a Government has a tendency to become more than
usually corrupt, because an evenly-measured contest
of Parties affords to unscrupulous men, desirous
of using their votes or political interest for their
own selfish advantage,* peculiar facilities for driving
hard bargains with the Administration.

* The following passage in Lord Derby's Speech in the House of
Lords, on the 8th of February, 1855, gives a striking description of
the position of a Minister not enjoying adequate Parliamentary
support :—

H 2

Nor is this all; our whole system of Parliamentary Government rests, as I have already remarked, upon the Ministers of the Crown possessing such authority in Parliament as to enable them generally to direct its proceedings, and espe-

"My Lords, I can conceive no object of higher or nobler ambition, none more worthy of the anxiety of a true patriot and lover of his country, than to stand in the high and honourable position of the Chief Minister of the Crown and Leader of the councils of this great Empire, assisted and supported by colleagues combined with him by unity of sentiment and mutual and personal respect, and with the knowledge that this and the other House of Parliament would give to such a Minister the assurance that, except on most extraordinary and unusual occasions, he would be enabled, with life and energy, to carry out his plans and to mature and accomplish his objects, and, practically as well as nominally, control and govern the legislation and internal economy of this great Country. On the other hand, to hold that highly responsible situation dependent for support from day to day upon precarious and uncertain majorities, compelled to cut down this measure, and to pare off that,—to consider with regard to each measure, not what was for the real welfare of the country, but what would conciliate some half-dozen men here, or obviate the objections of some half-dozen there, to regard as a great triumph of Parliamentary skill and Ministerial strength to scramble through the session of Parliament, and to boast of having met with few and insignificant defeats,—I say this is a state of things which cannot be satisfactory to any Minister, and which cannot be of advantage to the Crown, or to the People of this country. But, my Lords, to enter on the duties of office, not with a precarious majority, but with a sure minority of the other House of Parliament; to be aware that from day to day you were liable to defeats at any moment, by the combination of parties amounting to a sure majority, and only waiting for the moment when it would be most convenient to introduce motions for the attainment of such an end; to be a Minister on sufferance; to hold such a position without any

cially those of the House of Commons. This foundation would fail, and the system itself must fall into ruin, if it should become impossible, for any considerable time that an administration of proper strength should be formed. This might happen if the House of Commons, from the absence of any strong party-feeling or bond of union in the supporters of the Government, should show a disposition on light occasions to reject the advice of the Servants of the Crown, although the persons holding office had, upon the whole, more of its confidence than any other Ministers would be able to command. Should such a state of things arise, with parties in the country so divided as to afford no prospect of a House of a different character being obtained by a dissolution of Parliament, it would be impossible to escape the necessity of introducing new rules of political conduct, and a new mode of carrying on the public business. Hitherto it has been considered to be the duty of

security for enforcing your own views ; with the fear of exposing your own friends and the Country, your friends to perpetual mortification, and the Country to constant disappointment,—to undertake the responsibilities and the duties of office under such circumstances and in such a state of things, would be such an intolerable and galling servitude as no man of honour or character would voluntarily expose himself to, and such as no man would willingly submit to, except from motives of the purest patriotism and as proof of the absolute necessity of such self-sacrifice."

the Ministers of the Crown to resign, if they find
themselves without adequate support in the House
of Commons. Their doing so would be useless in
the case supposed ; and there would be no resource
but to tolerate the existence of an Administration
unable to guide the proceedings of Parliament.

But this would involve a complete abandonment
of the essential principle of a Parliamentary Government, even though it should continue to be
held, that an Administration against which a direct
vote of want of confidence had been carried must
retire. What particularly distinguishes our present
system of government, and constitutes, as I have
endeavoured to show, one of its main advantages,
is the responsibility which it imposes, both on Parliament and on the Servants of the Crown. Every
Member of the House of Commons feels, or ought
to feel, that it is a serious step to give a vote
which may compel the existing Government to
retire, without a reasonable prospect that another
better able to conduct the affairs of the Country
can be formed. The Ministers, on the other hand,
know that they are not held to be absolved from
responsibility for unwise measures, because they
have been forced upon them by the House of Commons ; but that, if they continue to administer
the affairs of the Country when powers they think

necessary have been refused, or a course they disapprove has, in spite of their advice, been adopted by the House, they are justly held answerable for the policy of which they consent to be the instruments. But if it should ever come to be regarded as not being wrong, that Ministers should retain office though they were no longer able to guide the proceedings of the House of Commons, there would cease to be in any quarter an effective responsibility for the prudence and judgment with which the affairs of the Nation are conducted in Parliament. Ministers could not be held answerable for the conduct of a Parliament they had no power to direct, and the only responsibility left would be that of the House collectively. Experience, as I have already remarked, proves, that a responsibility shared amongst so many is really felt by none; and that a popular assembly, which will not submit to follow the guidance of some leader, is ever uncertain in its conduct and unstable in its decisions.

After the Revolution of 1688, when the House of Commons had by that event acquired great power, and had not yet been brought under the discipline of our present system, these evils were grievously felt.* They would be far more so in

* See Macaulay's History of England, vol. iv. p. 434.

the present state of society, and we must expect to see the House of Commons arriving at many hasty and ill-judged decisions, and its Members giving their votes much oftener than they now do contrary to their judgment in deference to public clamour, if they were relieved from the apprehension of creating the difficulties that arise from a change of Government. Those who have watched the proceedings of Parliament, cannot be ignorant how many unwise votes have been prevented by a dread of the resignation of Ministers, and that the most effective check on factious conduct on the part of the Opposition, is the fear entertained by its leaders of driving the Government to resign on a question upon which, if they should themselves succeed to power, they would find insuperable difficulties in acting differently from their predecessors. The House of Commons would lose its distinguishing character; it would become more like the Congress of the United States,* but without the checks by which Congress is restrained; and we should have a government at once weak, capri-

---

* In the Life of Horace Greeley, editor of the 'New York Tribune' (a book which contains much curious information as to the working of the Constitution of the United States), there is a letter, in which the following passage affords a remarkable illustration of the effects of the absence of any individual responsibility for the decisions of the House of Representatives. "It was but yesterday

cious, and tyrannical, if the practice should ever grow up of regarding the Ministers, who are now the Servants of the Crown, as the servants of the House of Commons, and justified in pleading the will of that House as their excuse for adopting or acquiescing in measures of which their own judgment and conscience disapproved.

The political events of the last few years afford much ground for apprehending that the Country may be exposed to these very serious evils, from its becoming impossible that any Administration should be formed having sufficient strength in the House of Commons. Before the passing of the Reform Acts, there was little danger that such a state of things could arise. The former state of the Representation, together with the large means of influence which then existed, gave so much power to the Crown, that Ministers unacceptable to the Sovereign could seldom long maintain their position; and those who enjoyed the cordial support of their Royal Master were enabled to command so large a number of votes, that they could

---

that a Senator said to me, that though he was utterly opposed to any reduction of mileage, yet if the House did not stop passing Retrenchment Bills for Buncombe, and then running to the Senate and begging Members to stop them there, he for one would vote to put through the next Mileage Reduction Bill that came to the Senate, just to punish Members for their hypocrisy."—*Page 298.*

scarcely be left in a minority, except in cases when public opinion was declared against them with overwhelming force. Nothing can more clearly prove how completely the power of the Crown was at that time predominant in the House of Commons, than the well-known fact, that the combined opposition of Pitt and Fox, with all their Parliamentary talents and personal influence, would have failed to overthrow the Addington Administration, in spite of the general opinion entertained of its incompetence, if the state of mind of George the Third had not excited such just apprehension in his Minister, that he shrank from maintaining the contest.

The political condition of the Country, when such an Administration could be supported under such circumstances by the power of the Crown, was a very bad one, but its evils seem to have arisen less from the power of the Crown having been excessive in itself, than from the fact that this power depended in a great measure on the personal influence of the Sovereign, and was derived from sources which led naturally to its abuse. The personal influence of the Sovereign might be used, not to support, but to undermine his responsible Ministers; and we know that it was habitually so employed by George the Third, whenever he was compelled for a short time to accept the services of a Minister he disliked. It was the knowledge of this fact that contributed so much during that reign, to give undue power to those Administrations which were supposed to enjoy the royal favour, because every shabby politician (and unfortunately the class is a large one) shrank from joining an Opposition which was obnoxious to the Court, and which therefore could not hope for more than a very brief tenure of power, even if, by the strong support of public opinion, it should be enabled to attain it. The correspondence of the statesmen in the earlier part of the reign of George the Third, of which so much has now been published, presents a painful picture of the abuses and intrigues which prevailed when Court favour had so large a share in deciding the contest for political power; and Burke has described with just severity the system under which a party grew up and acquired so much strength, under the name of the King's Friends.

The means, also, by which the Ministers of the Crown were enabled to command the votes of a large number of Members of the House of Commons, before the passing of the Reform Bill, had grown to be very injurious and onerous to the country. So large a proportion of the whole House

was then returned by the influence of Borough proprietors and other powerful persons, instead of by
any really popular election, that Ministers were necessarily led to depend for the maintenance of their
power, less on meriting the confidence and appro-
bation of the Nation, than on the support of those
who possessed Parliamentary interest, which too
commonly could only be purchased at the expense
of the general good. This evil seems to have been
increased, (so far at least as regards the burden
upon the Nation,) instead of being diminished, by
the gradual discontinuance of the practice of giving
direct money bribes to the supporters of the Government in the House of Commons; because bribes
given in this form, from the votes for secret service,
were not really more immoral, and were far less
costly, to the nation than those which were accepted
in the form of jobs, and of places created, not for the
public service, but for the benefit of the holders.
But apart from the means by which it was obtained,
the command of a considerable number of votes in
the House of Commons by the Ministers was highly
useful, and its continuance would have been an
advantage, as conducing to the firm and vigorous
administration of affairs, if it had been preserved
in such a manner as to be enjoyed by the Advisers
of the Crown in virtue of their offices, irrespective

either of Court favour or of those sinister influences to which they were compelled to submit in order to secure it.

A comparison of the working of the Constitution, before and after the passing of the Reform Bill, must, I think, convince us that the question asked by the Duke of Wellington while it was in progress, " How is the King's Government in future to be carried on ? " deserved more consideration and a more practical answer than it received.   From the combined effect of the Acts of Parliamentary Reform and of the many other reforms, especially those of an economical character, which have been carried in the last forty years, the power of the Crown has been so much diminished, that there seem to be good grounds for believing that the state of things which, in 1780, amply justified Dunning's celebrated resolution against the increase of that power, has been reversed, and that the balance of the Constitution may now be in no slight danger of being deranged by the too great diminution of the influence in Parliament which the Servants of the Crown formerly enjoyed.

I am aware that so high an authority as Mr. Hallam has expressed an opinion, that there is no occasion for the Ministers of the Crown to possess any influence in Parliament beyond that which they would derive from a conscientious and effective discharge of their duties. He says: "There is no real cause to apprehend that a virtuous and enlightened Government would find difficulty in resting upon the reputation justly due to it, especially when we throw into the scale that species of influence which must ever subsist,—the sentiment of respect and loyalty to a Sovereign, of friendship and gratitude to a Minister, of habitual confidence in those entrusted with power, of averseness to confusion and untried change, which have in fact more extensive operation than any sordid motives, and which must almost always render them unnecessary."*

In giving this opinion, Mr. Hallam has, I fear, not made sufficient allowance for the effect of the various motives by which the Members of both Houses of Parliament are apt to be biassed in giving their votes. Discontent, ambition, the love of popularity, and even of notoriety, and various personal feelings, are found in practice to exercise so much influence, and must always be expected to array so many Members of the House of Commons in Opposition, that, unless the Government is enabled by some means or other to throw a considerable weight into the scale, by virtue of

* See Hallam's 'Constitutional History,' vol. iii. p. 355.

its official position, it is impossible it should exercise that authority which, as the very keystone of the whole system of Parliamentary Government, it ought to possess in the decision of questions submitted to the House of Commons. Hitherto, the undue diminution of this kind of authority in the Government, since the passing of the Reform Acts, has not been so seriously felt as it is likely to be hereafter. Until lately, various circumstances, and especially the existence of Parties formed previously to the alteration in the constitution of the House of Commons, have combined to avert, or at least greatly to mitigate, the inconvenience that might have been apprehended from this source. We cannot however expect this to continue, and already there are clear indications of the approach of a different order of things, in which, from the dissolution of ancient Party ties, and the great curtailment of the indirect influence of the Government, the existence of weak Administrations may become habitual. The fact, of all the most important public questions on which Parties were formerly divided having been finally settled, has contributed to increase the difficulty of maintaining the authority of the Government in the House of Commons. While these questions were still at issue, they served as a bond of union both to the

Party which supported, and to that which resisted, the measures in dispute, and helped to keep up the Party discipline upon which the strength of a Ministry, as well as that of an Opposition, greatly depends.*

The present state of things seems tending to bring about the injurious alteration in the Constitution which would result from the loss of the authority of the Administration in Parliament. There is the greater danger of this, because no change of the law is necessary to bring about such a change

---

* There is another consequence of the settlement of these questions which deserves to be remarked. Since the various reforms which thirty years ago were so strenuously contended for by one Party, and no less strenuously opposed by another, have been successively carried, it would be difficult to draw any clear distinction between parties from their opinions on public questions, and thus the division between them is made to depend more than formerly on personal feelings and interests. This tends both to lower the tone of Parliamentary warfare, and to diminish the wholesome authority formerly exercised by the leaders of Parties. Although the accomplishment of these reforms is in itself a great advantage to the Nation, it cannot be denied that new dangers have arisen from the termination of the struggle by which they were won. While that struggle lasted, it helped to keep politics in a healthy state, as the peril of her mortal strife with Carthage is said to have preserved Rome from that flood of corruption which soon set in after her final triumph over her formidable enemy. The consequences in this respect of the termination of our old Parliamentary contests, only add another to the many proofs to be everywhere found, how vain it is in human affairs to look for the quiet continuance of a state of things with which we may sit down contented.

in the character of our Government. The principle, that the confidence of the House of Commons is necessary to a Ministry, was established by no legal enactment, but by opinion and usage, which grew up by degrees. These may be altered as gradually and insensibly as they were originally formed; and the more easily, as there has never at any time been a uniform and unbending rule that Ministers ought to retire whenever they meet with a Parliamentary defeat. The strongest Governments have all occasionally experienced such defeats, under circumstances that have been regarded as making it their

To be in a constant conflict with evil in some shape or other, is obviously the condition appointed by Providence both for men and nations, and the moment that struggles for improvement cease, corruption and decay commence. The following are M. de Tocqueville's admirable remarks on "little Parties,"—the designation he applies to those that are formed in free countries when all great questions are settled, and only minor points remain at issue:—"Les petits Partis sont en général sans foi politique. Comme ils ne se sentent pas élevés et contenus par de grands objets, leur caractère est empreint d'un égoïsme qui se produit ostensiblement à chacun de leurs actes. Ils s'échauffent toujours au froid; leur langage est violent, mais leur marche est timide et incertaine. Les moyens qu'ils emploient sont misérables comme le but même qu'ils se proposent. De là vient que quand un temps de calme succède à une révolution violente, les grands hommes semblent disparaître tout-à-coup, et les âmes se renfermer en elles-mêmes. Les grands Partis bouleversent la société, les petits l'agitent; les uns la déchirent, et les autres la dépravent; les premiers la sauvent quelquefois en l'ébranlant, les seconds la troublent toujours sans profit."—*Démocratie en Amérique*, vol. i. pp. 208–9.

duty to bow to the decision of Parliament. The
government of the country could hardly be carried
on, and the just weight of the House of Commons
at the same time maintained, if the Administration
were not allowed on certain occasions thus to submit to it without retiring. But hitherto the rule
has been the other way, and it is only of late that
there has appeared to be a disposition to multi-
ply exceptions in a manner which may break down
the rule. As it becomes more difficult to constitute strong Governments, this disposition is likely
to increase. A weak Ministry, when a popular
clamour is raised in favour of measures they know
to be wrong, is in danger of being tempted to
take shelter from responsibility in a sham resistance
to them. The House of Commons and the Public,
on the other hand, may also be frequently tempted
to acquiesce in the continuance of a Government on
these terms, as the easiest mode of carrying some
object in favour of which the passions or prejudices of the People may be excited, in opposition
to the sober judgment of enlightened and right-
minded men.

Any diminution of Ministerial responsibility
would be peculiarly dangerous on questions affecting the pecuniary interests of individuals, since no
jobs are so bad as those perpetrated by a popular

PARLIAMENTARY REFORM. 115

assembly, through private canvass. A wholesome rule of Parliamentary law debars the House of Commons from making any grants of money without the previous recommendation of the Crown through its responsible Servants ; but unfortunately this rule may be evaded by addresses from the House to the Crown, praying that certain grants may be made, and promising to provide for them. Such addresses have been too often moved of late years ; and if the House of Commons should fall into the habit of thus virtually setting aside the wise principle of our Constitution, which makes the Ministers of the Crown responsible for originating all grants of money, a door will be opened to the very worst corruption. Symptoms may be detected in the Parliamentary proceedings of recent Sessions of there being some danger that the habitual weakness of the Government may also be the means of introducing another and very pernicious form of corruption. In France, before the Revolution of 1848, in the United States, and in some of our own Colonies, it has been matter of loud complaint that the appropriations made by the Legislature for public works have been often determined upon with less regard to the general good of the whole community, than to the object of purchasing parliamentary support for the Administration, or of enabling members of influence in the Legislature to secure their interest with their constituents by conferring pecuniary advantages upon them without cost to themselves. Abuses of this kind might soon spring up, and flourish as luxuriantly amongst ourselves as they have done elsewhere, if their growth were favoured by the same causes; and amongst these I know of none so powerful as that of the Government not possessing due authority in the Legislature, together with the responsibility that accompanies it.

Ministerial responsibility may also be injuriously weakened by the multiplication of open questions; that is to say, of questions on which Members holding office are allowed to take opposite sides without resigning. It is probably impossible altogether to dispense with open questions, but they must be regarded as an evil, and the public ought to be jealous of their multiplication. Every addition to the number of such questions tends to increase the risk of having divided Administrations, and also to relieve independent Members of Parliament who aspire to office from a wholesome responsibility. The fear of embarrassing their future career, by pledging themselves to impracticable measures, is a most useful check upon the votes of those who have not the responsibility of office; and it would be highly inexpedient to diminish the force with which this motive operates, in restraining Members of the House of Commons from voting in favour of what they know to be wrong or unwise, from deference to momentary clamour.

Secondly.—It was likewise, in my opinion, an error in the Reform Act (but in the circumstances of the time an inevitable one), that it gave the whole Representation of the country to constituencies which were everywhere so much of the same character. The former distinction, with respect to the nature of the Franchise between Counties and Boroughs, was indeed kept up, but the great diversity which had prevailed in the right of voting in different Boroughs was almost entirely done away with; and in spite of some reservation of vested rights, the £10 householders were made everywhere the masters of the town representation. It has been argued, and I think with justice, that though there were obvious and decisive objections to the capricious manner in which the Franchise varied in different Boroughs under the old constitution of the House of Commons, this arrangement, with all its faults, had yet the advantage of giving a better representation to some classes of society than they now enjoy. Thus it is said that by means of Boroughs where the right of voting was in potwallopers, or freemen, the working classes were enabled to return a certain number of Members, by whom they were more truly represented than they now are. As there were not a great many of these Boroughs, no dangerous amount of power was placed in the hands of this part of the population, and the comparatively small number of Members returned by these Boroughs practically represented the class to which the voters in them belonged throughout the country. In like manner, the higher class of the town population of the whole kingdom was probably better represented than it now is, by the Members returned for towns where close corporations had the disposal of the Seats. Under the Reform Act, the £10 householders are everywhere masters of the Borough elections, and thus the middle class to which they belong is invested not with a preponderance (which it is admitted it ought to have), but with a monopoly of political power, to the injury of the working class on the one side, and of the highest class of the town population on the other.

Thirdly.—Another fault, closely connected with that I have just adverted to, which may justly be found with the reformed House of Commons, is, that it fails to afford proper facilities for the admission of some of the classes of Members who were formerly returned by the close Boroughs. I have already admitted the force of the arguments urged in favour of these Boroughs, during the debates on the Reform Bill, on the ground of their having been the means of bringing into the House of Commons many of its most useful Members; and though, from the abuses to which they had also led, I cannot doubt its having been right, or rather absolutely necessary, at that time, to abolish Boroughs of this description, it is, I think, to be regretted that this was not done in such a manner as to provide some other means of bringing into Parliament certain classes of Members whose return by the close Boroughs had been attended with advantage. We miss in the reformed House of Commons the Members who virtually represented certain special interests, and those who, occupying an independent position, and not looking for the retention of their Seats to the favour of any numerous body of constituents, were able boldly to oppose any popular delusion of the day. My remark however on the want of a substitute for the close Boroughs, as regards some of the persons they were the means of bringing into Parliament, applies chiefly to the Ministers, and to those subordinate members of the Government who hold offices requiring that they should sit in the House of Commons.

While close Boroughs existed, the Administration of the day had no difficulty in appointing the fittest persons that could be found to those situations which, according to the existing practice, must be held by Members of the House of Commons. But it has now become difficult (except perhaps at a general Election) for a Minister to find Seats in the House of Commons for persons he may wish to appoint to Parliamentary offices ; his choice, therefore, in the selection of candidates for these places, is practically limited to men who are already in Parliament, or who have the means of obtaining admission to it.   He cannot even choose freely in the House of Commons itself, since it often happens that a Member who has been returned at the preceding general Election could not vacate his Seat afterwards, with any prospect of regaining it.

There can be no doubt that much practical evil has resulted from this state of things.   In the first place, it has been an obstacle to placing important offices in the Government in efficient hands ; and, if it were not invidious to do so, there would be no difficulty in pointing out very bad appointments which have been made solely from this difficulty. It has further, on more than one occasion, caused arrangements which had been made for filling the highest posts in the public service to be disturbed by the mere caprice of some local constituency, in rejecting as their representative a person selected for one of these posts by the Crown. Ministers have sometimes been thus driven to make arrangements of very questionable propriety, in order to obtain the Seats which were necessary for the performance of their duties; and at other times, have been exposed to a pernicious local influence in the discharge of their official functions. Indeed, it is so difficult for a Minister, who represents a large body of constituents, to exercise his judgment with proper freedom and to escape altogether from being biassed by their local interests and feelings, that it appears to me very desirable, that in general the Servants of the Crown should not hold Seats of this kind. Such seems to have been the opinion of Mr. Canning, who, when he became Secretary of State for Foreign Affairs, and Leader of the House of Commons, very wisely, as I think, resigned his Seat for Liverpool, and came in for a close Borough. In like manner, it was, I believe, a great advantage to Sir Robert Peel, as a Minister, that, after the passing of the Reform Act, he sat, not for a large and populous place, but for one of the smaller Boroughs, where he possessed a commanding influence; while, on the

other hand, it was a disadvantage to Lord John
Russell, in his Ministerial career, to represent the
City of London.

It is not however with regard to Cabinet offices
that the inconvenience I am now referring to is most
felt.   These offices are usually conferred on men
already known and distinguished, and to such men
it is not often a matter of much difficulty to obtain
a Seat in Parliament.   But it is far otherwise with
regard to the persons whom it would be most desirable to select for Law Officers of the Crown, for
Under-Secretaries of State, or for any of the subordinate Parliamentary offices.   For some of these situations, it is of great importance that the Government
should be able to choose the young men of whose
talents and acquirements they may think most
highly, not only in order that the duties of these
offices may be well performed at the time, but perhaps even more for the sake of providing, for the
future, a sufficient supply of men well trained for
the highest posts of the Government.   The task of
conducting the affairs of this great Nation in Parliament is one of so much difficulty, that few men can
be expected to become fit for it without that early
training which is generally required in order to
excel in any profession.   Unless, therefore, a constant succession of young men of ability can be

brought early into public life to acquire the knowledge and habits of business it requires, we must
be prepared for its becoming hard to find fit persons to fill the highest offices in the Government.

With respect to the Law Officers of the Crown,
it is of even greater consequence that they should
be chosen with the utmost care from the whole
Profession, since, both from the nature of their
duties, and from their supposed claims to be advanced to the highest judicial offices, the vital interests of the Nation, in the due administration of
justice, are deeply concerned in the appointments
that are made. The Law Officers should always,
if possible, be men who stand in the highest esti-
mation for professional knowledge and ability, and
who are also looked up to and respected as men of
honour and integrity. But it is most improbable,
that either the young men best qualified for subordinate political offices, or the lawyers most fit to
become Attorney or Solicitor-General, will always
be found in the House of Commons. Experience
has demonstrated, that the qualities which are required for these situations are not those which
most recommend men to the favour of electors.
With regard to the Law Officers of the Crown
more especially, I fear, that the necessity of selecting them from the ranks of the House of Com-

mons has already had an injurious effect on the whole legal Profession. It has taught the Bar generally to look for advancement, less to professional distinction and to high character, than to success in the House of Commons; and as lawyers have usually little opportunity of cultivating the favour of any body of electors in the legitimate exercise of their Profession, a competition has been created to gain Seats in Parliament by other, and often objectionable means. In this respect there is a change much for the worse from what was the state of things in the times before the Reform Bill. High professional distinction could then suffice to open for those who achieved it, both the doors of the House of Commons and the way to the legal offices in the Government. When Lord Lyndhurst, who has lately closed so brilliant a Parliamentary career, attracted the attention of Lord Liverpool, who was then Prime Minister, by the great ability he had displayed in a political trial, he was not in Parliament, but he was offered and accepted a Seat for a Treasury borough, became Solicitor-General, and in a few years rose to the Woolsack. It must be regretted that in these days no Minister can possess the facilities enjoyed by Lord Liverpool for enlisting the highest talent to be found at the Bar in the service of the State.

The injury to the public service arising from its being no longer in the power of the Government to secure Seats in the House of Commons for persons appointed to Parliamentary offices, has been much aggravated by the law under which the acceptance of office vacates the Seat of a Member of Parliament. While nomination Boroughs existed, no inconvenience could be occasioned by this provision of the law, and it was not an unreasonable security against having one of the comparatively few Seats then under popular influence withdrawn from it. But since the House of Commons has been reformed there has been no longer any real occasion for this security, while the law has worked badly by frequently preventing important offices in the public service from being conferred on the persons most fit to hold them, on account of their sitting in Parliament for places where they could not be secure of their re-election. The probability of this inconvenience was foreseen while the Reform Bill was under discussion, and the expediency of guarding against it by inserting in the Bill a clause for repealing the law in question was considered; but it was judged to be imprudent to risk giving additional strength to the opponents of the measure by attempting to introduce into it an amendment so open to misrepresentation.

Fourthly.—It must also, I think, be admitted that the Reform Act has failed to do as much towards putting down corruption as was desired and expected. Many persons go further, and assert that corruption has been actually increased by that measure; but I can see no grounds whatever for supposing this to be true. Corruption I believe to have been far more general before the passing of the Reform Acts than now; the mistake of supposing the reverse to be the case, seems to have arisen from overlooking the fact, that it could formerly escape detection much more easily than it can at present. The forms of proceeding before Election Committees, till within a few years, were such as to throw the greatest difficulty in the way of proving bribery, even in flagrant cases; whereas, by recent changes in the Law, the principle of using the most searching means to inquire into alleged corruption has been carried almost to an extreme. Many of the corrupt transactions of former days were also different in kind from what take place now; the sale of Boroughs by their proprietors, for instance, was practised openly and avowedly; and, though there is scarcely an instance of its attracting the notice or censure of Parliament, it was certainly not less corrupt than the sale of their votes by individual electors. The only difference between the two transactions is that in the one case the purchaser of the Seat bought it in gross from an individual proprietor, whereas in the other, he buys it in detail from the several persons among whom the right of disposing of it is shared. Perhaps the wholesale purchase was the most dangerous of the two, since in that case it not unfrequently happened that the Government was the buyer, and paid the price of the Seats in honours or in jobs. It is true that the owners of Boroughs often insisted on the purchasers of the Seats being of the same politics with themselves; but this was by no means the invariable practice, nor can it be regarded as altering the character of the transaction, even when it was followed. In many of the most corrupt Boroughs, the voters habitually accept in preference the bribes of candidates of their own Party, but it has never been held that they thus escape the guilt of corruption. But though corruption may have been considerably checked, as I believe that it has been, by the passing of the Reform Act, it would be absurd to pretend that it has been put down, or that the Measure has in this respect been as successful as was hoped.

Lastly. — The Reform Acts of 1832 were advisedly, and, as I think, wisely, framed in such a manner as to leave many anomalies and irregularities in our Representative system, and to keep within moderate limits the extension of political power to classes of the population which had not previously enjoyed it. Since those Acts were passed, the Nation has made much progress, and the state of things is greatly altered. The anomalies and irregularities still left in our Representation have thus become more striking than they were, and give greater offence, than thirty years ago, to the general sense of what is required by reason and justice. And though public opinion, I trust, recognizes (perhaps more distinctly than it did) the danger that would arise from giving a preponderance of political power to mere numbers, and the importance of securing to the most intelligent and best instructed portion of the Nation due weight in the conduct of its affairs; it seems also to recognize the want of some more effectual means for the working classes to make their opinions and feelings heard in Parliament. Hence the constitutional arrangement of 1832, when considered with reference to the circumstances of the present time, must, I think, be regarded as defective.

Such appear to me to be the chief defects, now requiring to be corrected, in our system of Representation, as it was settled by the celebrated Acts passed in 1832 ; but having freely acknowledged these faults, and not having attempted in any way to disguise or diminish them, I must conclude this Chapter as I began it, by expressing my opinion, that, in spite of its inevitable imperfections, the Measure was on the whole one of the greatest and most beneficial changes which any country ever effected in its institutions. We owe to it numberless other reforms, including the correction of abuses which were eating into the very vitals of the Nation, which nothing short of this alteration in the constitution of the House of Commons would have rendered it possible to extirpate, and which, if allowed to continue, must have led to some frightful convulsion ; we owe to it also more than a quarter of a century of domestic peace, and of the greatest prosperity and progress which as a Nation we have ever enjoyed.

It may justly be regarded as having been the means, under Providence, of securing these blessings to the country ; not merely because the Reformed Parliament has passed measures and supported a policy which could not have been looked for from the unreformed House of Commons, but also because the confidence of the People, which had been withdrawn from the latter, has been freely given to the former. This confidence has

K

given it strength, both for legislation and for
giving support to the Executive Government.
Some of the most useful Acts passed since 1832
would hardly have been accepted by the Nation
from a Parliament in which it did not feel that it
was really represented, even if such a Parliament
could have been induced to adopt them. And in
1848, amidst the crash of the old Governments of
Europe and of the revolutionary passions then
let loose, the Constitution and the Throne could
hardly have maintained their stability in this country, to the astonishment and admiration of the
world, if the great Measure of 1832 had not been
successful in recovering for the Legislature the
previously alienated affection and confidence of the
People.

It is quite consistent with holding this opinion,
as to the merits and beneficial results of the Reform Act, to believe that it has faults which it
would be highly desirable to remedy. Time, and
those changes which are always going on in every
human society, have rendered its original imperfections more obvious, and more injurious to the
working of our Government, than they were in
the first instance. I believe these imperfections to
be capable of being in some cases removed, and in
others diminished; but I am persuaded that the

utmost caution will be necessary in attempting to correct them, lest changes should be introduced, which, though plausible, and not perhaps apparently involving any departure from the principles of our Constitution, would yet be found, in practice, to obstruct the working of the complex machine of our Government.

CHAPTER VI.

THE REFORM BILLS OF 1859 AND 1860.

In the last Chapter, I have endeavoured to show that while the Parliamentary Reform of 1832 has been proved by its results to have been a wise and salutary measure, it was yet by no means free from faults. These, though far less serious than might have been expected from the circumstances under which it was passed, it would still be highly desirable to correct; I will therefore proceed to inquire whether it is probable that they would be cured or diminished, and that the constitution of the House of Commons would be really improved, by the passing of such a measure of Reform as either of those proposed by two successive Governments in the years 1859 and 1860. I will also inquire whether any changes of a different kind can be suggested which would be more likely to answer this purpose. In entering upon this inquiry, the first point to be considered is what we ought to look for in any Reform Bill.

It will, I presume, be universally admitted that the ultimate object of any measure of Parliamentary Reform should be to provide for the better government of the Nation, and to promote the welfare of the People at large. This indeed seems to be so clear, that it would scarcely have been worth while making the remark, were it not that the majority of the speakers who took part in the debates in Parliament on the Reform Bills of 1859 and 1860, showed themselves strangely apt to lose sight of so obvious a truth. Yet it is one which cannot be too steadily borne in mind, as affording our only safe guide in judging of plans for Reform, and as leading to the very important conclusion, that no measure of the kind ought to be adopted, either for the sake of gratifying a love of change, or for the purpose of bringing our constitution into more strict conformity with abstract notions of what it ought to be. For it is a trite remark, that Constitutions framed according to the speculative views of political philosophers have generally failed in practice; while, on the other hand, whatever may be the defects and anomalies of the British Constitution, it has secured to those who have the happiness to live under it, a larger measure of the blessings of real freedom and good government, than has been enjoyed by any other nation in the world for an equal period of time. The verdict of the best political writers, not only of our own, but of other countries, is almost unanimous upon this point.   I do not mean from hence to argue that all attempts to improve our Constitution, or correct its faults, are to be condemned; for I am well aware how true it is, that in human affairs to remain stationary is impossible, and that where improvement ceases, decay is sure to begin. But I do contend that, from the general failure of speculative Constitutions, and the comparative success of our own, we are entitled to infer that no changes should be admitted in a form of Government of which the results have on the whole been so good, except those called for by defects which have been practically felt in its working; and that, in seeking to correct even defects of this kind, we should take experience for our guide, cautiously avoiding the introduction of any alterations in our Constitution that are not in harmony with its principles, or that are calculated to derange its balance.   This caution is the more necessary, because

"There is some soul of goodness in things evil,
Would men observingly distil it out."

And even some of the most faulty parts of our present system of Representation incidentally serve useful purposes, good being so closely combined with evil in their results, that care is required lest we should lose the one in trying to get rid of the other. Nor ought it to be forgotten that, while no perfect Government ever has existed, or ever will exist, on earth, those Constitutions which have been most successful in practice, and especially our own, seem to have been partly indebted for their success to the fact that their opposite defects have, as it were, counterbalanced each other; so that, by correcting faults of one kind, without applying any remedy to those which act in an opposite direction, the equilibrium necessary for the safe working of the machine might be destroyed.

I hold, therefore, that in bringing forward any measure of Parliamentary Reform, its authors ought to be able to show that it has been suggested by experience, not by abstract speculation or a mere unreasoning desire for change; and that it is strictly consistent with the principles of our present Constitution, and is not calculated to derange its balance, or to interfere with its working. I would add, that no such measure can be considered worthy of acceptance unless it also affords a reasonable prospect of effecting a settlement of the question not likely to be very speedily again disturbed, at least so far as regards its main provisions. This is an essential condition of a good measure, because experience has shown that the habit of making frequent changes of this sort is one of the most dangerous which a people can acquire, and that nothing is more fatal to good Government and to the prosperity of a nation, than the constant agitation of questions as to the form of its Institutions. These questions are of so exciting a nature, that, while they are agitated, they absorb men's attention to the exclusion of all practical measures; and, while the construction of the machine by which the Country is to be governed is in debate, there is little leisure for considering how it is governed in the meantime by that which actually exists.

One of the first requisites also for a good Government is that it should possess that authority and moral force which nothing but a general assurance of its stability and permanence can confer; and the power of commanding the prescriptive reverence and confidence of its subjects which a Government derives from long duration in the same form, is an element of wholesome strength, of which it is impossible to supply the place, or overrate the value. Frequent changes in the Institutions of a nation prevent its Government from ever acquiring this strength, and render it impossible that a belief in the permanence of the authority they are called upon to obey, should take root in the minds of the people. Such changes also prevent the growth of that love of a nation for its Institutions, which may in a certain sense be called unreasoning, inasmuch as those who feel it would seldom be able to give a clear and precise reason for it, but which, as a popular sentiment, is of the highest importance, and when based on long experience, strictly conformable to reason.   As evils, and even great evils, must be suffered by the people under any form of Government, when that which is established among them is not supported by traditional feelings of reverence and love, they are apt to refer to it their inevitable sufferings, and to seek for an improvement in their condition from political revolutions.   They become afflicted with a restlessness like that of a sick man, who imagines that every change of position is to bring relief. ·

Hence ambitious and discontented men (such as are to be found in all countries) have a great advantage in attacking Institutions which have but lately taken the place of some other system of government, and which it is therefore believed may in their turn be made to give way to some newer scheme. Thus every fresh organic change in the government of a country tends to increase the difficulty of resisting the next which may be proposed: and there is the utmost danger that where such changes succeed each other rapidly, they may become more and more violent, and be attended with fiercer contests for power as they proceed, until at length the Nation is driven to submit to an authority resting upon force alone. The events of English history between 1640 and 1660, and those which have taken place in France from 1789 up to the present time, are full of instruction as to the process by which a nation, when it ceases to have respect for long-established authority and for prescription, may be brought into a state in which it can only be governed by a military despotism, and in which it becomes difficult, amidst the conflict of opinions and passions, to create any stable Government whatever.

Assuming that I have correctly described what is required to constitute a good Reform Bill, it will not be difficult to show that these conditions were far from being fulfilled by either of the measures submitted to Parliament in the Sessions of 1859 and 1860. The two Bills were essentially of the same character, the main object of both having been to increase the number of persons entitled to vote in the election of Members of Parliament, and to transfer some seats from small to large Constituencies.   The one would have carried these changes further than the other, but the limit assigned to them was in both cases arbitrary.

With respect to the Franchise, the principle adopted by the authors of both measures (if I rightly understand their language) was that the right of voting is of itself so great an advantage to the possessor, that justice requires its being extended to all to whom it can be granted without danger, while it was at least implied, that their unfitness to exercise the privilege requires to be proved, in the case of all to whom votes are refused.   Adopting this principle, both Bills proposed that the existing franchise should be considerably extended; but both at the same time recognized the necessity of maintaining a qualification for voters which might prevent the indiscriminate admission of the whole population to the exercise of political power.   The Bill of 1859 provided, with this view, that the existing qualifications from the possession or occupation of property should continue without being lowered; but by making the franchise the same in counties and in boroughs, it would have added the £10 occu-

piers of houses to the constituencies of the former;
and the forty-shilling freeholders to those of the
latter, and it would further have given the right
to persons possessed of a certain sum of money in
the Savings-banks, and to some other classes holding positions in society which were considered to
afford a presumption of their fitness to enjoy the
privilege of voting.   The contemptuous nickname
of the "fancy franchises" was somewhat unfairly
given to the rights of voting it was proposed thus
to create.   The Bill of 1860 was simpler in its
provisions; it merely lowered the household qualification in towns from £10 to £6, and gave £10
occupiers, under certain conditions, the right of
voting in counties.

Of these rival schemes, the first appears to be at
least the most logical and consistent with itself,
whatever may be the objections to it in other respects.   Assuming that fitness to exercise the
privilege ought to carry with it the possession of
a vote, it proposed that the same tests of this
fitness should be adopted in boroughs and in
counties, on the ground that these tests are equally
applicable in the one and in the other.   Again,
assuming that the possession or occupation of property, or of a house of a certain value, is a test,
though an imperfect one, of the intelligence and

independence which ought to qualify a man to
vote, it would have attempted to correct the defi-
ciency of this test, not by reducing the value of
the occupation which now confers the right, but by
creating new franchises to meet the case of persons
who are really well qualified to become electors,
without being the owners or occupiers of property,
under the conditions now necessary for acquiring
a vote. This mode of dealing with the question
was apparently suggested by the consideration, that
the fault of the existing qualification is not that
it is too high, but that it is uncertain. The possession of a forty-shilling freehold, or the occupation of a £10 house, can afford at best only a presumption that a man is sufficiently intelligent
and independent to be properly trusted with a
vote, and unfortunately it is a presumption which
is by no means to be relied upon. There are
notoriously many who become voters under both
these qualifications who have little claim to the
franchise from their character. On the other hand,
there are also many who are perfectly well fitted
by their character for the enjoyment of political
power, who do not obtain votes under the existing
law, and would still fail to do so if the present
franchise were only altered by being lowered, but
who might be admitted by the creation of the pro-

posed new qualifications. These reasons in favour
of the mode of regulating the franchise proposed by
the Bill of 1859 can by no means be regarded as
destitute of force ; but, on the other hand, there
was weight also in the objection, that taken altogether, the arrangements contemplated by that
Bill would have afforded dangerous facilities for
the creation of fictitious votes, and also for the
establishment of an undue control over the smaller
boroughs by great landholders.

The scheme for the extension of the franchise
proposed in 1860 was, as I have said, simpler than
that of the year before, but it was certainly less
consistent with itself, and one for which it was far
more difficult to assign grounds which will stand
examination. While its authors declared it to be
the principle of the measure, that none who are fit
for the exercise of political power should be excluded from its enjoyment, they were asked in vain
to show how this rule could be consistent with
giving the right of voting to £6 householders in
towns, but only to those whose holdings were of
the value of £10 in counties. This inconsistency,
it was argued, would be the more flagrant, because
house-rents being usually much higher in towns
than in the country, a £6 house in a rural district will generally be a very superior residence to

one of the same value in a borough, and be occupied by a person of a higher position in society. It was also repeatedly pointed out during the debates, that, under these provisions of the Bill, it would constantly happen that the inhabitants of one part of a street would be entitled to claim votes in a borough as occupying houses of £6 value, while their immediate neighbours in the same street, occupying houses of precisely the same description, would be excluded from the privilege because they were on the other side of the arbitrary line dividing the borough from the county.

Nor was any satisfactory explanation given of the reasons for extending the right of voting to the occupiers of houses of £6 instead of £10 value in boroughs. Yet such an explanation is certainly needed, if the principle of regarding the value of his house as a proper test of a man's fitness to be entrusted with a vote is to be retained at all. There is no difficulty in understanding the grounds upon which the Reform Act of 1832 proceeded in granting the borough franchise to every occupier of a house worth £10 a year who paid rates and taxes. The occupation of such a house, together with the fulfilment of the conditions required, was considered, reasonably enough, to afford a strong presumption that a man must hold a position in society, and be likely to have received an education, which would render him fit for the discharge of political duties. But by alterations in the law, and by judicial decisions which have taken place since 1832, the definition of a householder has been so extended, that it may now, in many cases, include the mere occupier of a single room at a weekly rent; the personal payment of rates and taxes is no longer necessary, but a constructive rating and payment of rates through the landlord are sufficient to found a claim to vote. Nor is this claim defeated by the fact, that the person who makes it may repeatedly change his abode during the year he must reside in a borough before he can be registered as a voter; he may move from one dwelling to another as often as he pleases without interfering with his claim, provided certain notices are given to the parish officers. The legal right to be placed on the register of voters, is not generally made use of by the lowest class of those who possess it by the law as it stands, unless when the agents of some political party undertake to put in the claim for them, and to give the notices required to establish it. The right nevertheless exists; and if in future it should be made to depend on the occupation of a £6 instead of a £10 house, the legal definition of a house, and the conditions on which a vote is admitted remaining the same as at present, a man who pays a rent of two shillings and fourpence a week for a room will be enabled to establish his right to vote in any borough (where the "Small Tenements Act" has been adopted) in which he has resided rather more than a year.* Considering that in London, and in the largest towns, the most miserable room in a house divided into tenements, is seldom let for less than half-a-crown a week, it can scarcely be contended that the proposed new franchise would have afforded any test whatever of the fitness for political power of those who might have claimed votes under it; nor is it easy to understand upon what grounds votes granted to such claimants could be refused to any portion of the population.

Both the Bills, besides providing for the exten-

---

* See the evidence taken by the Committee appointed by the House of Lords in 1860, to inquire what would be the probable increase of the number of Electors in the Counties and Boroughs in England and Wales from a reduction of the Franchise, and especially the evidence of Mr. S. Smith. But since the above statement was written, my attention has been called to a very recent decision of the Court of Common Pleas, in the case of Cook v. Humber, which may render it more difficult for the occupants of part of a house to acquire the franchise, than it was under the law as it was previously understood.

L

sion of the franchise in the way I have described, proposed to make some change in the manner in which the right of returning Members to Parliament is now distributed among different Constituencies. This question was dealt with precisely in the same manner by the two measures, except that the one carried the proposed change further than the other. Both abstained from the entire disfranchisement of any place now entitled to return Members to Parliament, but deprived some of the smaller boroughs of half the privilege they at present enjoy, and provided that they should each elect in future one Member of the House of Commons instead of two. The first Bill proposed to deal thus with fifteen, the second with twenty-five small boroughs, for the purpose of obtaining a like number of Seats for larger Constituencies. In both cases, the transfer of Seats was made simply on the ground that ' the Constituencies to be deprived of a part of their privilege were small, and that the Seats they were to lose were wanted for larger ones; no imputation whatever being cast on the places which were to be thus partially disfranchised. The proposed transfer was therefore a practical adoption of the principle that the present inequality of the distribution of the right of returning Members to Parliament, as compared to the importance of the several Constituencies, ought at least to be diminished. Such a recognition of this principle was exceedingly important, although its application was for the moment limited to a few Seats; and although the authors of the two Bills agreed in strenuously maintaining that the small boroughs ought to be preserved, and that no general plan for dividing the Country into new electoral districts ought to be accepted.

Except as to the extension of the franchise and the partial re-distribution of Seats, the Reform Bills of 1859 and 1860 contained no provisions of importance. Those of their clauses which were not directed to these objects, related only to minor matters; and neither Bill even professed to attempt the correction of any of those defects in the reformed House of Commons, which in a previous Chapter I have endeavoured to show that experience has brought to light.

From this description of the measures in question, it will be seen that they were entirely wanting in the qualities which I have pointed out as being, in my judgment, required in a Bill of Parliamentary Reform. They would have had no tendency, so far as I can perceive, to improve the House of Commons as an instrument for securing the good government of the Country; since there is no ground for supposing that the fifteen or twenty-five Seats it was proposed to take from the smallest boroughs would have been filled under the new arrangement by more useful Members than at present, and there is still less reason for believing that the increase of the number of electors would have improved the general character of the Members returned, either by counties or by boroughs. The best that was to be hoped was, that the addition to the existing Constituencies of a large number of voters of a lower rank in life than most of those who now possess the privilege, might not lead to a worse choice of Representatives being made for the future.

Perhaps it may be said that the object of these Bills was not so much to improve the composition of the House of Commons, as to give it a greater hold upon the confidence of the People, by enabling a larger proportion of the population to have a voice in choosing its Members, and to remove a sense of injustice created by the present state of the representation. I am far from denying that, if the House of Commons could be proved to fail in commanding the confidence of the great body of the People, in consequence of their not having sufficient influence in its election, this would be a legitimate reason for a change of system, even though the House, as now constituted, might not have shown itself wanting either in intelligence or honesty of purpose; since to give expression to the wishes and feelings of the nation is not less one of its duties than to pass good laws, and to exercise a wise superintendence over the Executive Government. A Reform of Parliament, however, proposed on grounds of this kind ought not to be accepted without even more caution than one intended to correct practical abuses in legislation and in government; and, above all, unless it can be shown that the measure recommended is calculated to answer the object it has in view, by removing the feeling of discontent which has made it necessary, instead of being likely to become the beginning of a series of changes. Far from their having been satisfactory in this respect, it was the great fault of the Bills I have been considering, that neither of them afforded the slightest ground for expecting that its passing would have effected a settlement of the question even for a single year. On the contrary, they could not have been better contrived to act as mere stepping-stones to further changes, had such been their design. What they would have done, and what they would have left undone, would have alike contributed to make them answer that purpose. They would have

tended to increase the number of Members of the
House of Commons prepared to support further
changes, and yet would have failed to satisfy any
of the sincere advocates of such measures. They
would have involved a practical admission of the
principles on which the most plausible objections
to the present constitution of the House of Commons are founded, and yet would have failed to
correct, or even to diminish, the anomalies from
which these objections are drawn.*

Such a recognition of their principles would
have been especially valuable to the Radical party
with reference to their great object—the correction
of the present inequality of the different Constituencies which enjoy the right of returning Members to Parliament. Even now it is not very easy
to answer Mr. Bright when he contends that it is
contrary to all reason and justice, to give the same
weight in the House of Commons to the county of
Rutland as to one of the divisions of Yorkshire,
to Calne as to Salford. But it would be far more
difficult to defend the distribution of Seats as it
would have been left, if either of the Bills of 1859

---

* These anomalies would indeed have been rather aggravated than
diminished, since the Constituencies which are already too large
would have been greatly increased by the proposed alteration of
the Franchise, while it would have made a comparatively slight addition to those which are too small.

or 1860 had been passed, and if Parliament had thus given its sanction to the principle of taking away the right of returning Members to the House of Commons now enjoyed by small Constituencies, in order to confer it upon large ones. After the ground of prescription in favour of the existing arrangements had been thus abandoned, and after an Act of the Legislature had recognized the propriety of altering these arrangements, with the view of rendering the share of Parliamentary power enjoyed by the inhabitants of different parts of the kingdom less unequal, it would have been impracticable long to maintain the arbitrary line by which it was proposed to limit the extent of change in this direction.

Little doubt can therefore be entertained that the passing of either of these Bills must have been followed at no long interval of time by further alterations, which would either at once, or by a few short steps, have effected a complete redistribution of the right of returning Members to Parliament, in such a manner as to make the number of Seats assigned to each Constituency bear a near proportion to its importance. But such a redistribution of Seats, even though unaccompanied by any further extension of the franchise than these Bills contemplated, would have been quite sufficient, under the arrangements they proposed, to change the whole character of our Constitution, by converting the House of Commons into a body representing the numerical majority of the population.

The danger that the adoption of either of the schemes of Parliamentary Reform lately proposed, would have proved only the first step towards an alteration of this sort in the character of the House of Commons, would probably have excited more alarm than it did, were it not that the fears entertained as to the probable effects of the Reform Act of 1832 have turned out to be so groundless. The event has signally falsified the predictions of the opponents of that great measure, that it would inevitably lead to further changes subversive of the Constitution, and it is hastily inferred that we may therefore dismiss from our minds any apprehension of such consequences from much smaller measures.   In truth, we ought rather to come to the very opposite conclusion, since the policy of these last measures was the direct reverse of that which had previously been successful.   The avowed object of the first Reform Bill was to accomplish a great change in the distribution of political power in the Nation, on the ground that the working of the House of Commons, as it was previously constituted, had proved such a change to be absolutely necessary for the public good. The unreformed House of Commons had for many years shown by its conduct that it was not sufficiently under the influence of public opinion, and that it was habitually biassed by the selfish interests of those who returned a majority of its Members, to the injury of the Nation at large. This evil the Reform Bill was designed to correct, and its authors declared that one of their main reasons for making the measure so large, was that they hoped by doing so to give permanence to the settlement of the Constitution, which it was intended to effect. They believed that it was so framed as to satisfy the great majority of honest Reformers, to secure the better government of the Country for the time to come, and thus to guard against the danger they foresaw, that a first change in the Constitution might become the prelude to further and more dangerous changes in the sequel. The justice of these anticipations, and the wisdom of this policy, have been established by the result. The Reformed House of Commons has proved to be an effectual instrument for promoting better legislation and the better government of the Nation; while at the end of more than thirty years the settlement of the Constitution accomplished in 1832 remains essentially undisturbed.

The Reform Bills of 1859 and 1860 had very different objects, and were founded upon very different views. They were not brought forward on the ground that a change in the distribution of political power was necessary in consequence of great abuses in the Government; on the contrary, the authors of these measures distinctly admitted that the House of Commons, as now constituted, has worked well, and, instead of professing to have framed them so as to guard against the danger of frequent changes in the Constitution, by accomplishing at once all that is required, and thus giving satisfaction to the majority of Reformers, their great argument in favour of their Bills was that they would be so moderate that they would be free from danger. But this boasted moderation implied that they were so obviously incomplete as to afford no standing-ground for maintaining the arrangement they proposed to effect, and was thus in itself a source of danger. Indeed, there is, perhaps, nothing we ought to fear so much as what is called a very moderate measure, since it is only by successive steps, beginning with some measure of this character, that there is any probability of an ultra-democratic character being ever given to our Constitution. The sense of the Nation would be delcared so decidedly against such

a change, if proposed directly, that there can be
no doubt that it would be rejected.   But a series
of measures, each apparently of no great consequence, might accomplish by degrees what would
be scouted if proposed at once.   Their moderation,
as it was called, was therefore the reverse of a recommendation of the Bills of 1859 and 1860, and
only served to render either of them well fitted to
become the first step (proverbially the most difficult) in that slippery descent which leads to complete Democracy.

It is by this process that complete Democracy
has generally been established in those nations
where it has gained the ascendancy.   M. de Tocqueville has pointed out that, in the first years of
the independence of the United States, there was
far from being that complete and unbalanced
ascendancy of the Democratic principle, either in
the Constitutions of the separate States or in that
of the General Government, which he found existing when he visited America; and that it was by
successive changes, each preparing the way for that
which was to follow, that this alteration in the
character of the Government was accomplished.
He has justly remarked, that when a nation once
enters upon this course of gradual change, especially with respect to the extension of the franchise,

it is scarcely possible for it to stop, or to find ground on which a permanent stand can be made, till every restriction on Democratic power has been swept away.

We have for the present escaped from taking the first steps in such a downward career by the failure of the Reform Bills of 1859 and 1860, but the same causes which induced two successive Administrations of opposite parties to bring forward these Bills, may again lead to the introduction of another of the same character, and perhaps with a different result. It is a question therefore deserving the most serious consideration, whether the transfer of supreme political power to the numerical majority of the People (to which the passing of such a measure would manifestly tend) would be likely to promote the welfare and happiness of the Nation. For my own part, I regard it as not in the slightest degree inconsistent with a firm attachment to free Institutions and to popular liberty, to express my conviction that such a change in the character of our Government would be one of the greatest misfortunes that could befall the Country. I believe that it would prove injurious to all classes of society, and perhaps to none more than to that which might seem at first to be the most direct gainer by it.

The mere possession of political power is of itself no advantage to the People at large; indeed,
it is impossible that such power should be directly
exercised by the People of a great Nation.   Under
the most Democratic Constitution it must be dele-
gated, either avowedly or virtually, to a few individuals.   The privilege of choosing these holders
of power, is all that such a Constitution can even
profess to confer upon the People; and it has been
found that there is no security that this privilege
shall be more than a delusion.   Dexterous management almost invariably gives the real control of
elections, under a system of Universal Suffrage and
Vote by Ballot, to small knots of irresponsible and
unscrupulous intriguers, and often enables them to
impose upon the community rulers who possess its
confidence as little as they deserve it.   Thus, a few
years ago there was seen in California the extraordinary spectacle of an armed insurrection of the
inhabitants virtually deposing the authorities of
the State so elected by themselves, in order to
execute the decisions of a self-constituted Vigi-
lance Committee.

The possession of political power is valuable to
the People, not for its own sake, but as the means
of ensuring good Government; their real interest,
therefore, is not that they should have the largest

possible share of power, but that they should have
such a measure of it, and that the Government
should be so constituted, as to afford them the
best security for its being well conducted. And
a Government is to be considered as well conducted when wise laws are passed and impartially
enforced ; when public employments are placed in
the hands of honest and capable men; when the
relations of the State with foreign nations are managed with firmness, in a conciliatory spirit and
with a regard for justice; and when every member of the community is effectually protected
against wrong from any quarter, without unnecessary interference with the freedom of thought or
action on the part of individuals, or undue or unequal pressure of taxation.

A Government is to be considered better or
worse in proportion as it more or less perfectly
fulfils these conditions; and adopting this as the
test, good government has not been found, either
in ancient or in modern times, to be the result of
extreme Democracy, any more than of Oligarchy or
of Despotism. The great political philosophers of
antiquity formed, as we know, a highly unfavourable judgment of the nature and effects of unbalanced Democracy from what had been observed
when they wrote, of the working of Governments

of this character. Though it has of late become
the fashion among some political speculators to
treat the works of these authors as no longer
worthy of attention, I believe that the results of
their experience are still well deserving of the
consideration so long paid to them, and that their
writings contain lessons of wisdom not less applicable to our days than to theirs. The discovery
that the People may act through their representatives, instead of directly, in public affairs, has
indeed removed one of the difficulties which in
ancient times obstructed the working of purely Democratic Governments, and rendered them only
practicable on a small scale ; but I see no reason
for supposing that the nature of this kind of
Government is altered, from its being carried into
operation on a much larger scale by the machinery of representative bodies. On the contrary,
there is an almost marvellous resemblance between
the characteristics of Democratic Governments in
ancient and modern times, considering how completely the state of society is changed. In France,
and in some other European countries, those brief
periods during which unrestricted Democracy has
obtained the ascendancy in the last seventy years,
have afforded examples of abuses and excesses,
singularly like those which are described as having

followed Democratic revolutions in ancient times, and have led much in the same manner to the the extinction, for a time at least, of political liberty.

But the United States of America, which afford such an instructive lesson as to the process by which complete Democracy may be established in a Nation, afford also the best example of its working. And much as it was the custom of the admirers of Democracy to boast of its success in the United States before the breaking out of the present civil war, I can discover much less to recommend this system of Government than to warn us against it, in the experience of that great Republic.* Up to the time of the violent disruption of the United States, their Government had indeed proved highly favourable to the material prosperity of the Nation, to its being preserved from the undue pressure of taxation, and to the accumulation of wealth. Even in these respects it may well be questioned whether it had been really superior to

* Even during their highest prosperity the vices of the Government of the United States, and the consequences to which they would probably lead, were perceived by some observers. In the 'Life and Correspondence of Southey,' there is a letter written by him so long ago as November 16, 1833, in which he says:—" The time cannot be far distant when the United States of America, instead of being held up to us as an example, will be looked to as a warning."— Vol. vi. p. 233.

the Government of this Country since the passing
of the Reform Act, if we take into consideration
the burthen of Local and State taxes, as well as of
those imposed by Congress, and also the advantage
the American Union had enjoyed from its large extent of unoccupied territory, and from its geographical position, which had given it little temptation
or opportunity to engage in expensive wars, such
as those of which the charges are still the cause
of so large a part of our public burdens.   Granting, however, that the Government of the United
States had been highly favourable to the material
prosperity of the People so long as the Union was
maintained entire, it would be difficult to show in
what other particular it answered the description
of a good Government.   Far from having tended
to throw power into the hands of the best and
wisest members of the community, it was matter
of general and just complaint that the system
which prevailed practically excluded the most honest and enlightened citizens of the United States
from all share in the Government, and even from
the exercise of any influence in the conduct of
public affairs.   For many years both Legislative
and Executive power had been completely en-
grossed by those who had least scruple in flattering the passions of the mob, and most skill in the

M

arts of intrigue.   The effects of this were manifest in the character and conduct both of the Executive Government and of the Legislature.   With respect to the latter, it is notorious that the proceedings of Congress and of the State Legislatures have been alike remarkable for their habitual coarseness and vulgarity, and have sometimes even been disgraced by scenes of actual violence.*

* " Lorsque vous entrez dans la salle des Représentants à Washington, vous vous sentez frappé de l'aspect vulgaire de cette grande assemblée.   L'œil cherche en vain dans son sein un homme célèbre. Presque tous ses membres sont des personnages obscurs dont le nom ne fournit aucune image à la pensée: Ce sont pour la plupart des avocats de village, des commerçants, ou même des hommes appartenant aux dernières classes.   Dans un pays où l'instruction est presque universellement répandue, on dit que les représentants du peuple ne savent pas toujours écrire."—Démocratie en Amérique, vol. i. p. 284 (13th edition).

Horace Greeley, in a letter in the ' Tribune,' describing the usual proceedings of the House of Representatives, says that a person having made his way to the gallery " can only look down on the noisy Bedlam below him, somebody speaking and nobody listening ; but a buzz of conversation, the trotting of boys, the walking about of Members, the writing and folding of letters, calls to order, cries of question, calls for ' yeas ' and ' nays,' etc., give him large opportunities for headache—meagre ones for edification.   Half an hour will usually cure him of all passion for listening to debates in the House.   There are, of course, occasions when it is a privilege to be here, but I speak of the general scene and impression.

" To-day, but more especially yesterday, a deplorable spectacle has been presented here—a glaring exemplification of the terrible growth and diffusion of office-begging.   The Loco-Foco house has ordered a clean sweep of all its underlings—door-keepers, porters, mes-

Their measures also have shown little trace of an enlightened desire to promote the welfare of the Nation at large, but, on the contrary, seem to have had for their object to gratify the short-sighted selfishness of those who have succeeded in acquiring the chief influence in these assemblies. Nothing can afford a more striking instance of this than the commercial and financial Legislation of Congress, and it is curious to observe the contrast which it presents to the measures of our own Parliament on similar subjects.   In our Parliament, public opinion,—that is, the opinion, not of mere numbers, but of the enlightened and educated part of the Nation, has been strong enough to enforce the application of sound political science in matters of finance and trade.   It has swept away all Protection, and has provided for raising

sengers, wood-carriers, etc, etc.   I care nothing for this so far as the turned-out are concerned ; let them earn a living like other folks ; but the swarms of aspirants that invaded every avenue and hall of the Capitol, making doubly hideous the dissonance of its hundred echoes, were dreadful to contemplate.   Here were hundreds of young boys, from twenty down to twelve years of age, deep in the agonies of debasing earwigging and button-holding, talking of the services of their fathers or brothers to ' the party,' and getting Members to intercede for them with the appointing power.   The new doorkeeper was in distraction, and had to hide behind the Speaker's chair, where he could not be hunted except by proxy."— *H. Greeley's Life*, p. 246.

the revenue required for the public service by
taxes, which are admitted to be on the whole wise
and not needlessly burdensome to the People. But
while public opinion was able to do this in England, contrary to the wishes, and contrary to the
supposed interests of that landed Aristocracy which
is said to possess an undue power in Parliament,
and to abuse it for the oppression of the Nation,
Congress, on the contrary, continued to maintain
the very narrowest system of Protection ; and no
man having the slightest knowledge of the subject
could doubt that even before the monstrous
measures suggested by the civil war were adopted,
the Revenue laws of the United States were directly opposed to the first principles of political
economy, and calculated to lay a useless load on
the mass of the community for the benefit of a
few.

The Executive Government has been conducted
in a manner equally unsatisfactory. During the
half-century preceding the civil war, the bearing
of the United States towards other Nations was
marked by habitual arrogance, and a too frequent
disregard for the obligations of truth or justice.
Had any European Power acted in the same spirit,
it could hardly, even for a single year, have escaped
from being involved in war. The whole system

of internal administration during the same period
was one of notorious corruption.   Patronage was
avowedly exercised, not for the public good, but for
the sole purpose of serving the interests of the do-
minant party ; the shameless maxim, that " to the
victors belong the spoils " having been acted upon
each time that a new President came into office, by
the dismissal of the whole body of public servants,
down even to the village postmasters and the lowest officers of customs, for the purpose of giving
their places to those who had taken an active part
in the election that had raised the Chief Magistrate
of the Republic to power.   All the great departments
of the State were administered in a similar spirit.*

* The biographer of Horace Greeley, when speaking of the
Presidential election in which Jackson defeated Adams, says,
" Hurrah for Jackson ! carried the day.   The last of the gentlemen
of the revolutionary school retired.   The era of wire-pulling began.
That deadly element was introduced into our political system which
rendered it so exquisitely vicious that henceforth it worked to corruption by an irresistible necessity.   It is called rotation in office.
It is embodied in the maxim, ' To the victors belong the spoils.'   It
has made the word *office-holder* synonymous with the word *sneak.*
It has thronged the Capitol with greedy sycophants.   It has made
politics a game of cunning, with enough of chance in it to render it
interesting to the low crew that play.   It has made the President a
pawn, with which to make the first move,—a puppet, to keep the
people amused while their pockets are picked.   It has excluded
from the service of the State nearly every man of ability and worth,
and enabled bloated and beastly demagogues, without a ray of
talent—without a sentiment of magnanimity, illiterate, vulgar, in-

Towards the close of Mr. Buchanan's administration, an inquiry by a Committee of Congress into
the state of the Navy, brought to light the fact
that in making contracts for the Public service, the

sensible to shame,—to exert a power in this Republic which its greatest Statesmen in their greatest days never wielded."—*Greeley's Life*, p. 100. We are not, of course, to accept this description as being literally correct; it is obviously written under the influence of excited feelings, which must probably have led to a good deal of exaggeration; but, making all allowance for this, the state of things which could be viewed in this light by an American citizen must be very bad. There is also abundant other evidence as to the main fact of the general prevalence of corruption.

Mr. Baxter, in his 'America and the Americans' (page 59), speaking of several Americans having been heard to declare, "that they believed their own Government to be the most corrupt on the earth," says,—"This appears to me too strong a condemnation; but the disease prevails in the State Legislatures, and in the Councils of the various cities, just as much as at Washington. No one in New York seemed for a moment to doubt the alleged jobbery and trickery resorted to in obtaining privileges from the civic rulers. Leading men of every shade in politics, informed me that offices and favours were there openly bought and sold; that aldermen and councilmen accepted these situations for the avowed purpose of getting quickly rich; and that jobs every week were there perpetrated with impunity, which, in this country, would bring to disgrace every person connected with them. I believe that as great corruption exists in the government of that city as was ever brought to light in the days of the Stuarts; and what is more, I have heard people defend it, on the ground that in America all can, at one time or other, share in the plunder, whereas in Europe public robbery was the privilege of the few. Within the limits of the municipality murders are of frequent occurrence, prisoners constantly escape, and highway robberies are neither few nor far between; whilst the police force, in 1853, cost more than a million of dollars."

main object had been to put money into the
pockets of political partisans.   Thus, a contract for
the supply of coals was shown to have been given to
a physician, who had nothing to do with the coal
trade, who never took any part in the purchase of
the coals he was supposed to supply, but merely
signed the certificates brought to him by those
who really did so, in order to enable him to share
in the profit derived from the contract.   Among
the documents laid before this committee was a
letter addressed to the President, strongly urging
that the contract for the machinery for a steam-
sloop should be assigned to a certain firm in Phi-
ladelphia, in order to obtain their influence in the
approaching election.   There was no attempt to
disguise the object for which he was asked to give
the contract to this particular house; it was put
openly, on the ground of its being of importance in
the then state of the election, and the letter containing this request bore the President's own in-
dorsement, submitting it to the attention of the
Secretary of the Navy.

The Chief Magistrate who could deal thus with
such an application cannot have been very nice as
to political corruption, yet even he was shocked
with that which he found to prevail; and a very
remarkable letter of Mr. Buchanan's, dated Fe-

bruary 23, 1857, has been published, in which he speaks of " the disastrous influence which excessive and lavish expenditure of the Public money may exert on the character of our free institutions ;" and he goes on to complain that money from the National Treasury is "continually demanded to enrich contractors, speculators, and agents, and these projects are gilded with every allurement which can be imparted to them by ingenuity and talent. Claims which had been condemned by former decisions, and which had become rusty with age, have been again revived, and have been paid principal and interest. Indeed, there seems to be a general rush to obtain money from the Treasury on any and every pretence."

This passage alludes to a practice which seems of late years to have been introduced into the United States, by which members of Congress and of the Government combine in admitting extravagant and untenable claims of contractors and others on the Public purse, under an understanding that they are to have a share in the booty.*

* How completely carrying jobs of this and of other descriptions through Congress and the State Legislatures has become a regular art may be judged from the fact, that the cant name of " log rolling". has been invented for one of the most effective devices made use of for the purpose. It is thus explained by Mr. Tremenheere :—" The term ' log rolling' is derived from the backwoodsman's craft, and

But the most extraordinary proof of the height to which corruption had grown in the few years that preceded the Civil War is to be found in the report of a Committee of the Legislature of Wisconsin, in which it is shown that the passing of a Railway Bill had been carried by the wholesale bribery of a preceding Legislature, and of the members of the Government. The Governor of the State received the lion's share of £10,000, while his private Secretary, the Lieutenant-Governor, the Controller of the Bank, thirteen Members of the Senate, and sixty of the House of Representatives, together with the Clerks of the House, were proved each to have received sums varying from £1000 to £5000 for their assistance in passing the measure, which, it is stated, only four Members of the House of Representatives voted for without being paid. In addition to all these sums, another of £50,000 was put down in gross as having been paid to "outsiders," that is, to lobby agents, and

from the neighbourly assistance common on the outskirts of civilization. When a settler has cut down his timber, and sawn it into convenient lengths for getting it off the land, his neighbours assemble with their oxen and chains, and in a few hours drag the whole off his ' clearing.' When summoned, he is ready to do them the same turn. Political and Electioneering 'log rolling' means, therefore, ' help me in my job and I will help you in yours.' "—*Notes on Public Subjects made during a Tour in the United States and in Canada*, p. 125.

for various other undefined expenses,—to so enormous an amount was the Public plundered by the persons to whom they had entrusted the administration of their affairs.

Such corruption, and especially such an avowed disregard of all but party interests in the selection of the public servants, could not exist without affecting that first interest of society, the pure administration of justice. When first established, and up to a comparatively recent period, the Supreme Court of the United States was a tribunal which both deserved and enjoyed the highest respect. Its Judges were enlightened and honourable men, whose opinions were often quoted, and still have high authority in our own Courts. For some years before the Civil War, there had been a lamentable change for the worse in the character of this Court, owing to the manner in which vacancies in its Bench had been filled up, and its decisions had ceased to command the same confidence as in its better days. But, though the Federal Courts had fallen off, their deterioration was nothing in comparison with that of the Courts of the several States. In the Federal Courts, the Judges are still appointed by the President, with the sanction of the Senate, and hold their offices during good behaviour. But in the Courts of most

of the States, the Judges are now elected by the
People, generally for short periods, their salaries
also being in many cases voted annually by the
Assemblies. From Judges so appointed, and constantly looking forward to having soon to solicit
their re-election, it is obvious that a firm and
impartial administration of the law was not to be
looked for; we cannot therefore be surprised to find
it stated by the American newspapers (and the
assertion is confirmed by many disinterested observers), that in the United States the laws had
already, before the War, become mere cobwebs to
resist either rich men or the popular feeling of the
moment.

While the upper classes were practically excluded
from any legitimate influence in the Government of
the country, the illegitimate influence of money had
become almost irresistible, so that rich men are said
to have had little to fear from the law; and not a
few instances might be cited of its having proved still
more powerless to restrain the People when their
passions are excited.* One of these it may be worth

* "It is painful to observe that in many instances mob violence
even yet interferes with justice in the Western Republic, and that
wealth and station procure acquittals far more readily there than they
do in aristocratic England. So many American citizens admitted
and mourned over these evils to me, that I shall not occupy my space
in adducing proof." . . . "Europeans will never believe that a

while to mention, as an example of the manner in which the law may be defied under a system of Government which rests upon the principle that the will of the majority, whether right or wrong, is always to be obeyed.   In the autumn of 1858, there existed a quarantine establishment in a situation near New York, where it had been placed by the authority of the Legislature and Government of the State.   There were many villas in the neighbourhood of this quarantine establishment, to which it was considered a nuisance.   For this reason, the inhabitants of the district endeavoured to get it removed, but finding that this could not be accomplished by legal means, the course they took was to assemble in open day and burn the building to the ground.   No secret was made beforehand of the intended outrage ; on the contrary, the time when it was to be committed was openly announced.

country is really free, so long as rowdyism reigns rampant in civilized cities, and social rank, partisanship, or pecuniary bribes corrupt the fountain-head of justice.   It is mockery for citizens of these States, where punishment seldom or ever overtakes the rich, to talk of liberty and equality.   Under the shadow of ultra-democratic Governments in the other hemisphere, every year judicial decisions are given without exciting attention, so unrighteous and so strongly marked by a mean subserviency to wealth and station, that were they pronounced in monarchical Britain, no matter how high the authority, the consequences would endanger the peace of the nation, and shake the very pillars of the throne."—*Baxter's America and the Americans,* pp. 100, 101.

At the appointed hour the rioters assembled, and deliberately set fire to and destroyed the building, first removing the sick, some of whom, however, it is believed, lost their lives by exposure to the weather. The authorities took no step whatever to resist the outrage they knew to be intended, and there was a mere nominal attempt to punish the perpetrators. Legal proceedings were indeed taken against them, but are described in a local newspaper as having been a protracted farce. The result was a decision from the Bench, that, as the quarantine establishment had been presented as a nuisance by the Grand Jury, the rioters were justified in burning it down.

But, while legitimate authority was thus weak, and the Government possessed so little power to discharge its first duty of maintaining the Public peace, and protecting its subjects in the enjoyment of their legal rights, it was far from being true that men enjoyed an excess of personal freedom in the United States, even in the good days of the Republic. On the contrary, thirty years ago (and the evil increased afterwards) it was already complained by the ablest of the writers on American Institutions, that men did not enjoy under them the real liberty they ought, because the tyrannical pressure of the majority cramped the freedom of thought and action of individuals.* No graver objection than this can be brought against a system of Government, because the freedom of thought and a state of society which encourages the free utterance and discussion of conflicting opinions is

* "L'Amérique est donc un pays de liberté où, pour ne blesser personne, l'étranger ne doit parler ni des particuliers, ni de l'État, ni des gouvernés, ni des gouvernements, ni des entreprises publiques, ni des entreprises privées, de rien enfin de ce qu'on y rencontre sinon peut-être du climat et du sol; encore trouve-t-on des Américains prêts à défendre l'un et l'autre, comme s'ils avaient concouru à les former."—*Démocratie en Amérique,* vol. i. p. 284. (13th edit.)

"Je ne connais pas de pays où il règne en général moins d'indépendance d'esprit et de véritable liberté de discussion qu'en Amérique."—*Ibid.,* p. 307.

"En Amérique la majorité trace un cercle formidable autour de la pensée. Au dedans de ces limites l'écrivain est libre, mais malheur à lui s'il ose en sortir. Ce n'est pas qu'il ait à craindre un auto-da-fé, mais il est en butte à des dégoûts de tous genres, et à des persécutions de tous les jours. La carrière politique lui est fermée; il a offensé la seule puissance qui ait la faculté de l'ouvrir. On lui refuse tout, jusqu'à la gloire. Avant de publier ses opinions, il croyait avoir des partisans; il lui semble qu'il n'en a plus maintenant qu'il s'est découvert à tous; car ceux qui le blâment s'expriment hautement, et ceux qui pensent comme lui, sans avoir son courage, se taisent et s'éloignent. Il cède, il plie enfin sous l'effort de chaque jour, et rentre dans le silence comme s'il éprouvait des remords d'avoir dit vrai."—*Ibid.,* p. 308.

"Les monarchies absolues avaient déshonoré le despotisme, prenons garde que les républiques démocratiques ne le réhabilitent, et qu'en le rendant plus lourd pour quelques-uns, elles ne lui ôtent, aux yeux du plus grand nombre, son aspect odieux et son caractère avilissant."—*Ibid.,* p. 309.

the first requisite for the mental advancement of
a Nation; and Mr. Mill, in his admirable work on
Representative Government, has well observed, that
" the most important point of excellence which
any form of Government can possess is to promote
the virtue and intelligence of the people themselves," and that the merit of Political Institutions
" consists partly of the degree in which they promote the general mental advancement of the community, including under that phrase advancement
in intellect, in virtue, and in practical activity and
efficiency; and partly of the degree of perfection
with which they organize the moral, intellectual,
and active worth already existing, so as to operate
with the greatest effect on public affairs. A Government is to be judged by its action upon men,
and by its action upon things; by what it makes of
the citizens, and what it does with them; its tendency to improve or deteriorate the People themselves, and the goodness or badness of the work it
performs for them, and by means of them. Government is at once a great influence acting on the human mind, and a set of organized arrangements for
public business; in the first capacity, its beneficial
action is chiefly indirect, but not therefore less
vital, while its mischievous action may be direct."*

* Mill's ' Considerations on Representative Government,' pp. 30
and 33.

Judged by this rule, the Political Institutions of
the United States cannot be regarded as successful.
As I have endeavoured to show, they have failed
to "organize the moral, intellectual, and active
worth already existing so as to operate with the
greatest effect on public affairs;" and they have
still more conspicuously failed "to promote the
general mental advancement of the community."
For many years, the striking change for the worse
in the moral tone and character of American
Statesmen since the first days of the Republic has
been generally remarked, and the Civil War has
brought to light the lamentable fact, that this
change for the worse has extended, far more than
was previously supposed, to the People.*

* The following extract from an address delivered in 1854 by Dr.
Hopkins, Bishop of Vermont, to the convocation of Trinity College,
Hartford, United States, shows what is the opinion of an American,
of high authority from his character and position, and a great ad-
mirer of the American Constitution, as to the deterioration of the
people since its establishment.

"Those eminent sages and patriots who settled the Government
of the United States some seventy years ago, came to their task
with the knowledge and experience of the Old World to guide them.
They improved upon all their models by adopting the good and
avoiding the evil in every previous system; they struck out a new
and admirable scheme, by which each State might fully provide for
its own internal administration, while the whole were bound together in all that related to war and peace, and general commerce
and mutual rights, by a general Federal Constitution. They guarded
against despotism by making the rulers elective. They excluded

Looking to the high qualities shown by the American People in the War of Independence, I have been no less surprised than shocked by observing how differently they have borne themselves in the present struggle. The manner in which they have submitted to all that has been done by the Government since the beginning of the contest, argues a sad deterioration in the character of the Nation.

the pride of aristocracy by prohibiting all titles of nobility and the entailment of estates. They cut away the roots of religious intolerance by giving equal rights to all religious sects, and refusing a special establishment to any Church or denomination. They made the people sovereign. And by these and other provisions framed in a kindred spirit they earned the praise of being the wise master-builders of the noblest republic in the world.

"But no Government can execute itself. Theory is one thing, and practice is another. . . . How do we abide the test after seventy years of our brief experience?

"First then, we hear on every side the charge of political corruption. Bribery is practised in all our elections. The spoils of office are expected as a matter of course by the victorious party. The President of the United States dares not to be impartial; for if he were, he would lose the confidence of his friends without gaining the confidence of his enemies. The oldest statesmen and most prominent, cannot follow the dictates of their judgment and conscience without being reproached as if they were laying a trap for the Presidential chair. The very laws of Congress are set down as the results of personal venality or ambition. The House of Representatives and even the Senate Chamber are disgraced every year by fierce passion and violent denunciations. The barbarous and unchristian duel is anticipated as quite inevitable, unless it be averted by explanation which may satisfy worldly honour in utter contempt of all religious principle. And no member of either House can go to the performance of public duties with any security that he may

N

The accounts that have been published of the corruption prevailing in the departments entrusted with the conduct of the war, and of the plunder of the Public by grossly fraudulent contracts, are too clear and too well supported to leave any doubt of their truth.   And we know that the measures taken by the Government and by Congress to provide for the enormous expenditure thus incurred, have been directly contrary, not only to the first principles of Political Science, but to the plainest dictates of common sense.   We know also that personal liberty was suspended throughout the Northern States, not at first by an act of the Legis-

not be insulted by coarse invective before the day is closed.   Yet our rulers are never weary of lauding the character of Washington, as if they were quite convinced that the time had passed by when they might be expected to verify the language of praise by the act of imitation.   When we look into the other classes of the community, the same charge of venality and corruption meets us again.   Our merchants are accused of all sorts of dishonest management; our brokers, of stock-jobbing; our city aldermen, of bribery; our lawyers, of knavery; our Justices, of complicity with the guilty.   The same worship of Mammon seems to govern the whole, and the current phrase of 'the almighty dollar' is a sad but powerful exponent of the universal sin which involves the mass of our population."

The Bishop afterwards refers to the falling off in the number of candidates for the Ministry as a symptom of the decay of religion, and says,—

" The population is growing with wonderful speed, and the teachers of religion, instead of multiplying in an equal proportion, are actually less than they were twenty years ago."

lature, but by an apparently unauthorized assumption of power by the Executive Government, and that the power so assumed has been largely and arbitrarily exercised. Yet none of these things seem to have met with the disapproval of the People,—some of them have even been applauded; and the most notorious abuses have provoked no such expression of public indignation as they have deserved, and have called forth no attempt to put an end to the scandal. But the worst symptom of the demoralization of the People is the tone in which they have usually been addressed at Public Meetings, as well as in Congress and in the State Legislatures, by those who are courting their favour. To those who have not read these speeches, it would be impossible to give an idea of the depth of political ignorance, the morbid craving for the most nauseous flattery, and the unreasoning violence against all opponents, which those who could use such language must have calculated upon finding in their hearers. Nor does it seem that they have been mistaken in their calculations, judging from the applause with which their worst sallies are reported to have been received. There are grounds for hoping that the rural population has been far less corrupted by the system of government in the United States than the inhabitants of the towns.

Unfortunately, the latter appear to possess a preponderance of power.

Perhaps I may be accused of having shown a want of good feeling towards the Americans, by describing at so much length, and with so much harshness, the defects of their system of government, while they are suffering so grievously under the calamity of civil war. I can, however, truly assert that the foregoing pages have not been dictated by any want of good will to them as a People, nor do they imply any indifference to their sufferings. On the contrary, I have watched with painful interest the progress of this lamentable war, and I entertain the most earnest desire for its early termination, and for the welfare of a Nation, in which, with all its faults, I see much to admire. But I think that to expose the vices of the system of government they have adopted, is not to act an unfriendly part towards the Americans, but rather to render them a service, especially at the present time. With all its evils, the Civil War has at least this advantage, that it is likely to lead to a revision of the Political Institutions of the United States; and, if a wise reform of those Institutions (which discussion may tend to promote) should be the fruit of their present sufferings, the Americans will not have endured them in vain. Goodwill and consideration for a kindred nation did not therefore forbid my speaking freely of the character of their Government, and stating the facts which tend to prove that it has worked badly, while it was essential to my argument that I should do so.

My object in this Chapter has been to show that the adoption of either of the Reform Bills lately submitted to Parliament would have been a misfortune to the Nation, because it would have been a step, and an important step, towards altering our Constitution, by introducing the principle of giving equal political power to all the members of the community, and of placing the supreme control of the Government in the hands of the numerical majority.   But this is the very principle, which, though by no means admitted on the first establishment of the Republic, has now for many years been loudly proclaimed by the leading Statesmen of the United States, and has been fully acted upon by the Nation.   I consider it to be a principle equally unsound in theory and mischievous in practice.   It is not the mere will of the majority that ought to govern a Nation, but justice and reason.*   The measures of a Government ought,

* This is so well explained by M. Guizot, in his 'Histoire des Origines du Gouvernement Représentatif,' that I cannot forbear quoting the passage, though it is rather a long one.   Speaking of

in the first place, to be just, and in the next, to be such as to promote the true interests of the whole community. To secure justice to all, it is necessary the system of Government which gives supreme authority to the numerical majority of the People, he says :—

"Son principe est que la majorité a droit par cela seul qu'elle est majorité. Mais dans l'idée de majorité entrent deux éléments très-différents : l'idée d'une opinion qui est accréditée, et celle d'une force qui est prépondérante. Comme force, la majorité n'a aucun droit que celui de la force même, qui ne peut être, à ce titre seul, la souveraineté légitime. Comme opinion, la majorité est-elle infaillible ? suit-elle et veut-elle toujours la raison, la justice, qui sont la vraie loi et confèrent seules la souveraineté légitime ? L'expérience démontre du contraire. La majorité, en tant que majorité, ne possède donc la souveraineté légitime ni en vertu de la force, qui ne la confère jamais, ni en vertu de l'infaillibilité, qu'elle n'a point.

"Le principe de la souveraineté du peuple part de la supposition que chaque homme possède, par son droit de naissance, non-seulement un droit égal à être bien gouverné, mais encore un droit égal à gouverner les autres. . . . Le principe de la souveraineté du peuple, c'est-à-dire le droit égal des individus à l'exercice de la souveraineté, ou seulement le droit de tous les individus de concourir à l'exercice de la souveraineté, est donc radicalement faux ; car sous prétexte de maintenir l'égalité légitime, il introduit violemment l'égalité où elle n'est pas, et viole l'inégalité légitime. Les conséquences de ce principe sont le despotisme du nombre, la domination des infériorités sur les supériorités, c'est-à-dire la plus violente et la plus inique des tyrannies.

". . . Tel ne peut pas être le principe du Gouvernement Représentatif. Personne ne conteste que la vraie loi du gouvernement c'est la raison, la vérité, la justice, que nul ne possède, mais que certains hommes sont plus capables que d'autres de chercher et de découvrir. Fidèle à ce but, le Gouvernement Représentatif repose sur la répartition du pouvoir de fait, en raison de la capacité d'agir selon la raison et la justice, d'où découle le pouvoir de droit."—*Tome I.* pp. 107–109.

that no class of society should be excluded from its
due share of power, because experience teaches us
that the class so excluded would be liable to oppression.   But even if the experiment had never
been tried, we should surely have little right to
expect that placing supreme power in the hands of
the numerical majority of the population, and carefully. removing every obstacle to the accomplishment of their will so soon as it is pronounced,
would conduce to such a wise administration of a
nation's affairs as would be calculated to advance
its welfare.   In every country the working classes
must largely outnumber all the other classes of the
community united; and from the mere fact of almost their whole time being occupied by their daily
labour, it is impossible that labouring men should
in general be equally well instructed with those
who have greater advantages of fortune.   Hence,
if the conduct of the Government is to be determined by the pleasure of the numerical majority
of the population, it follows that the policy of the
Nation will be directed by those who, being the
least enlightened, are the least competent to form
a sound judgment as to what that policy ought to
be.   We might also have inferred beforehand, that
if unchecked power were given to the majority of
the People, there would not only be danger of

error from want of knowledge, but that the multitude would be exposed to the still greater danger of being led astray by men who would have an interest in deceiving them and in flattering their passions.

These conclusions as to the probable effects of a system of Government founded upon this principle, are amply confirmed by the experience both of ancient and modern times. Nowhere has that experience been so complete and so instructive as in the United States, and it is on this account that I have thought it necessary to describe somewhat at length the working of their institutions. We may hope that the impressive warning to be drawn from the results of the mode of Government adopted in the great American Republic, may, at least for some time, prevent any countenance being given in this Country to a fresh attempt to effect a change in our Constitution in the spirit of either of the Reform Bills that have happily failed. It remains to be considered whether a Reform of Parliament of a different character may not be required, and might not be accomplished, if proper means were taken for the purpose. To this inquiry I shall address myself in the next Chapter.

CHAPTER VII.

SUGGESTIONS FOR A REFORM BILL.

HAVING explained my reasons for disapproving of
the Reform Bills of 1859 and 1860, I have now
to undertake the far more difficult task of offering
some suggestions as to how a measure might be
framed which should not be open to similar objections, and which should be calculated to effect
a practical improvement in our Constitution. These
suggestions will have no pretension to being a
complete plan of Parliamentary Reform, for to
draw up such a plan would be a task to which I
have not the presumption to suppose that I should
be equal, even if I possessed the information and
the materials that would be required for its execution. All I shall attempt will be to give a general description of the kind of measure I believe
to be wanted, with an explanation of some of the
changes by which the most serious faults in our

present system of Representation might, I think, be
corrected.   Before going further, I must however
remark that a Reform Bill, in order to be a good
and safe measure, must, I am persuaded, involve
larger changes than seem to be generally contemplated.   Our experience of the two last Reform
Bills, affords convincing proof that it is impossible
to devise a satisfactory scheme for amending our
Representation, while keeping its general frame-
work unaltered.   The existing arrangements are
so complicated, and their defects and anomalies are
so bound up with what is useful in them, that no
mere patching of these arrangements, or improvements in their details, could answer.   Partial alterations would only make the faults that would be
left more glaring, and would inevitably shake the
whole fabric.   Hence, if any change whatever is to
be made, our whole system of Representation ought
to undergo a complete revision.

Nor is this opinion at all inconsistent with that
which I have expressed in the last Chapter as to its
being wise to take experience for our guide, and
to observe extreme caution in making constitutional changes.   In order to apply this rule when
we are considering how to amend an ancient Constitution, we ought carefully to distinguish between
the useful purposes which the various parts of the

Constitution have really served, and the means by which these results have been accomplished. Some changes may be suggested which, though seemingly mere modifications of existing arrangements, would make a total alteration in their effect, and in the working of the Constitution. On the other hand, there may be cases in which apparently startling innovations would really be calculated to preserve the true balance, and the former character of the Government; because, from a change of circumstances, the particular means by which certain results had been produced, may have ceased to accomplish their object, and the adoption of entirely new methods may be necessary for attaining the same ends. The guidance of experience will, in such cases, be more truly followed by introducing extensive but well-considered changes, than by only venturing upon petty ones. It is, in short, the spirit of Institutions that have been found to answer that we should endeavour to preserve, not their mere outward form.

Having guarded myself by this preliminary remark, I will proceed without further preface to consider what are the amendments it would be expedient to make in the laws under which the House of Commons is now elected; and the first question to which I will direct my attention is, whether the right of voting in the election of Members of Parliament ought, or ought not, to be more widely extended than at present? Arguments entitled to serious consideration have not been wanting on either side of this question. In favour of an extension of the Franchise, it has been urged that our existing system of Representation affords to the working classes no means of making their wishes and opinions heard with effect in the House of Commons; that there can be no doubt that a large number of persons perfectly qualified for the exercise of political power are not admitted to the right of voting, and that this exclusion is unjust; that advantage would arise from allowing a larger proportion of the community to take a part in public affairs by voting in the election of Members of Parliament, because the exercise of this power would tend to make those to whom it was granted feel a more lively interest in the concerns of the Nation, and thus exercise a useful influence on their character;—much importance is attached to political discussions as the means of promoting the intellectual and moral improvement of the working classes, while "political discussions," it is said, "fly over the heads of those who have no votes, and are not endeavouring to acquire them."*

* Mill, on Representative Government, p. 158.

On the other side, it is contended that it is not true that the law as it stands excludes the working classes from political power, for in the counties many labouring men have votes as 40s. freeholders, and in the boroughs, with the relaxation that has taken place in the rules established by the Reform Act as to rating, there is scarcely any industrious and well-conducted working man that may not look forward to acquiring a vote if he does not already possess one ; and in point of fact, in some manufacturing boroughs, working men now form a large proportion of the constituency, as was clearly proved by evidence taken before a Committee of the House of Lords in the Session of 1860.*   It is further contended, that if a pecuniary qualification for voting is to be retained at all, its reduction would either fail to confer the right on any considerable number of the working classes, or else would admit so many of them as to give them the complete control of elections, to the exclusion of the higher ranks of society. This, it is said, would be inevitable, because the higher ranks are so few as compared to the working men, while the circumstances of the latter are so much alike, that a pe-

---

* See Evidence taken by the Committee appointed to inquire into the probable operation of a reduction of the Franchise, Questions 184–6, 2360–3, 2435–7, 2524, 2657.

cuniary Franchise which would make any considerable addition to the number of their class who now possess the right of voting, would admit nearly the whole body. Hence a measure of this sort would tend to throw predominant power into the hands of the least educated part of the community. A simple reduction of the value required to make a house or property confer a vote, would further have the effect of extending the Franchise not only to the intelligent and deserving of the working class, but to those of an opposite character, and in some cases principally to the latter. In towns where wages are high the best-conducted of the working classes generally inhabit houses which give the right of voting under the existing law, while houses of lower value are often occupied by men who spend great part of their earnings in drink.

Again, it is said that, admitting the truth of what has been urged by Mr. Mill as to the importance of seeking to interest as large a portion as possible of the population in public affairs, we may fairly doubt whether this object will be attained by a very wide extension of the Franchise,— at least, if elections continue to be conducted in the same manner as at present. When the Franchise is very widely distributed, each individual vote becomes of so little consequence that it ceases to be much valued by its possessor. We find, practically, that in some of the largest towns, and especially in the Metropolis (where from house-rent being high, the constituencies are very numerous, and include persons holding a comparatively low position in the community), the privilege is so little regarded, that it is only by very laborious exertions on the part of candidates, that even one-half of the electors can be prevailed upon to give their votes. And it is further to be observed, that this unwillingness to exercise their Franchise is always much the strongest in the most intelligent and cultivated classes ; so that these elections are left, in fact, in the hands of the lowest and most ignorant of the constituencies. Experience also proves that these large constituencies afford facilities for the personation of electors and other serious frauds, and give great scope for the corrupting arts of vulgar electioneering, by means of which they are apt to be brought under the dominion of men who make a profession of managing these elections, and are thus enabled to exercise and abuse a great and irresponsible power. Perhaps a larger proportion of the community, or at all events of its most intelligent members, may be led to take an active interest in elections, and in public affairs, by a system

under which the electors form a less numerous
and more select body, yet one which is sufficiently
large to be powerfully acted upon by the opinion
of the non-electors, and from which no man is per-
emptorily excluded, since, when the country is in
its usual state of prosperity, a working man of industrious and provident habits is likely to have
little difficulty in sooner or later acquiring a vote
as the occupier of a £10 house.   It is a mistake
likewise to regard the privilege of voting as an advantage to those who possess it, which cannot justly
be withheld from any members of the community
unless it can be proved that danger would arise
from their having it.   No personal benefit can be
derived from his vote by an elector except through
a breach of his duty.   It is a trust committed to
. him for the public good, and for his personal advantage only so far as that advantage is involved in
the general welfare of the nation.   It follows that
the object to be kept in view in regulating the franchise ought to be that of providing for the members of the House of Commons being well chosen.
Nor is it consistent with truth to describe (as is so
often done) those who do not possess votes as being
excluded from the benefit of the constitution. That
benefit is shared in by all who enjoy the security
and freedom which are the fruits of good govern-

ment. More than this, a man may even have very considerable political power without possessing the franchise, since it would be wrong to suppose that giving a vote once in four or five years in the election of a Member of Parliament is the only or the principal mode of exercising political power in this country. A man who feels a real interest in public affairs, and has qualified himself to take part in them by the knowledge he has acquired, can generally exertise a much more important influence by acting on the opinion of others, than by giving a single vote in a constituency of some thousands of electors.

On a careful balance of these conflicting arguments, I am led to conclude that a simple extension of the Franchise passed by itself must certainly prove injurious to the Nation; but that advantage might perhaps result from granting to the working classes additional means of making themselves heard in Parliament, provided that this were done in a judicious manner, and that the concession were accompanied by other measures calculated to guard against the dangers to be expected from it if it stood alone. What would be the best mode of providing for a better representation of the working classes, and by what other measures this concession ought to be accompanied if it should be determined upon, are questions that may be better discussed after considering another of the principal demands of the Democratic party, —I refer to the revision for which they call, of the existing distribution of the right of returning Members of Parliament, among the different constituencies that now possess it.

Upon this question there is a strong conflict of opinion. Mr. Bright, and the Reformers of his School, contend that any reform of Parliament without a complete re-apportionment of the right of returning Members to the House of Commons, would be a mockery. They dwell on the absurdity and injustice of giving no more weight in the House of Commons to such great and wealthy cities as Liverpool and Manchester, than to petty towns like Thetford and Ripon, and of allowing the county of Rutland to count for as much in deciding on the questions brought before Parliament as one of the divisions of Yorksire. They prove by elaborate statistics that Members representing towns and counties, containing together only a small fraction of either the population or the wealth of the country, form a large majority of the whole House of Commons; while a small minority of that House would include all the Members returned to it by constituencies forming collectively a great majority of the Nation, and the richest and most energetic part of it.

On the other hand, in the debates on the last Reform Bill, some of its most distinguished advocates, and especially Lord John Russell, Mr. Gladstone, and Sir James Graham, argued with much force on the important purposes which the smaller boroughs had served in our Constitution, by bringing into the House of Commons many of its ablest and most useful Members, and by providing for the representation of various classes and interests, which would otherwise have failed to obtain the weight they ought to possess in Parliament.

There is, I think, much truth in what has been said on both sides in this controversy. I cannot doubt, on the one side, that practically the small boroughs have answered purposes of the highest importance in our Constitution, and that a simple re-distribution of the Representation, either according to population, or even according to property and population combined, would fatally alter the whole character of the House of Commons, by giving predominant power to the numerical majority of the population. But in admitting this to be true, I find it impossible to contest its being equally true that the anomalies in the present distribution of the right of returning Members to

Parliament, and the extreme inequality in the shares of political power assigned to different individuals and to different portions of the Nation, without any reference to their respective fitness for the exercise of such power, cannot be defended on the principles of common-sense and justice. I must add, that while, on the whole, the returns made by the small boroughs have done much to render the House of Commons better fitted than it otherwise would have been to fill its proper place in the Constitution, these returns have been obtained by means both very objectionable in themselves, and also very uncertain in their working.

When I say that the means by which the Members who sit for the smaller boroughs are generally returned, are in themselves objectionable, I mean that the great majority of the elections for these boroughs are carried by the influence of money, or of money's worth. Probably this assertion will be met by a clamorous denial of the fact by those who are interested in the smaller boroughs; I am nevertheless prepared to maintain that it is strictly true. The venality of many of these places is too notorious to be contested, and even in those in which bribery, in the coarse form of direct gifts of money to the voters, is nearly or altogether unknown, the influence of pecuniary interest, in some shape or other, will be generally found, on close investigation, to be what really determines the choice of the electors among the rival candidates for their favour. How, indeed, can this be otherwise? Seats in Parliament are objects of eager desire to many wealthy men, ready and anxious to spend large sums of money in obtaining them. On the other hand, the power of disposing of these much-coveted seats is, in the smaller boroughs, placed in the hands of perhaps not more than three or four hundred electors, for the most part in a very humble condition of life, many of them needy men, and, unfortunately, many of them also men who stand by no means high among their own class either for character or intelligence. Can we be surprised that in such circumstances appeals should often be made to the pecuniary interest of the electors, rather than to their sense of public duty, and that these appeals should often be successful? We find accordingly, that there are innumerable modes of bringing the interests of the electors to bear upon their votes.

Sometimes this is done by procuring political or other advantages for some of the chief persons in the borough, while they on their part, by loans and gifts of money to their poorer neighbours, by giving them employment or other favours, obtain such a hold over them before the time for an election comes, that when it arrives they can practically command their votes. Sometimes it is by large subscriptions to local charities, or works for the benefit of the town, or by some other expenditure of the same sort, that the Member for a borough virtually pays for his Seat. More often, pecuniary interest is brought to bear upon electors through the owners of the land, or of the houses they occupy. This is the kind of influence which is most commonly exercised over those boroughs which are still under the dominion of some great proprietor, and it is obvious that this merely amounts to paying for votes by money's worth instead of with actual money. Whether a man sells his vote for £10 once in every four or five years, or gives his vote to the candidate recommended to him by the landlord from whom he holds a house or field, worth to him £1 or £2 a year more than his rent, it is equally his pecuniary interest which determines the use he makes of his right as an elector. A more sentimental explanation is indeed often given of the influence over some boroughs enjoyed by landowners who have succeeded to it from their ancestors; but that explanation is scarcely consistent with the fact that this influence, hereditary though it may be, is generally found to be transferable with the property which gives it, and may thus be acquired by the most upstart purchaser.

I need not however pursue this topic any further, nor attempt to trace out more in detail the various modes by which the power of money is brought to bear upon elections; it is enough to say that I believe no candid man can look closely into the preseut system of borough elections without being convinced that this is the power by which they are generally determined. Bribery is not worse than other modes of improperly influencing electors (on the contrary, I regard it as less immoral, because less injurious to the public than a demagogue's appeal to men's passions and prejudices); still, it is in itself undoubtedly an evil. I am therefore justified in asserting that although the Members sent to Parliament by the smaller boroughs may in general be well selected, and though they form as a class an important and useful element in the House of Commons, the means by which they are returned to it are in themselves objectionable.*

* This is well stated in the following extract from a very able article " On English Politics and Parties," which appeared in the first number of a new Quarterly Review, which was begun three or four years ago, but did not long go on :—

" It is not sufficiently remembered in discussions on this subject

Nor must I omit to observe, that, while it is true
that on the whole a useful body of Members are
introduced into Parliament by these objectionable
means, those means are by no means uniformly
employed to bring into the House of Commons
men whose presence there is desirable. On the
contrary, they are often used to secure the return
of Members of an opposite description ; and these
boroughs may be objected to, not only as producing
a good result by bad means, but also as frequently
failing to answer those purposes, which they are
said by their admirers to be so useful in accomplishing. No doubt distinguished lawyers, who

that the main business of Parliament is to decide what taxes shall
be levied, who are to pay them, and how they shall be spent. . . .
Now, on the levy and application of taxes, it is clear that the owners
of property, who pay most taxes, have most right to be represented.
Indeed, if the owners of property are not adequately represented in
the governing body, their property is scarcely safe. As the Representation stands at present, there are safeguards enough for property. The misfortune is, that they are indirect and circuitous, and
shock the increasing straightforwardness and honesty of the age.
Constituencies that can be bought, and constituencies that can be
frightened, are an effective, but not a very dignified mode of securing their due influence to the educated classes. But before we
sweep them away, we are bound to see that their place in the Constitution is filled up. If the employment of bribery and intimida-
tion, as constitutional guarantees, seems to us immoral; if the existence of a large unenfranchised class is inconsistent with the self-
respect which the citizens of a free state should feel,—at all events
we must provide new guarantees less objectionable, but as efficacious
as the old."

eventually become law officers of the Crown, and
rise to the Woolsack or to the Bench; great merchants, and men eminent for their knowledge of
political affairs, or for their intellectual endowments, are often indebted to the small boroughs
for an entrance into the House of Commons, which,
under the present system of elections, they would
have found it difficult to obtain by means of a
metropolitan borough, or of a county, or a large
town. But the means by which Members of this
kind obtain their return for the small boroughs,
may be used with equal success to procure the
election of unscrupulous adventurers both of the
legal and of other professions,—men who, having
virtually bought their seats, intend to use them in
order to sell themselves to the best advantage. So
also the patron of a borough (for there are still
boroughs that have patrons) may use his influence
to bring into Parliament some person appointed to
an important office under the Crown, or he may
give a seat to some young man whom he believes
to have talents that will make him a useful acquisition to the party he belongs to; and thus an
introduction into public life, and the opportunity
of being trained for future eminence, may be furnished to one destined hereafter to become an or-
nament to the House of Commons, and to render

good service to the Crown and to the Nation. But the power of the patron may equally be used to secure a Seat for some incapable relation or hanger-on, who must at best be useless in the House of Commons, and may possibly become an instrument for promoting the selfish or corrupt objects of the person who has sent him there.

These considerations lead me to believe that the existing distribution of the right of returning Members to the House of Commons among different constituencies cannot be maintained with advantage, and that it ought to undergo a complete revision; but that such a revision would not be expedient, or even safe, unless accompanied by other changes. A revision of the present distribution of Seats implies that a tolerably equal share of political power should be given to the several constituencies in proportion to their respective importance, and that the privilege of sending Members to Parliament should not be left to any constituency so small as to be necessarily subjected to some irregular influence. But a measure of this sort, if adopted singly, (much more if coupled only with an extension of the Franchise,) would sweep away what is good and useful as well as what is mischievous in the results of our present irregular system, would aggravate most of the faults which I have described in a former Chapter* as having been shown by experience to exist in that system as settled by the Parliamentary Reform of 1832, and would convert our Constitution into an unbalanced Democracy. If, therefore, these changes are necessary, (as, if not now, I believe they soon will be,) they ought to be accompanied by other amendments of our Constitution, calculated by their Conservative tendency to maintain its balance.   Nor do I believe that it would be so difficult, as might at first sight be supposed, to devise measures answering this description, if we keep steadily in view the precise results we desire to arrive at, and if, taking experience for our guide, we carefully examine in what respects good has been worked, even by those parts of our Constitution which we are prepared to alter because we recognize their faults.

The first of the Reforms of a Conservative tendency which I should suggest, and one which I should consider a great improvement under any circumstances, but quite indispensable if any changes favourable to Democratic power are to be admitted, would be the adoption of what Mr. James Marshall has called the " cumulative vote ;"† that is to say,

---

* See Chapter V.

† See his excellent pamphlet ' Minorities and Majorities, their Relative Rights,' published in 1857.

the principle of giving to every elector as many votes as there are Members to be elected by the constituency to which he belongs, with the right of either giving all these votes to a single candidate, or of dividing them, as he may prefer. The object of adopting this rule would be to secure to minorities a fair opportunity of making their opinions and wishes heard in the House of Commons. In order that it might fully answer this purpose, the right of returning Members to Parliament ought to be so distributed that each constituency should not have less than three representatives to choose. Supposing that three Members were to be elected together, and that each elector were entitled to three votes, which he might unite in favour of a single candidate, it is obvious that a minority *exceeding* a fourth of the whole constituency would have the power of securing the election of one Member.* It is probable that in general three

---

* To make this clear, suppose that there is a constituency of 3000 electors having to return three Members to Parliament, and each elector having a right to give three votes on the cumulative principle? There will be 9000 votes therefore to be given in all, and if these were equally divided among four candidates, each of them would poll 2250. But 750 electors, or one-fourth of the whole, if they gave all their votes to one candidate, would give him just 2250 votes; so that if even a single additional vote were given in his favour, the remaining votes could not be so divided as to enable three candidates to poll as many as himself; that is to say, he could

Members would be thus returned, each representing a different shade of opinion among the voters.

The advantages this mode of voting would be calculated to produce, and the justice of making some such provision for the representation of minorities, or rather, the flagrant injustice of omitting to do so, have been so well shown by Mr. Marshall in the pamphlet I have already referred to, and by Mr. Mill* in his highly philosophical treatise on

---

not stand lower than third on the poll, and must therefore be returned. In like manner, if four Members were to be elected by voters each giving four votes on the cumulative principle, a minority *exceeding* one-fifth of the whole body would be enabled to return one Member.

* Mr. Mill, in declaring his approval of this mode of voting, has however expressed a decided preference for another arrangement suggested by Mr. Hare, which would carry much further the principle of providing for the representation of various opinions in the House of Commons. Mr. Hare's plan may be described as one for virtually uniting into a single constituency all the separate constituencies in the Kingdom, by enabling every voter to have his vote entered as being given, not for any local candidate, but for one of a list of national candidates. By this arrangement, every candidate who could command the support of a sufficient number of electors from the whole body of a national constituency would be returned to Parliament, and men of almost every variety of opinion, by combining together, would be enabled to have a Member to represent them in the House of Commons. I entirely concur with Mr. Mill in regarding the object aimed at by Mr. Hare as one which it would be desirable to accomplish, and I also think the plan he has proposed for this purpose highly ingenious, and well calculated to obviate many of the difficulties to be apprehended in carrying it into execution. The scheme however, with all its merits, is open in my

Representative Government, that it is quite needless for me to argue the question as one of principle. But I may observe, that in addition to its being right in principle, this measure would be in strict accordance with the lessons of experience, if read in their true spririt. One of the most remarkable peculiarities of the British House of Commons, as compared to other representative bodies, is, that it has always had within its walls Members representing most of the different classes of society, and of the various and conflicting opinions and interests to be found in the Nation. Much of the acknowledged success with which the House of Commons has played its part in the Government of the Country has been attributed (I believe most justly) to this peculiarity. The changes made by the Reform Act, and especially the abolition of the various rights of voting formerly to be found in different towns, and the establishment of one uniform Franchise in all the English boroughs, (with only a small exception in favour of certain classes of freemen,) tended somewhat to impair the cha-

opinion to the insurmountable objection of being too complicated, and of being therefore calculated to give a preponderance of power rather to the best organized political party than to that in which the most intelligent part of the Nation has the greatest confidence.— *See Mr. Mill on Representative Government, p. 141; and Mr. Hare's Treatise on Representation.*

racter of the House in this respect. The greatly increased intercourse between different parts of the country, and the rapidity with which opinions are propagated from one extremity of the Kingdom to another, have had a similar tendency; and there is no longer the same probability as formerly, that different opinions will be found to prevail in different places, so as to enable all parties to find somewhere the means of gaining an entrance to Parliament for at least enough of their adherents to give expression to their feelings.

Hence there is a danger that the House of Commons may cease to enjoy, to the same extent as formerly, the great advantage of representing the various classes and opinions to be found in the Nation. That danger would be greatly aggravated by rendering the constituencies more nearly equal than they are; but the simple change involved in adopting the "cumulative vote" would do much towards guarding against it, since, with this mode of voting, it would be impossible that any considerable party in the country should be left unrepresented in Parliament. The tendency of the alteration would be Conservative in the best sense of the word, while at the same time in many cases it would have the effect of relieving Liberal politicians from a disadvantage to which they are unfairly subjected.

On the one side, it would prevent the Representation of the large town constituencies from being monopolized, as at present, by candidates ready to pledge themselves to the support of Democratic measures.   Even in the metropolitan boroughs we might reasonably expect that some Members would be returned really representing the higher and most educated classes of their inhabitants, who are now practically without any Representation at all, except that which they obtain indirectly, by means of Members chosen by other constituencies. Thus, in the large towns it would put an end to an unjust monopoly on the part of Radical politicians, and on the other hand, in those counties where a Conservative majority now excludes a strong Liberal minority from any share in the Representation, it would correct a similar tendency in the opposite direction.   In both cases this system of voting would be calculated to give more weight to the independent electors who are not thorough-going partisans on either side, and to favour the return of candidates deserving their confidence.*

Valuable as this change in the mode of voting

---

* In the Constitution given to the Cape of Good Hope in 1850, this system of voting was introduced in the election of the Upper Chamber, and I understand that it has been found to work very well.

would be, it is by no means the only provision of
a Conservative tendency which would be required
in a large measure of Reform.

Those who have studied the composition of the
House of Commons, must be aware that it has generally numbered among its most valuable Members some who are so little fitted to obtain success
as candidates in great popular elections, that they
could never have gained an entrance to it except
through the small constituencies of which I have
been contemplating the abolition. These Members have been most useful, not only by the ability
and knowledge they have brought into the House,
but also by practically representing various classes
and interests, which ought to have the means of
making their wishes and opinions heard within its
walls. To guard against the exclusion of Members of this description from Parliament, I am of
opinion that in revising the present distribution
of Seats among different constituencies, a certain
number ought to be set apart, and not given to
any local constituencies whatever. The principle
of a Franchise not of a local character, is at present only known in the University elections, but
in these it is completely established. The graduates
of Oxford and Cambridge, and of the University
of Dublin, wherever they reside, are entitled to vote

P

in the election of Members for these Universities. The Franchise does not depend upon the possession or occupation of property, or upon residence in any particular places, but upon having obtained a degree,—that is, a certificate of having received an education of the first class. The Members so chosen may therefore be fairly considered as representing the most cultivated minds in the Nation. When the opportunities for gaining admittance into the House of Commons now afforded to men of ability, but wanting the qualifications required by popular candidates, are diminished in one direction, it would surely be wise to increase them in another; I should therefore propose that each of our great English Universities should have four Members instead of two, the University of Dublin three, and that new constituencies of the same character should be created. This increase in the number for Members of the Universities would be open to objection, as being calculated to give too much advantage to the party which has hitherto been all-powerful in their elections, if it were not coupled with the adoption of the " cumulative vote;" but with this condition, I am persuaded that it would be liable to no such drawback, none of the great parties into which the Nation is divided would be likely to gain an advantage over its adversaries, and we might be pretty sure that able and well-informed men of different political opinions would be sent into the House of Commons by these learned bodies.

In addition to the Universities which already possess Members, representatives might be given to the London and Durham Universities (uniting them for the purpose), to the Universities of Scotland, which also might make together a single constituency, and the Queen's Colleges in Ireland. The learned professions might also furnish constituencies, by which a further addition would be made to the share given to knowledge and intelligence, in the representation. That this ought to be done, and that more political power ought to be given to men of high education than to others, is a principle which has been maintained by most of our best writers on such subjects, and by none more strongly than by Mr. Mill.* Indeed, it seems self-evident that if we desire to see the Nation well and wisely governed, the representation ought to be so arranged that while no class is excluded from making its voice heard in Parliament, the preponderating power should be given to those who have acquired the knowledge necessary to enable them to form a sound judgment as to the true in-

* 'Considerations on Representative Government,' pp. 165–170.

terest of the country in the various questions that arise. But the object of giving additional weight in the National councils to men of cultivated minds, would be more effectually answered by creating special constituencies of the kind I have described, than by conferring additional votes, in the ordinary local elections, on persons who possessed some high educational qualification, as suggested by Mr. Mill. If those who voted in respect of the Educational Franchise, were merely entitled to give more votes than others in the elections for the places where they lived, their influence, scattered through the whole Nation, would be comparatively little felt, and there would be no certainty that they would anywhere be able to secure the return of the candidates they would prefer; whereas by concentrating their influence, and forming them into separate constituencies, a direct representation would be ensured to them. The manner in which these Constituencies should be formed, and the number of Members to be assigned to them, could not be properly determined without much previous inquiry and consideration, but I entertain a strong conviction that the principle of creating them is right, and that there would be no real difficulty in applying it in practice.

Nor is it only for the purpose of giving increased

weight to the most educated part of the Nation that it would be desirable to create Constituencies not of a local character.   It might also be useful in bringing into Parliament Members to represent certain classes and interests who might otherwise fail in making themselves properly heard in the House of Commons.   Constituencies might be formed of persons engaged in some of our great branches of industry irrespective of the places of their abode.   More especially working men, as such, might be enabled to send to Parliament a limited number of Members who would directly represent them.   I am not aware of any reason why those who have worked in certain trades for a given time should not be registered and formed into a corporate body with the right of electing Members of the House of Commons.   By that arrangement the working class might have the power given to them of choosing enough Representatives fairly to express their wishes and feelings in Parliament without the risk of giving them a monopoly of the Representation by a large reduction of the Franchise.

It has been suggested that this object of giving them a sufficient representation without overwhelming power, might be attained by returning to what existed before the Reform Act, and making the Franchise vary in different towns.   In some towns it has been said Universal Suffrage, or something nearly approaching to it, might be established, while in others the present Franchise or even a higher one might be maintained. Thus each class would be represented somewhere, as they were in old times by means of the Close Corporations in some towns, and the Potwallopers in others. The fact that the former variety in the rights of voting did, at least to a certain degree, answer the purpose described, cannot be denied, but it would scarcely be practicable in the present state of society to return to the system of allowing such arbitrary differences to exist between different places; and, if the object is a good one, why not take the most direct means of attaining it? With the present facilities for communication, there is no reason why men united together not by living in one place, but by being engaged in some common pursuit, should not be enabled to vote in their respective places of abode, in the choice of their common Representative.

There is another object for which it is of still greater importance to provide, that namely of securing the most distinguished Members of the House of Commons from being excluded from it by a dissolution of Parliament at a moment when they have become unpopular from the line of conduct they may have adopted on some question which has greatly excited the passions of the Nation.   Formerly the nomination boroughs, some of which were under the control of each party in the State, effectually secured the chief ornaments of the House of Commons from being excluded from it, when the current of popular feeling turned against them.   Nor was such a security unnecessary. On the dissolution of Parliament in 1780, Burke lost his Seat for Bristol, in consequence of what all now admit to have been his wise resistance to the American War, and his advocacy of an enlightened commercial policy; he was again returned to Parliament by Malton, on the nomination of Lord Rockingham.   When, in the general election which followed the overthrow of the Coalition Ministry, the party of Fox was defeated so signally (and I freely admit deservedly), it was mainly by means of the nomination boroughs that it escaped being absolutely extinguished in the House of Commons.

Now in these and in similar cases these boroughs have been highly useful.   The House of Commons cannot afford to lose its most distinguished Members when they happen to become unpopular for the moment, even if this should be the consequence of their having been betrayed into some serious error of conduct.   When popu-

lar opinion is running strongly in one direction, it
is most important that those who believe it to be
misled should have full opportunity of making
their arguments heard in Parliament.   They ought
to be heard, even if it were clear that they were in
the wrong; but with the example of Burke before
us, we cannot doubt that sometimes at least it may
be the minority that is in the right.   To guard the
Nation as far as possible from being led away into
fatal errors, it is indispensable that the voices which
are raised against the prevailing opinion of the day
should not be silenced in the House of Commons,
and further, that there should be some of its ablest
Members placed in a position in which they may
faithfully discharge the difficult and painful duty of
opposing what they believe to be a popular delusion,
without the risk of being for that reason deprived
of their Seats.   Even if instead of agreeing with
Mr. Cobden and Mr. Bright with respect to the
Chinese War of 1857, I had differed from them as
widely upon this question as I do upon many others,
I should have regarded their temporary exclusion
from Parliament in consequence of the honest stand
they made against what they considered to be
wrong, as having been a misfortune to the Nation.

For these reasons, I think that if Parliament
should undergo an extensive Reform, tending in

some respects to bring it more under the influence of the opinions and feelings of the people, it would be most desirable to provide that a few of the Members of the House of Commons should hold their Seats by a tenure, which would make them independent of the sudden variations to which these opinions and feelings are liable. What I mean is, that they should hold their Seats for life. I shall be by no means surprised if this proposal should be scouted as a novelty too monstrous to be listened to for a moment, but I would submit, that though it may be novel in form, it is not so in substance. Walpole, Burke, Pitt, Fox, and other leaders of the unreformed Parliament practically held their Seats by a tenure not dependent on popular caprice, because they knew that if the larger Constituencies were to reject them, they had a secure refuge in the nomination boroughs under the control of some of their party adherents. Nor is it, I think, possible to doubt that this security with respect to their personal position, and the absence of any necessity for deferring to the prejudices of a popular Constituency, enabled these great men to serve their country with more effect than they could otherwise have done.*

---

* Even in the reformed House of Commons there have been a few leading men who have held a position of equal security, and I be-

Perhaps it may be asked how the independence of popular control possessed by some Members of the unreformed House of Commons can be represented as having been an advantage, when it is admitted that the great fault of that House was its not being sufficiently amenable to public opinion. The answer is obvious: in the House of Commons of that day, not merely a few of its leaders, but so large a proportion of all its Members were free from responsibility to popular Constituencies, that the House, as a body, was rendered far too little alive to public opinion, and to the public interest. In recognizing the evil of such a state of things we may recognize also the partial good with which it was attended, in securing those men whose talents and experience made them most useful to the House of Commons, against being excluded from it by popular caprice. If this was a real and great advantage, (of which even a slight study of our Parliamentary history can hardly leave a doubt,) surely it would be wise to endeavour to make provision for retaining it disentangled from the evil by which it was formerly accompanied.

lieve with the same advantage. The commanding influence of Sir R. Peel in the little borough of Tamworth made his return for it a matter of certainty, and this independence contributed, I believe, very powerfully to his utility in the House of Commons between the passing of the Reform Act and his death.

With this view I would suggest that a limited number of Members, say from twelve to fifteen, might be chosen for life by the House of Commons itself by "cumulative vote," not less than three being elected together. In the first instance, either the whole of the fifteen original Life Members might be elected together, or (what would probably be more convenient) they might be named in the Reform Bill, of which this provision would form a part, with a due regard to the claims of different parties in the House. Future vacancies should not be filled up until at least three had occurred.* By this arrangement each of the most important of the different parties in the House would be enabled to secure a share of the Life Members, and it may fairly be presumed that the choice of these parties would fall on their ablest men, and that the important object would be gained of guarding the House against the risk of losing the services of its most distinguished and experienced Members if they should become unpopular in consequence of the fearless discharge of their duty, and yet the House as a whole would be left under the effective control of public opinion.

* If Parliament were sitting when three Seats for life became vacant, they should be filled up at once. But it might happen that when there were already two vacancies, more than one Life Member might die during the recess.

Lastly, it is indispensable in a good Reform Bill that it should contain some provision against the danger of habitual weakness in the Government. Among the defects of the Reform Act of 1832, I have, in a former Chapter,* mentioned, as the first and most important, its tendency to leave the Ministers of the Crown without due authority in the House of Commons, and I have stated my reasons for considering their possessing such authority to be essential to the proper working of Parliamentary Government. Since those pages were written for the first edition of this Essay, the course of events in the political world, and further reflection, have not merely confirmed the opinion I have there expressed, but have convinced me that in this respect the faults of the present constitution of the House of Commons are even greater than I had supposed, and are the source of still more serious dangers than I had apprehended. As I am anxious to avoid saying anything that can be construed into censure of any political party or its leaders, I must abstain from attempting to support this view of the subject by a scrutiny of the proceedings of the House of Commons in its recent sessions; but without entering into particulars as to the Parliamentary transactions of these

* See Chapter V., p. 98.

years, I may assert, with little fear of contradiction, that they prove the evils arising from the want of power in the House of Commons on the part of the Ministers, to be gradually increasing. Already it has produced a marked effect both upon their management of affairs in Parliament, and upon their conduct in the discharge of their executive functions. In Parliament, its operation may be traced in the manner in which Ministers have dealt with questions like that of church-rates, on which strong differences of opinion prevail ; in their reluctance to propose, in the face of serious opposition, or their inability to carry many of the improvements that are needed in the laws affecting the social condition of the country, and the welfare of the people ; and perhaps most of all, in the extent to which the votes of the House of Commons for some branches of the National expenditure have become the expression, less of the deliberate views of the servants of the Crown as to what would be best for the public service, than of the opinion entertained at the moment by a fluctuating majority.*   In the conduct of the Executive Govern-

* The subject upon which the House of Commons has shown the strongest inclination to reject the guidance of the Government of the day, has been that of granting money for Metropolitan buildings and improvements. Votes upon questions of this kind have been regarded as of no political significance, while almost every

ment, the effects of the insufficient Parliamentary
power of the Ministry may be detected in the want
of firmness and consistency in their measures, produced apparently by the fear of giving plausible
grounds of objection to opponents, or of running
counter to any of the varying currents of popular
feeling.

A careful examination of the political events of
some years past must, I think, convince any impartial inquirer that I have not gone beyond the
truth in describing the injurious consequences of

Member has had his own particular notions as to what ought
to be done, and the decisions to which the House has come, have in
consequence been fluctuating and uncertain. The effect of this
upon the public interest has been described by Mr. Gladstone to
the House of Commons. After referring to what he admitted to
be a just complaint, as to the delay there had been in deciding
what use should be made of Burlington House since its purchase
for the public, he proceeded to say, " That this, and other circumstances of a like kind, were entirely owing to the lamentable and
deplorable state of our whole arrangement with regard to the management of our public works. Vacillation, uncertainty, costliness,
extravagance, meanness, and all the conflicting vices that could be
enumerated, were united in our present system. There was a total
want of authority to direct and guide. When anything was to be
done, they had to go from department to department—from the
Executive to the House of Commons, from the House of Commons
to a committee, from a committee to a commission, and from a
commission back to a committee—so that years passed away, the
public were disappointed, and the money of the country was wasted.
He believed such were the evils of the system that nothing short of
a revolutionary reform would ever be sufficient to rectify it."—*See*
Hansard, vol. clx. p. 1360.

the weakness of the present and some preceding
Administrations.   Nor is this state of things to be
attributed to the faults of the particular men who
have filled prominent places on the political stage.
They cannot, indeed, be regarded as having been
blameless in this matter; but they have probably, on
the whole, acted much as might have been expected
in the circumstances in which they have been placed,
and the real root of the evil lies deeper than the
accidental failings of individuals.   Judging from
the general character of Representative Assemblies,
whether in our own Colonies or in other countries,
it seems to be the natural tendency of these bodies,
when invested with a control of the Government,
to split themselves into separate parties, no one of
which is strong enough to hold its ground against
a combination of the others; while such a combination is easily formed for the purpose of driving
out the actual holders of power, but can seldom
be maintained in support of the party that may
thus be raised to it.*   The consequence is, that

* In France, the Chamber of Deputies, for some years after the
Revolution of 1830, showed much of this tendency to split itself into
a variety of parties, none of them strong enough to form a stable
administration.   M. Guizot at length succeeded in forming a Ministry of great Parliamentary strength, but this was accomplished
by a large use of the great influence, which the system of centrali-
zation established in France, enabled the Government to exercise
over the very restricted Constituency then entrusted with the

where there is nothing to counteract this tendency, ephemeral Administrations are found to succeed each other rapidly, all being equally powerless, and equally incapable of discharging their proper duties with effect.   Parliamentary Government, in such a state of things, becomes one of the very worst systems of Government to which a country can be subject.   Indeed, it can scarcely be called a Government at all, for under such conditions it is inconsistent with the existence of any authority capable of ruling a nation (and mankind require to be ruled), or of steadily directing the measures either of the Executive Government or of the Legislature, to any clearly defined and well-considered objects of public good.   Instead of being so directed, these measures will vary with every change in the game of party politics, and will generally have for their aim to gain a fleeting popularity by flattering the passions and prejudices of the people, or of some particular section of it.

We have had conspicuous examples of these evils in our Australian Colonies since the establish-

power of electing the Chamber; and the extreme narrowness of the Franchise, together with the means by which a majority of the Chamber was secured for the Minister, had this fatal consequence, that neither the Chamber nor the Government (as distinguished from the Administration of the day) possessed the moral power arising from public confidence, and both fell, almost without a struggle, before the first breath of revolutionary violence.

ment of what is called " responsible Government;"
nor can there be much difference of opinion as to
the injurious consequences to a nation under Parliamentary Government, of its being impossible to
form a stable administration of proper authority.
But if the danger of such a state of things is admitted, and also the fact that it is one which is
likely to arise from the very nature of Representative Assemblies, if no means are taken to guard
against it, is it to be inferred that for that purpose we must tolerate a system of corruption? At
first sight, such might appear to be the conclusion to be drawn from the facts before us.   In a
former Chapter* I have admitted that the power
of the Ministers of the Crown, in the unreformed
Parliament, rested upon the exercise of an influence, which, though far from being altogether corrupt, was yet strongly tainted with corruption.
And it is the reduction of this influence by Parliamentary reform, and by the various economic
reforms which have grown out of it, that has created the difficulty now complained of. For although
before the passing of the Reform Act, accidental
causes sometimes produced a temporary difficulty
in forming a strong Administration, the general
tendency was the other way, and Administrations

* Chapter III., p. 41.

supported by the Crown had usually more power in Parliament than was desirable. Now, on the contrary, the servants of the Crown have for several years been growing less and less able to guide the proceedings of the House of Commons, and there is reason to anticipate a further progressive diminution of their authority.

These are facts which I believe it to be impossible to dispute, but it does not follow that nothing can be done to strengthen the hands of the Government in Parliament without a return to old abuses. Other means might be discovered of accomplishing that object, and it is possible that if we examine how it was that the Government of the day exercised so much power in the unreformed House of Commons, we may find that some of the elements of that power might admit of being separated from the abuses out of which they grew. On looking into the subject with this view, our attention can hardly fail to be attracted by the circumstance, that the Government for the time being derived from its official position the power of conferring Seats in Parliament on a considerable number of its adherents. By means of what were called Treasury Boroughs, and boroughs belonging to patrons who habitually sold the Seats to the existing Administration, every Administration in succession nominated a considerable number of Members of the unreformed House of Commons, who, in return for their nomination, were expected to vote for the Minister to whom they were indebted for it. So completely was this practice established, that a change of Administration was almost uniformly followed by a dissolution of Parliament,* in order that the new one might gain the Seats in question ; and it was considered a point of honour for the holders to resign them, when, from any change of circumstances, they became unwilling to vote as they were expected. I have no means of ascertaining what was the number of its friends that a Government could thus bring into the Unreformed House of Commons,—indeed, it must have varied greatly from time to time ; but I believe it was commonly supposed, that if no disturbing circumstances interfered, the Ministers actually in power might in those days reckon upon being able to command from forty to fifty Seats in a new Parliament by virtue of their official position, in addition to the natural strength of their party.

* Thus the appointment of the Grenville Administration, on the death of Mr. Pitt, in the beginning of 1806, led to the dissolution of the existing Parliament after the termination of the session ; and the new Parliament, which met in the winter, was in its turn dissolved almost immediately after the accession to power of a new Ministry, on the dismissal of the previous one by the King, in April, 1807.

This was not the sole, or perhaps even the principal source of the power exercised by the Administration in the House of Commons at the time I have been speaking of; but there can be no doubt that being thus enabled to reckon on the steady support of a compact body of adherents, sure to be always in their places when required, contributed greatly to give strength to the Government. The fact also, that with a change of Administration this support was usually transferred by a dissolution of Parliament to the new Ministers, rendered it unlikely that a Government should ever exist with a bare majority over its opponents. Transferring forty or fifty Seats from one party to the other would make a difference of double that number in a division. A party therefore, which had been strong enough to drive an Administration from power when the Government Seats were held by its adversaries, might expect a considerable majority when these Seats were made over to its friends.

Looking to the manner in which it formerly worked, the power of securing by their official influence the return of a limited number of Mem bers of the House of Commons, is one which I consider it desirable to restore to the servants of the Crown. The re-establishment of Treasury Boroughs is not, of course, to be thought of, still

less any contrivance to enable the Government to
purchase Seats in Parliament for its friends by
money or patronage. But the same result might
be obtained by an arrangement for which there is
a precedent in the Municipal Reform Act, and to
which I can see no valid objection. By that Act
it is provided that a part of the Municipal Council
in every borough shall consist of Aldermen elected
by the Council itself. This provision has the effect
(which I believe was neither intended nor foreseen when it was adopted, but which I consider to
have been highly beneficial) of tending to give to
whatever party may be the strongest for the moment in one of these Councils, a sufficient majority
for the satisfactory transaction of business.

In like manner it might be one of the enactments
of another Reform Bill, that at the beginning of
every new Parliament the House of Commons
should elect a limited number of Members for the
Parliament, not by " cumulative vote," but by lists,
so that the majority of the House, by acting in concert, would have the power of naming the whole.
This would in effect give the nomination of these
Members to the Ministers of the Crown, for though
Ministers of late years have seldom been able to
command what is called a good working majority,
it is still necessary that they should have a majority

on those important questions on which their existence as a Ministry depends; and no question could
be more clearly one of confidence or no confidence,
than that of whether their list of Members to be
chosen by the House should be accepted or not.
At the same time, the necessity of so framing their
list as to prevent its being open to just objection on
the part of their supporters, would check the disposition to favouritism which might lead to an improper selection of names to be put upon it, if the
direct power of nominating these Members were
given to the Government. This arrangement would
do much towards preventing that equal division of
parties which has of late years been so great an
obstacle to good Government, and towards restoring
to the servants of the Crown their proper weight
and authority in the House of Commons, by giving
back to them their old power of bringing a certain
number of their friends into Parliament without
the old taint of corruption in the means of doing so.
It would also enable them to provide Seats in the
House of Commons for any of the holders of Parliamentary offices who might fail to obtain them
otherwise,* and likewise to bring into Parliament
young men possessing talents calculated to render

* The proposed arrangement would answer this purpose in the
middle of a Parliament as well as at the time of a dissolution, be-

them useful to the Administration, to whom the opportunity would thus be afforded of making themselves known, and of acquiring that early training which is so great an advantage to those who are to take an active part in public affairs.   As power, in the common course of things, would sometimes be in the hands of one party, sometimes of another, each would in succession have the means of introducing its most promising young men into political life, and this would meet another of the difficulties which have arisen out of the Reform Act.

It may perhaps be urged as an objection to the suggestion I have made, that its adoption would render a dissolution of Parliament almost a necessary consequence of every change of Administration. Such undoubtedly would be its operation; but in my opinion this would be no evil, but rather the reverse.   In old times, a dissolution of Parliament (as I have already observed) generally followed a change of Government, and the expectation of its doing so had the good effect of causing the House of Commons to be cautious in coming to a vote calculated to force the existing Ministry to retire.

A more plausible objection to the proposal is, that

cause some one of the friends of the Government who had been thus brought into the House of Commons would always be found willing to resign his Seat in order that it might be conferred on a person appointed to office.

it is in direct contradiction to the views of our best
and wisest Statesmen, who, from the earliest days of
Parliamentary Government, have concurred in laying the greatest stress upon preserving the entire
independence of the House of Commons, and in representing the power of the Crown within its walls
as requiring to be guarded against with the utmost
jealousy.   Up to the time of the passing of the
Reform Act, this was undoubtedly the prevailing
opinion among statesmen and political writers; but
we must bear in mind that in those days the power
of the Crown in the House of Commons really was
excessive, was maintained by corruption, and was
used to extend the means of corruption on which it
depended.   We cannot be surprised therefore, that
those who only saw these abuses, should have failed
to perceive that going too far in diminishing the
power that had produced them, would give rise to
other evils of which they had had no experience;
nor can their authority be properly pleaded against
measures suggested by a state of things totally unlike any they were acquainted with.

I must add, that it was against the corruption by
which the influence of the Government was maintained that their objections were chiefly, and very
justly, directed; but now there is far more danger
of corruption from the Administration having too

little power in the House of Commons than from
its having too much. Jobs of the kind formerly
common in this country are no longer easily perpetrated by a Government in the face of the much
greater publicity that now attaches to all its acts,
and of the increased power of public opinion.
On the other hand, we may learn from the experience of the United States the serious danger there
is of a different kind of corruption being produced,
by giving a control over the pecuniary concerns of
a great Nation to a Representative Assembly not
acting under the guidance of acknowledged leaders, and therefore relieved from the wholesome restraint produced by the sense of individual responsibility. Private canvass, intrigue, and combination,
—the arts known in America under the name of
" lobbying " and " log-rolling,"—have free scope in
an Assembly where this guidance is wanting, and
are used to carry, for the benefit of those who are
skilled in them, measures injurious to the Public,
or to procure the recognition of unfounded claims
against the National Treasury.

From the nature of its business and the extent
of its authority, the House of Commons would
be peculiarly liable to influences of this sort; and
it is difficult to set limits to the corruption that
might be expected to disgrace its proceedings, if

they were no longer under the check of an effective responsibility on the part of the Ministers of the Crown, arising from the power they are able to exercise over its measures. Already we have seen, in the last few years, formidable symptoms of the influence which a well-organized system of canvass may acquire in supporting private interests in the House of Commons at the expense of the Public. This has been particularly striking in the attempts which have been made to overrule by Parliamentary pressure the decisions of the Queen's Government with respect to the claims of Naval and of Military Officers, and of some classes of the Civil Servants. Those who have carefully watched the proceedings of the last few sessions must have observed the strong disposition that has been shown indirectly to set aside the old rule, that favours and remuneration for public service should come from the Crown, while the part of the House of Commons is to check profusion. A rule that was full of wisdom, since it did not permit demands to be made on the public purse except on the recommendation of Ministers, who are responsible for what they propose; while private Members, acting under no such responsibility, are liable to the temptation of trying to earn a false popularity by urging an injudicious and improvident grant of favours.

This can only be checked by the Government having sufficient strength to resist such motions, and therefore a measure calculated to secure to the Ministers of the Crown the possession of a moderate amount of power in the House of Commons, would tend, not to promote corruption, but to guard against it.   And this would be still more the case if in giving this power directly, provision were also made against its being indirectly and irregularly increased.   With this view, it would be reasonable that the law which prohibits persons engaged in the collection of the revenue from voting or taking part in elections should be extended to all who are employed in the permanent Civil Service of the State.   There is no reason why the prohibition should apply to one only out of the various branches of that service ; it should be made applicable to all.   This would have the advantage of not only diminishing the means possessed by the Government for the exercise of an improper influence, but also of marking distinctly the duty of public servants (not holding political offices) to observe a strict neutrality in party politics.

The mode I have suggested of adding to the Parliamentary strength of the Servants of the Crown may be open to more objections than have occurred to me, but whatever may be the force of these objections to the particular proposal I have made, I am convinced that it is a matter of urgent necessity to provide, by some means or other, for a moderate increase of the power now possessed by Ministers in the House of Commons. Our Constitution brings the whole conduct of the Government under the virtual control of the House of Commons; unless therefore the Ministers, as its leaders, are enabled to exercise within its walls an authority that cannot easily be shaken, and to command a majority on all ordinary occasions, it is obvious that the policy of the Government must fall under the direction of a fluctuating majority of the House. But the measures of a Government directed by the fluctuating majority of a popular Assembly, will necessarily be ruled by popular passion and feeling instead of by reason and prudence. These can only exercise their proper authority when the National Councils are guided by Ministers not too numerous for calm deliberation and possessing a real power which cannot be hastily withdrawn from them by the caprice of the People or of their Representatives. It cannot be expected that the Ministers to whom the duty of conducting the policy of the Nation is entrusted, will perform their task with firmness and judgment, if they are liable to be deprived of power and to have their decisions overruled the moment they fail to satisfy the popular feeling of the day. The want of some strong and stable authority to conduct its affairs is very injurious to a nation even in quiet times, much more so in times of difficulty and adversity. Recent events in Denmark afford an instructive lesson as to the calamities which in such seasons my be caused by the people themselves, exercising either through their Representatives, or by less regular means, too direct a control over the measures of their Government. There can be no doubt that Denmark might have escaped no small part of what it has suffered, if the feelings naturally excited in the minds of the Danes by their cruel wrongs, had not been allowed so much influence over the manner of conducting both the war and the negotiations, and if the King and his Ministers had been more free to act upon their own judgment as to what it would be best to do in the unhappy circumstances in which the country was placed. On the other hand, a no less instructive lesson as to the advantage a people may derive from giving large powers to able leaders, is afforded by the wonderful success with which the Seceding States of the American Union have for more than three years maintained the unequal conflict in which they are engaged.

These considerations lead me to the conclusion,

that it is absolutely necessary for the welfare and even for the safety of the Nation, that the Ministers of the Crown should be enabled to exercise a substantial power within the walls of the House of Commons. When I say a substantial power, I do not mean such a power as would enable a Ministry to maintain itself in office in spite of its being strongly and decidedly condemned by public opinion, but one that need only yield to such a settled opinion, not to mere passing clamour. Formerly (as I have already admitted) the servants of the Crown, when cordially supported by their Master, had probably too much Parliamentary power* (although even in those times there was more reason for objecting to the sources from which their power was derived than to its amount), but now the fault is certainly the other way. What we have now to fear is not that a bad Ministry will be able to govern in defiance of public opinion, but that the Ministers (be they Tories, Whigs, or Radicals) will not, while they are in office, have sufficient power to act according to their own deliberate judgment, instead of being compelled to follow the shifting currents of the popular will.

Lastly, I think it would clearly be expedient, that any new Reform Bill should contain a clause

* See page 106.

relieving Members of the House of Commons from the necessity of being re-elected on their appointment to Parliamentary Offices. I am far from desiring to see an increase in the number of placeholders in the House of Commons; but those whose presence there is required, and is now sanctioned by the law, ought not to be compelled to go through the ordeal of a re-election.* I have already observed, that this has proved in practice a serious obstacle to the appointment of the fittest persons to important posts in the public service. The law also, as it stands, is the mere accidental result of a struggle between two opposite opinions, and is singularly inconsistent and capricious in its operation. While the Junior Lords of the Treasury and Admiralty vacate their seats by accepting these offices, the rule does not apply to the more important and better-paid offices of the Secretaries to these Boards and of the Under-Secretaries of State, merely because the latter are not technically appointed by the Crown.

If such measures as I have now described for preserving the balance of the Constitution should be adopted, the views of the Democratic party might, I think, be met by assenting to the principle of a redistribution of the right of returning

* See Chapter V., p. 125.

Members to Parliament, and of providing for a better representation of the working classes in the House of Commons. The last object would be attained to some extent, by creating a limited number of special constituencies, composed of these classes in the manner I have already described, and by adopting the cumulative vote, which would give them the command of at least one seat in many boroughs with the existing Franchise. Beyond this, I should propose to assimilate the right of voting in towns and counties. I can see no reason why, if the possession of a 40s. freehold is considered a sufficient test of a man's fitness to vote in a county, it should not equally qualify him to exercise the same privilege in a borough; and in like manner, a householder who is fit to vote in a borough, is equally fit to do so in a county. This would of itself involve a large increase in the number of voters, especially as the improvement that is going on in the condition of the people, is daily augmenting the proportion borne by the inhabitants of £10 houses to the rest of the population.* Independently of any change in the law, a gradual extension of the Franchise is thus taking place, which I am inclined to believe would be sufficient.

* See Report of the Committee on the Elective Franchise, Questions 3580-2, 3586.

At all events I should deprecate a simple lowering of the existing occupation Franchise in boroughs. By the "Small Tenements Act" it has been provided, that in order to establish a claim either to the municipal or Parliamentary Franchise in places where this law has been adopted, rates paid by landlords who compound for their rates shall be regarded as being paid by their tenants, if the latter give notices to the Overseers requiring their names to be entered in the rate-book. The clauses of the Reform Act requiring claimants of votes to be rated, have thus been virtually repealed; for though they remain nominally in force, their operation can be defeated by notices served on the Overseers.* As I have pointed out in the last Chapter, to extend the right of voting in this state of the law to the occupiers of houses of lower value than at present, would be nearly equivalent to giving it indiscriminately to the whole population; while the concession

---

* There is this further disadvantage in the present state of the law, that while it has removed whatever real security for the respectability of borough electors was afforded by the necessity for their being personally rated, it only dispenses with this necessity in favour of those who comply with formalities which are very apt to be neglected, unless when attended to by the paid agents of a political party. The consequence is, that an organized party will generally place all its adherents, respectable or unrespectable, on the register, but many really independent persons will fail to establish the right they possess.

would be illusory if the rule of the Reform Act as to personal rating were reverted to under the present practice of allowing rates to be compounded for. Perhaps the objections to a reduction of the occupation Franchise might be obviated, and the problem of making votes more easily obtainable by the working classes, without conferring them indiscriminately upon all, might be solved by adopting the suggestion of Mr. Mill, and making the payment of some small amount of direct taxation a necessary condition for enjoying the right of voting.* As the primary function of the House of Commons, from which all its other powers have been derived, is to impose taxes for the public service, it would not be unreasonable to require that all who take part in choosing the Members of that House, should themselves be direct contributors to the taxation it imposes ; and it might fairly be presumed, that the Franchise would be fitly bestowed on persons who valued it enough to be willing to pay a tax in order to obtain it. The proposal of Mr. Mill seems therefore to be sound in principle, but experience does not encourage the expectation that it would be favourably received by the people. The provision of the Reform Act of 1832 which required every voter to pay a shilling towards the

* See his ' Representative Government,' p. 163.

expense of registration, was so unpopular, that Parliament was induced to repeal it. The object of imposing the tax might also be defeated by candidates for Seats in the House of Commons taking upon themselves the payment for voters who supported them.

I have next to consider to what extent, and in what manner, the distribution of the right of returning Members to Parliament among different constituencies should be altered. I have already said that I do not think the existing arrangements upon this subject ought to be interfered with at all, unless we are prepared to go so far in the way of change as to get rid of all the glaring anomalies that now exist. But I do not mean to imply that an attempt ought to be made to divide the Nation into constituencies, each returning a number of Members exactly proportioned to that of the voters. This would be inexpedient, because it would involve an amount of change and an abandonment of existing local divisions which would be highly inconvenient, while it is not, as I conceive, required by the true principles of Representative Government. The House of Commons is not a body of delegates, or, to use the words of Burke, " a congress of Ambassadors from different and hostile interests," in which it is necessary carefully to measure the amount of influence given to each of these rival interests. And even if this were admitted to be necessary, it may well be doubted whether that object would be accomplished by adopting the rule that the number of Representatives should be exactly in proportion to that of the Constituencies by which they are returned. Such a rule would probably give a larger share of political power to the metropolis, and to the great centres of manufactures and commerce, than would be desirable or even just. It must be borne in mind that a population collected closely together, and for the most part engaged in the same pursuit, derives from that circumstance, and from the facility for joint action growing out of it, the means of exercising far greater influence upon the Government than a population equally numerous but scattered over a much wider area. Hence, in order to maintain a really just balance of political power, a somewhat larger representation in proportion to the number of their inhabitants should be given to the less than to the more populous districts.

The anomalies and extreme inequality of the existing division of the country for electoral purposes would be removed sufficiently for all practical objects, by adopting the principle of allowing no separate constituency to fall below some minimum, or to exceed some maximum, both to be determined after due inquiry. Assuming that the Franchise were made the same in counties and in boroughs (as I have already proposed), no elector now entitled to a vote need be disfranchised in consequence of the adoption of this rule, though it would be necessary that some boroughs should be merged in the counties to which they belong, and that some places which now return Members separately should be joined together for that purpose. This would be the more necessary, because, with a view to the adoption of the "cumulative vote," I contemplate that, as a general rule, not less than three Members should be elected together, and in some cases a greater number.

By merging the small boroughs in the counties of which they form part, a considerable number of Seats would be rendered disposable, if the minimum determined upon for constituencies were fixed as high as I think it ought to be, and the constituencies of some of the less populous counties would thus receive the augmentation which they would probably be found to require. On the other hand, by giving some of the Seats thus rendered disposable to large towns in the populous manufacturing counties, and at the same time considerably enlarging the borough boundaries, the constituencies of these counties might be brought within the maximum appointed. Perhaps I shall make my meaning clearer by pointing out the sort of arrangement which might be adopted in a case of each kind. I will suppose (and I need hardly observe that this is merely a supposition by way of explaining how the scheme would work, as I have no means of ascertaining the actual facts) that the northern division of the county of Northumberland would be found to have less than the minimum of electors required for a separate constituency, but that the addition of the two boroughs of Berwick and of Morpeth would bring the number of voters up to the required amount. In this case, these two boroughs might be merged in the county, three Members being assigned to the enlarged constituency. As the three places now return five Members,* two Seats would thus become disposable. On the other hand, it is not improbable that, notwithstanding the Act of 1862, the West Riding of Yorkshire might be found to form two constituencies exceeding the prescribed maximum. If so, a few of the Seats set at liberty by merging small boroughs in the counties they belong to, might be given to some of the large Yorkshire towns, in such a manner as to reduce the above-named large con-

* 2 for Northumberland; 2 for Berwick; 1 for Morpeth.

stituencies within the appointed limits. Leeds, with some of the largest of the present boroughs of the Riding, and perhaps some of the towns not now separately represented, such as Doncaster, might each be given three Members, enough of the surrounding country being attached to them to form in each case an adequate constituency, which would, of course, be deducted from that of the county. By a proper regulation of the limits of the towns, there would be no difficulty in thus bringing the constituencies of the two divisions of the Riding within the appointed maximum. The arrangement would also naturally include either merging the smaller boroughs, such as Ripon and Pontefract, in the county constituencies, or uniting them with the larger towns.

Considering how many small boroughs there are in some counties, I can hardly doubt that the general application of this principle would set free a sufficient number of Seats to make room for the Members I have proposed to bring into the House of Commons by other modes than local elections, after providing for all local claims, and without putting the minimum of electors for a separate Constituency extravagantly high. And though this arrangement would not get rid of all inequality in the share of political power given to the different local Constituencies, in the proportion to their numbers, it would reduce that inequality (now so shocking to every notion of fairness) within certain and comparatively moderate limits. No Constituency would exceed the maximum, or fall short of the minimum, which might be adopted after due inquiry ; and at the same time there would be no unnecessary interference with existing local divisions, and especially with that distribution of the Kingdom into counties, which it is desirable to maintain on account of its long-standing, and its historical associations. .

The arrangements I have suggested would also correct other anomalies besides that of the extreme inequality of the existing Constituencies. It has long been recognized as an absurdity, that the occupation of a £10 house should be considered as a sufficient qualification for a borough voter, while in a county no occupier can, in that character, claim the same privilege unless the property he holds is worth £50 a year. So long as the boroughs were really towns, and their Members represented a town as distinguished from a country population, and while the county Members were elected by the freeholders only, and thus represented property, the distinction in the Franchise between the one and the other was at least intel-

ligiblc. But now, many of our small boroughs
include large rural districts, the inhabitants of
which almost swamp those of the original town,
while they are also represented by the Members
for the counties to which they belong. In these
places the £10 occupiers vote for the borough, the
£50 occupiers of land without a house upon it, and
the freeholders (if their freeholds are not such as
to give votes for the borough) for the county.
Under certain circumstances the £10 householders,
who have also separate £50 farms or freeholds,
may vote both for the borough and for the county.
Thus it might happen that in a strictly rural district, a man might occupy a small farm just under
£50 a year immediately without the boundary of a
borough, and would have no vote because his qualification would be insufficient for a county elector;
and yet his next neighbour, only differing from him
by being in a somewhat lower condition of life, and
holding an adjoining house and field worth £10
a year, from the same landlord and by the same
yearly tenure, might enjoy the privilege denied to
himself, because the smaller property was within
the boundary of a district added to some borough
five or six miles off, in order to make up a reasonable Constituency. There might be a third inhabi-
tant of the same district, differing little in circum

stances from the other two, and entitled to vote both for the county and for the borough, because he occupied a £10 house, and possessed a separate 40s. freehold within the limits of the latter. The freeholders in boroughs vote in the county in which the town is included, and that places like Manchester and Liverpool have not only their own legitimate representatives, but are also able to exercise an influence in the elections for the counties, which may often be sufficient to overpower that of their agricultural inhabitants.

Making the Franchise the same in counties and in boroughs, and requiring that votes should be given where they arise, would at once put an end to these anomalies, which are, indeed, worse than anomalies, since they involve extreme unfairness in the capricious distribution of political power, and in arbitrarily withholding the right of voting from some men, and bestowing it upon others, without the slightest reference to their respective fitness or unfitness for the exercise of the privilege. I am aware that strong objections were made to the regulation as to the Franchise which I have now suggested when it was proposed as part of the Reform Bill of 1859, nor do I dispute the force of some of the arguments urged against the arrangement as contemplated by that Bill. The assimi-

lation of the county and borough Franchise in
the manner proposed, if unaccompanied by other
changes would have have been calculated to give
undue power to great landowners in the smaller
boroughs, and also to impair the provision wisely
made by our constitution for securing a distinct
representation to the two very distinct classes of
the community, consisting of the inhabitants of
towns on the one hand, and of the country on the
other. But these objections would not apply to the
proposal as part of a larger measure.   Landowners
would not be likely to exercise a dangerous influence in constituencies no longer restricted in numbers like those of the present small boroughs. And
though it is true that much advantage formerly resulted from securing its due share of the representation to each of the classes represented by the counties and boroughs respectively, it must be borne
in mind that circumstances are now greatly altered.
There is still a difference in the character and circumstances of different portions of the Nation, corresponding to that which of old existed between the
borough and county populations, but the division is
far less local than formerly, owing to the new facilities created in recent times for intercourse between
different places, and to the growing up of what, in
character, is a town population beyond the limits

of the Parliamentary boroughs. In this state of things, the proper representation of each of the different classes in the community is far less likely to be attained by keeping up a distinction between counties and boroughs with respect to the Franchise, than by adopting a uniform Franchise, together with the system of the " cumulative vote." I have already pointed out that this system would, both in counties and in boroughs, tend to secure representation to those who are now practically unrepresented.

Another, and no slight advantage, that would result from revising the present division of the country for the purpose of elections, would be its tendency to relieve Parliament from the reproach of being guilty of hypocrisy and inconsistency with respect to electoral corruption. It now deliberately, and with its eyes open, maintains a system, of which the inevitable effect is to bring a very large number of electors under the direct or indirect dominion of money, and at the same time it legislates severely against bribery; and when any unfortunate borough is proved to have yielded to the almost irresistible temptation of allowing bribery to carry its return, Parliament, which has wilfully exposed it to that temptation, makes a great parade of virtuous indignation, and passes an Act for its disfranchisement. Thus we have seen St. Albans and Ipswich deprived of their Members, after proceedings very costly, not only in money, but in far more valuable time. There is gross inconsistency in this mode of dealing with the subject of corruption in elections. If the desire to put it down were sincere, some attempt at least would be made to remove the causes which produce it; and of these it is notorious that none is more powerful than leaving the power of disposing of Seats in Parliament to small bodies of electors, of a class which makes it morally certain that they will exercise the privilege for their own pecuniary benefit. By revising the present distribution of the right of returning Members to the House of Commons, so as to prevent its being enjoyed by any Constituency not likely, from its numbers and circumstances, to be independent of money influence, we might not succeed in putting down corruption in elections (and I am not visionary enough to suppose that it can ever be entirely suppressed), but we could hardly fail to diminish its prevalence, and at all events Parliament would be relieved from the disgrace of virtually maintaining the evil practices against which it professes to legislate with severity.

How the votes at elections ought to be taken will

also require to be carefully considered in framing a new Reform Bill.   One question of course will be, whether the system of voting by ballot ought to adopted, for it is not to be supposed that this old article of the radical faith will be abandoned, or that it will fail even now to command the support of many eager partisans.   But there are strong signs that the more than ample discussion the subject has undergone has brought the majority of the public to the conclusion, that the opponents of secret voting have had the best of the argument, and the weight of authority inclines to the same side, especially since it has been so decidedly adopted by Mr. Mill in his work on Representative Government.   It is needless, therefore, for me to enter into a question which has been completely exhausted, and I will content myself with observing that even if the arguments against the ballot upon principle were less conclusive than I consider them to be, there would be a strong objection to it on the ground of the facilities it affords for abuse and partiality in the conduct of elections.   Even with the best system of registration, a discretion must unavoidably be entrusted to Returning Officers, as to admitting or rejecting the votes of those who present themselves as electors; and when the franchise is widely extended, and the constituency is very numerous, it is not easy to ascertain whether all who come to the poll are really the electors they profess to be, or are fraudulently personating registered voters who are dead or absent. The Returning Officer can alone determine, at the moment, whether votes objected to on this ground are to be admitted or not. But if the voting is open, his decision is not without appeal, since votes he has improperly admitted or rejected, may be afterwards struck off or added to the poll by an Election Committee, which can thus correct a wrong return. If, on the other hand, the voting is secret, this cannot be done; there is nothing to show from which candidate votes improperly admitted are to be taken away, nor can new votes be added without giving up the rule of secrecy. The Returning Officer may therefore have notoriously admitted fictitious votes on one side, and rejected good ones on the other, and a colourable majority may thus have been obtained for the candidate who would have stood lowest on the poll if it had been fairly conducted; and yet the return cannot be corrected. All that can be done in the clearest case of abuse is to quash the election, and perhaps punish the Returning Officer; but this, which makes a new election, and probably another contest, necessary, is no redress of the injustice done to the candidate improperly rejected, or to the electors whose real opinion has been over-ruled by fraud. From the best accounts we possess of Australian and American elections, it appears that abuses of this kind, to which the system of ballot is calculated to lead, have in fact been very common.

Supposing the scheme of voting by ballot to be rejected, it would remain to be considered whether any other changes in the mode of taking votes should be introduced, in order to enable electors to exercise their right with more convenience and less expense than at present. Two suggestions have been made with this view: one, that electors should be allowed to give their votes by voting-papers transmitted to the Returning Officer; the other, that some mode of indirect voting should be adopted. The use of voting-papers would certainly diminish the trouble and expense of giving votes, especially for electors living at a distance from the place of election, and it is presumed that this conside-ration has lately induced Parliament to pass an Act by which this mode of voting has been sanc-tioned for the Universities. As the University Electors are so generally non-resident, and belong to a class comparatively little exposed to the in-fluence of bribery, there is both more need for the change, and less risk of its leading to abuse in these elections than there would be in other cases. The

experiment is, therefore, one there was fair reason
for trying so far as the Universities are concerned;
but it is much to be feared that the extension of
the same system to all elections would give dangerous facilities for bribery and for other abuses.
Perhaps one of its chief objects, that of enabling
distant voters to give their votes without the heavy
expense of going to the poll, might be attained by
providing that a registered elector, not being within
easy reach of the place where an election was about
to take place, should be allowed to appear before
any Court of Petty Sessions, and there publicly sign
a declaration of the vote he desired to give, and
that this declaration being transmitted by the Court
to the Returning Officer, should be entered as a vote
on the poll.

The system of indirect voting has been condemned
by most writers of authority, and especially by Mr.
Mill in his Essay on Representative Government;
but I cannot think that it deserves to be so sum-
marily rejected as it has been by him. His chapter
upon this subject seems to me to be greatly inferior
to the rest of his valuable Essay, and to be far from
satisfactory; for whether the conclusion to which he
comes is right or not (a question on which I am
not prepared to express a decided opinion, as there
is so much to be said on both sides), it is at all

events clear, that in his enumeration of the recommendations of indirect voting he has omitted some of the most important. He has failed to notice, among other arguments in its favour, that a well-arranged system of indirect voting might afford the means of obviating some of the worst of the very serious difficulties and inconveniences which arise from having exceedingly numerous Constituencies. With an extension of the Franchise the number of electors must be increased, and when it becomes very large, it is impossible that they should all be known by sight, either by the persons appointed to take the poll, or even by those employed by candidates to check the tender of false votes. From the same cause it also becomes difficult to prevent confusion and disorder at the polling places, and to secure to the electors the means of giving their votes without personal inconvenience, and without the risk of incurring violence or insult if they happen to support an unpopular candidate. The best arrangements it has hitherto been practicable to make have very imperfectly met these difficulties, and even precautions attended with considerable expense have not proved sufficient to guard effectually against the personation of electors and other abuses. A still more serious evil, resulting from the excessive number of some Constituencies, is the little interest it has made electors take in the exercise of their privilege, from their knowing how small an influence their individual votes can have on the result of the elections. This want of interest makes them unwilling to incur even a slight amount of trouble for the purpose of giving their votes, and the consequence is, that a very small proportion of such Constituencies as those of the Metropolitan Boroughs can usually be induced to vote at all; and, what is worse, the apathy of the electors throws undue power into the hands of small knots of intriguers, who, by skilful organization and canvass, are generally enabled virtually to control the elections.

Indirect voting, by reducing the number of persons entitled to vote at the final election of Members of the House of Commons, would certainly tend to correct these evils; it therefore deserves to be considered whether this system of voting might not be introduced in such a manner as to make it free from the objections generally urged against it. It has been argued that if all who enjoy the Franchise are not allowed to vote directly in the election of their Representatives, but only to choose those by whose voices the final election is to be determined, the primary electors will either take no interest in the exercise of their restricted privilege, or else they will convert the division of the election into two stages into a mere form, by choosing electors pledged to support the candidates they prefer in the final election. The elections of Presidents in the United States are referred to as proving that this last is the natural working of election by two stages. There is no doubt that these elections have in reality been merely a roundabout way of taking the votes of the whole population of the United States in favour of this or that candidate for the Presidency, and the preliminary choice of electors has been a vain form; but it is by no means clear that a similar result must follow under different arrangements. The electors who are afterwards to decide who is to be President of the United States, are not chosen till long after the different candidates for the Presidency have been declared, and their respective claims have been discussed and canvassed throughout the whole Republic; they are chosen likewise with reference to an election which is to be held at a definite and not distant time after the primary election. In such circumstances it is not surprising that the primary electors vote " for the Lincoln ticket" or the " Breckenridge ticket," and that the choice of the future President is virtually decided by the primary election.

But the case would be very different if the electors who were eventually to choose the Members of the House of Commons were themselves chosen, not after a dissolution of Parliament, and immediately before the final election, but while it was still uncertain when they might be called upon to exercise their privilege.   Some such arrangement as the following might be adopted.   The proportion which the electors are to bear to the primary voters should first be determined, and supposing it to be one elector for every twenty voters (though this is merely a supposition for the sake of explaining the suggestion), it might then be provided that so soon as the annual register is complete, any twenty registered voters who should think fit to join together for the purpose, should have the right of appointing one elector by a declaration bearing their signatures (with their numbers on the register), that they wished the person therein named to vote in their behalf.   A day should be fixed (as soon after the completion of the register as might be consistent with convenience) before which such declarations should be sent to the Returning Officer, and after a proper investigation of their authenticity, the names thus sent in should be published as those of the Parliamentary electors for the Constituency for the ensuing year.

Those electors who did not think fit to join in appointing some one to vote in their behalf would of course lose the benefit of their franchise. By an arrangement of this kind, even if the number of voters were largely increased by an extension of the Franchise, the great evils resulting from over-grown Constituencies under the existing system would be effectually prevented, and the number of votes to be given at the poll would be reduced within such a compass, as to make it easy to guard against confusion or personation. Nor is it likely that the appointment of electors would degenerate into a mere form, while the interest taken in elections by the voters at large would be thus rather increased than diminished. No doubt great efforts would generally be made to nominate as electors known supporters of the sitting Members, and of persons who had already declared themselves candidates for various places; but even electors so chosen would be influenced by circumstances that might arise between the time of their appointment and a Parliamentary election, and would be quite free to consider the claims of any new candidates that might come forward. And as the electors would represent small bodies of voters voluntarily joined together, on the principle suggested by Mr. Hare, it might reasonably be expected that each elector

would consult those by whom he had been nominated, and to whom he must look for being nominated again another year, before he decided upon
the vote he was to give in their behalf.   The division of the whole Constituency into small bodies
of this kind, having a motive for discussing among
themselves the pretensions of different candidates,
and their political opinions, would have a tendency
to diffuse amongst the population a more general
and more intelligent interest in these matters than
is now found to exist.   A poor man who is one of
10,000 voters for a large town, feels that his single
vote can have so little effect upon the result of the
election, that he is apt either to neglect giving it
at all, or to give it to the party most skilful in
bringing some irregular influence to bear upon him.
But if he were one of twenty friends joined together
by their general concurrence of opinion to depute
one of their number to give a vote in a Constituency thus reduced to 500, he would know that that
vote would have an appreciable importance, and
he would be likely to take an interest in considering and discussing, with those who shared it with
him, how it should be bestowed.

By this, or perhaps by some better · arrangement, indirect voting might be made to produce
some considerable advantages ; still, I am aware

that these advantages would not be unmixed, and that it is hardly to be expected that any scheme of the kind should be free from serious objections. Amongst these, it might be urged that none but the devoted adherents of some political party would have a chance of being chosen electors, and that the most independent men would be excluded from all share in choosing the Members of the House of Commons. To a certain extent this might be true, but it may be doubted whether, in very large Constituencies, organization, and the arts of professional politicians, will not have undue influence, whether the voting be direct or indirect. At this moment it is certain that they are almost irresistible in such Constituencies as those of the Metropolitan boroughs.* The considerations I have now mentioned, together with other reasons which may be urged both for and against indirect voting, would require to be very carefully weighed before any satisfactory decision could be come to on the question whether this system ought, or ought not, to be adopted.

In the preceding pages I have stated my views as to the general character of the amendments required in the constitution of the House of Com-

---

* See the evidence of Mr. Albert James before the Committee of the House of Lords on the Elective Franchise.

mons; and though there would be several other points to be considered whenever the subject may have to be practically dealt with, there is no occasion for my noticing them here, since my design has been rather to show what are the main objects to be aimed at in a Bill of Parliamentary Reform, than to propose a detailed scheme for their accomplishment. Indeed, I should wish to be understood not as expressing a fixed opinion, but as offering only suggestions for consideration, even in recommending the changes I have described. They are what the information at present within my reach has led me to regard as the amendments of the Constitution best calculated to improve the House of Commons, according to what I take to be its true ancient character, of a body representing all the different classes of the community, but in which a decided preponderance is given to education and intelligence. Better methods of attaining this result than have occurred to myself will in all probability be devised by others, and I desire to keep my judgment free to consider what they may propose.

There remains one important question, to which I must advert before closing this Chapter. Assuming it to be desirable that a Reform of Parliament, calculated to amend our Constitution without changing its principle, should be carried, how is it possible that this should be accomplished? I have already given my reasons for believing that though no large measure of Parliamentary Reform could at this moment be attempted with any prospect of success, this state of opinion is not likely to be lasting, and that the time cannot be far distant when an urgent demand will arise for the improvement of our representative system. But even in that case there would be great difficulties to be overcome before any Reform Bill could be carried, and scarcely a possibility of passing one calculated to effect a real improvement in our Constitution, without a departure from the usual practice in bringing the question under the consideration of Parliament. No Ministers, however able they might be, could be expected to succeed in drawing up a project that would be really satisfactory, without more assistance than they could command by the ordinary machinery of the Government. Careful inquiry, and much consultation with men of various knowledge and experience, would be required, before this could be accomplished. And even if a good Bill were prepared, there would be little hope that any Administration would be able to carry it if they submitted it to Parliament without concert with other political parties.

In the first edition of this Essay I pointed out

that the jealousy and suspicion with which such a
Bill would be regarded, if brought forward by a
Conservative Government, would be almost sure to
lead to its defeat; while a Ministry of what is called
the Liberal Party would hardly have any better
prospect of success in a similar attempt, because if
it were to propose a moderate measure, it would
fail to command the popular support necessary to
overcome a powerful opposition ; and, on the other
hand, a measure of an ultra-Democratic character,
likely to enlist the passions of the People in its
favour, would probably provoke a strong Conservative reaction.   The result has verified these anticipations, and after the failure of the Reform Bills of
1859 and 1860, neither of the great parties which
have successively governed the State are likely to
repeat the experiment of bringing forward a com-
prehensive Bill of Reform, with the prospect of its
being resisted by the adverse party. It is therefore
only by the consent of different parties that we can
hope that a Reform Bill will be passed, and yet
the need for one is daily becoming greater.   It is
wanted, as I have already endeavoured to show,
both as a safeguard against the gradual deterioration of our Constitution by successive petty changes,
and to correct faults in our present system which
cannot fail to become more and more felt; and it is

also wanted (perhaps scarcely less urgently) for the purpose of removing what is likely to become a most serious obstacle to the existence of any strong and durable Administration. While the question of Reform remains unsettled, every Liberal Government must be placed in a false position, in which no course will be open to it not beset with difficulties and dangers. Such a Government cannot (as experience has proved) bring forward a measure of Reform with any hopes of success.* Yet it cannot oppose motions like that of Mr. Locke King for the extension of the county Franchise, or that

* The following is the opinion of a writer in the ' Morning Star' (the organ of the Radical party), as to the difficulty of carrying a Reform Bill :—"I should say, taking Conservatism to mean those who are opposed to the Ballot and any real extension of the Suffrage, that it comprises within its ranks nineteen-twentieths of the House of Lords, nine-tenths of the large landed proprietors, nineteen-twentieths of the Church of England clergy, seven-eighths of the county magistrates of the kingdom, five-sixths of the lawyers seven-eights of the officers of the Army and Navy, and four-fifths f all the men owning above two thousand a year. This is the permanent staff of the army of Conservatism, or by whatever name it calls itself. In times of political enthusiasm, when great principles are at stake, the ten-pounders, with the whole body of the working class behind them, can hold their own against this mighty array of social influence ; but this can only be done when there is some public object to gain, that unites these numerous classes in support of each other, and reconciles the poorer electors to the sacrifices which it always costs them to maintain their principles. The present state of things offers no motive to small shopkeepers and other dependent voters to expose themselves to petty martyrdom."

of Mr. Berkeley for the Ballot, without finding itself divided from its usual supporters, and compelled to depend upon its opponents, at the same time bringing the Seats of many of its members and adherents into jeopardy. Nor can it, without extreme discredit,* either treat such motions as open questions, or yet support them, while declining to pledge itself as a Government to carry the measures it has agreed to, with the very serious consequences to which giving a pledge of this kind must lead. To a Conservative Administration, the present state of this question must be a source of still greater embarrassment, not only from the Parliamentary difficulties to which it exposes them, but from its placing their supporters under so much disadvantage in many elections, and especially in those for all considerable towns.

* This was written before the debates in the House of Commons in the last Session, on the Bills of Mr. Locke King and Mr. Baines for enlarging the County and Borough constituencies. What occurred on these occasions has confirmed my opinion as to the discredit brought upon a Liberal Government by the manner in which it is compelled to deal with questions of this kind. Ministers had declared this to be an improper time, in their opinion, for Parliament to attempt any improvement of our Representative system, and had accordingly declined to propose measures for that purpose on their own responsibility. Yet, when these bills were brought forward by private members of Parliament, and the second reading was opposed by moving the previous question, Ministers in both cases voted that the Bills should then be proceeded with.

For these reasons I believe it would be equally for the interest of the Nation at large and of all political parties to pass a new Reform Bill calculated to correct the real faults of our present representation, but that it is only by the consent of the most powerful at least of these parties having been secured beforehand, that a Bill of this kind could be submitted to Parliament with any chance of being carried. What is wanted, therefore, is that the leaders of the various parties into which Parliament and the Nation is divided should be induced to meet to consider the subject in a spirit of mutual forbearance, and with a sincere desire to settle the question.

In the first edition of this Essay I ventured to suggest that the best mode of attempting to bring the leaders of the chief parties in the State to an agreement as to the provisions of a Reform Bill which they might all support, would be for the Queen to nominate a Committee of Her Privy Council, composed of Members taken from different political parties, and instructed to consider and report to Her Majesty what measures of Reform it would be expedient to propose to Parliament. Though this suggestion found no favour when it was made, what subsequently occurred, and the discredit brought upon Parliament by the proceedings with reference to Reform in 1859 and 1860, go far, as I think, to show that it would have been well if it had been adopted. And the same reasons which weighed with me at that time lead me still to believe, that the course I then recommended would afford the best chance of effecting a satisfactory settlement of this difficult question. It seems more and more clear that it is indispensable for the success of any good measure of Reform, that, before it is submitted to Parliament, there should be an understanding with regard to it among different parties; and yet it would obviously be unsafe and improper for the leaders of these parties to endeavour to come to such an understanding by means of private and unauthorized consultations among themselves. The holding of such consultations would certainly be denounced (and not without reason) as an odious cabal, and an objectionable attempt to control the deliberations of Parliament by a secret conspiracy, and any conclusion so come to would have no authority whatever with the Public. The appointment of a Committee of the Privy Council would, on the contrary, be a mode of proceeding open to no such objection, and in strict conformity with the principles of the Constitution.

From the earliest times of our history the Crown has been in the habit of calling on the Privy Coun-

cil for advice on all matters of importance. The
Privy Council has also long been accustomed to
act in many cases by Committees, the Cabinet itself
being only one, though by far the most important
of these Committees. Since the Revolution and
the establishment of our present system of Parliamentary Government, it has become usual, except
on some rare occasions, to summon to meetings of
the Privy Council, and of its Committees, only those
Members of the Board who are connected with the
Administration of the day; but this practice is prescribed by convenience only, not by law, and was
not that anciently followed, nor has it been uniformly adhered to even in modern times. Thus in
the year 1850 the Queen was advised to refer the
consideration of the changes it would be expedient
to make in the Constitutions of the Australian Colonies to a Committee of the Privy Council, two
Members of which did not hold office in the Government. The Report of that Committee was laid
before the Queen in Council, and having been approved by Her Majesty, on the advice of her Ministers, a Bill founded upon it was submitted by them
to Parliament, and eventually passed. I am not
aware that any objection was taken to this mode of
proceeding, which was obviously highly convenient,
since, while it left the full responsibility for the

measure brought before Parliament upon the Ministers of the Crown, it afforded them very useful assistance in the preparation of the measure, and also the means of bringing formally before Parliament a full explanation of their reasons for recommending it.

I suggested, in 1858, that this precedent should be strictly followed with respect to the question of Parliamentary Reform, except that I proposed that the Committee of the Privy Council to which this subject should be referred should be a larger one, and should include Members of various political parties. No doubt this exception is an important one, and there would be a wide departure from what is usual in attempting to bring together the Ministers, and the Leaders of the parties opposed to them, for the purpose of deliberating upon a great public question, and advising Her Majesty as to the provisions of a Bill to be submitted to Parliament. But the peculiar circumstances of the case afford grounds for this departure from the ordinary practice. In considering the question of Parliamentary Reform, there are two things to be ascertained : first, what are the changes which would be best calculated to improve the working of our Constitution ; and, secondly, what are those to which Parliament could be brought to assent ? Now the

T

first of these branches of inquiry might perhaps be conducted as efficiently, or almost as efficiently, by a well-selected Royal Commission (such as that which proved so successful in the Reform of the Poor Law), as by a Committee of the Privy Council. From the nature of the subject, however, it would be difficult to name a Royal Commission which, even in inquiring what ought to be done, would not be under some disadvantage as compared to a Committee of the Privy Council composed of men who had themselves been engaged in the contests of public life and in the business of Parliament, and who would thus have the benefit of their own experience, in addition to all they might learn from the deepest thinkers and ablest political writers, on whom they would doubtless call for advice and assistance. And in the second branch of the inquiry, —that as to what changes Parliament might be brought to agree to,—a Royal Commission would probably be able to render no assistance whatever, while there would be little difficulty in ascertaining what could or could not be carried by the aid of a well-selected Committee of the Privy Council, having among its Members some of the Leaders of all the great parties in the State, including the Radical party. The chiefs of this party, who ought to represent it in such a Committee, may not at present be Privy Councillors; but I am aware of no objection to their being made so, since they are men on whom this honour would be very fitly bestowed. Should it be practicable to bring a Committee, or a considerable majority of a Committee so constituted, to concur in a report recommending a plan of Parliamentary Reform suited to the present state of the country, there would be little doubt as to the success of a Bill founded on this report and submitted to Parliament by Her Majesty's Ministers.

I am aware this suggestion assumes that rival politicians might be brought to treat the question of Reform as one which ought not to be made the subject of party contests, and to join in honestly and fairly endeavouring to settle it; but why should this be despaired of? I am persuaded there is no ground whatever for thinking so ill of public men in this country as to suppose that amidst all their personal differences and ambitious contests, they do not feel a sincere desire to promote the welfare of the Nation; and in this case, in doing what would be for the public good, they would also be best serving their party interests, which, for the reasons I have already explained, require that this question of Parliamentary Reform should be settled. If it is not settled by consent, it cannot fail sooner or later to give rise to another great political conflict, and the history of the Reform Act of 1832 affords an impressive lesson as to the importance of averting such a conflict and preventing a change in the Constitution from again becoming a subject of party strife. The struggle by which that measure was carried, was one of which the full danger and difficulty were not generally known; but those who are aware of the truth must, I am sure, concur with me in believing that a nation has seldom passed safely through such peril of a fearful convulsion. Though it would not become me to enlarge upon the subject, I trust I may without impropriety express my conviction, that, under Providence, we owe our escape from that great peril to the judgment and firmness with which the helm of the Government was held by its Chief, and to the steady course which he steered, in spite both of the bitter opposition to which he was exposed on the one side, and of the violent counsels so urgently pressed upon him by almost all his friends on the other. To engage the Nation again in a contest of the same kind, without the same urgent necessity, would be an act either of the most reckless folly or of the deepest guilt.

Nor is it only as to the danger of such a contest that the events of 1831 and 1832 are instructive. If we carefully consider the whole course of the proceedings in the Reform Bills, we must, I think, come to the conclusion that these measures might have been greatly improved, and that three much better Acts might have been passed (for the three divisions of the United Kingdom), if, instead of being carried as they were, they had been settled by temperate and candid discussion between the leaders of different parties. Instead of making a life-and-death battle for the maintenance of existing abuses, the Tory party, had they been wise, would have frankly accepted, as unavoidable, the transfer of a large measure of political power from the hands of the borough-holders to those of the people at large, and would have confined their efforts to the improvement of the measure, so as to obviate the most reasonable of their objections to it. If they had shown a disposition to take this course, I feel convinced that the Ministers of that day would not have refused to meet them in a conciliatory spirit. As it was, the violence of the opposition which the measure encountered, made it utterly impossible that the question of amending it should be calmly considered; and unfortunately, the changes which to ensure its success were made in it during its progress, were for the most part changes for the worse.

At the same time it would be most unjust to

throw the whole blame of the struggle by which the Reform Bill was carried upon the Tory party. It must in fairness be admitted that the violence of some of the partisans of the measure was well calculated to increase the alarm which its magnitude might reasonably create, even in men influenced by no selfish considerations, but only by an honest concern for the good of the country. Sufficient anxiety was not felt by many of the Reformers, to reconcile adversaries of this class to what was, in truth, a hazardous experiment,—an experiment which I believe it to have been absolutely necessary to make, but of which the result could not fail to be matter of anxiety not alone to its opponents, but also to those of its supporters who understood its real character.*

* What I regard as the just view of the Reform Bill, and of the opposition it encountered, is so well stated in an article in the ' North British Review,' that I cannot forbear quoting the passage. " The Reform Bill, it is impossible to deny, was a transfer of power and political influence from the aristocracy to the middle classes. Who now will not acknowledge that this was a revolution, at the magnitude of which genuine patriots might well stand aghast, which cautious men might well deem wild and perilous, which even men who loved progress, if they loved safety likewise, might well deprecate and dread? Those who loved the People might not unreasonably doubt the wisdom of entrusting this new weapon to the People's hands. No one will now deny that it was a great experiment. No one will deny that in some respects its opponents judged it more truly, and saw further into its consequences, than its pro-

Both the recollection of what occurred when the last great change in our Constitution was accomplished, and a consideration of the difficulties to be encountered in attempting a new one, lead therefore to the conclusion, that a reference of the question of Parliamentary Reform to a Committee of the Privy Council, would afford the best prospect of arriving at its satisfactory settlement. But it would be an almost indispensable preliminary to such a reference, that it should be recommended by Parliament, and that the two Houses should concur, not only in asking the Crown to appoint a Committee of the Privy Council to consider what amendments are required in the constitution of the House of Commons, but also in declaring their

moters. For ourselves, we confess that, approving it as we did and do,—believing it to be a just, a wise, and a necessary measure,—tracing in the main to its secondary influences the rapid progress of reforms in other lines,—we yet see in it several dangers, drawbacks, and extensive seeds of future and questionable change, which we did not see when it was passed; we acknowledge much weight and wisdom in many of the hostile arguments which at the time we scouted as the mere dictates of selfishness and folly; and we look back with something like remorse and shame at the violence of our language, the acrimony of our feelings, the imperfection of our philosophy, and the shortness of our vision. We were blind to much that our adversaries saw; we were obstinately deaf to many representations that ought to have been listened to with deference and profit; and if the thing had to be done again, we should act with greater modesty and temperance, with far less confidence, and far more misgiving."—*North British Review for August*, 1854, p. 573.

views as to the objects to which these amendments
should be directed.   Nor do I think it would be
impossible to define these objects by a few short
resolutions, to which a majority of both Houses
might agree.   Though very conflicting opinions
have been expressed on the propositions that have
been brought before the House of Commons for
altering the law under which it is elected, there is
reason to believe, that its Members have differed
from each other more as to the manner in which
the changes they have been asked to adopt would
be likely to work, than as to the results it would
be desirable to obtain.   Few probably, even of those
holding the most popular opinions, would be prepared to contend that a Reform of Parliament
ought to throw a predominance of political power
into the hands of the numerical majority of the
population.   In theory, at least, it would be admitted, that any alteration in our Representative
System ought to provide, not only for enabling all
classes of the community to make their opinion and
wishes heard in Parliament, but also for giving due
weight to knowledge and intelligence, and for making the House of Commons act as nearly as may be
in accordance with the deliberate judgment of those
most able to form a sound judgment as to the true
interests of the Nation.   Probably it would also

be recognized as desirable, that some arrangement should be made to secure to the Ministers of the Crown that authority in Parliament which the system of Parliamentary Government requires them to exercise.   And lastly, there could be no difference of opinion as to the necessity of so arranging the system of representation, as to avoid giving any encouragement to corruption.   Resolutions declaring these to be the objects to which a Reform of Parliament ought to be directed, might therefore be expected to command the assent of both Houses. If passed, they would afford good Parliamentary grounds for an Address to the Crown praying for the appointment of a Committee of the Privy Council to consider by what arrangements these— the deliberately avowed purposes of the Legislature —might best be attained.   Such resolutions as I have described, if adopted with this view, would not be open to the objections which may in general be justly taken to the passing of abstract resolutions by either House of Parliament.   They would indeed be abstract in their character, but they would have a practical and most important object, since they would serve for the guidance of those to whom the high duty of preparing a scheme of Reform for the consideration of Parliament would be entrusted.

I have only to add, in concluding this Chapter, that it will cause me no surprise if the views which it explains should generally be regarded as visionary and impracticable. I am quite prepared to find that of the changes I have suggested, some will be pronounced wild and dangerous by Conservatives, others as attacks on the liberties of the People, by politicians of opposite opinions. But though I have little expectation that there will be many by whom my views will be accepted, I am sanguine enough to hope that these pages will not prove altogether useless. They will fully accomplish the object with which they have been written, if they should serve to provoke the further discussion which is so much needed of the principles on which a Reform in Parliament ought to be attempted, and if they should be found not altogether barren of suggestions deserving the notice of those who desire to consider this most important subject in a spirit of serious inquiry, and without reference to party interests.

CHAPTER VIII.

ON THE EXERCISE OF PATRONAGE UNDER PARLIAMENTARY GOVERNMENT.

THE working of Parliamentary Government in this Country has been much affected by the greater or less amount of patronage possessed by the Crown at different times, and by alterations of practice as to the exercise of that patronage which have taken place in the last century and a half; and it must also be much influenced hereafter by any changes which may be made on these points. It does not therefore seem foreign to the subject of this Essay, to consider the nature and effects of the system which has prevailed in this country, in making appointments to the civil and military offices which are not held by the Members of the Administration.

Under all forms of government, from despotism to unbridled democracy, complaints have been common, that the servants of the State have not been wisely and honestly selected, but that merit has been habitually passed by, and the public interest sacrificed, by the appointment of incompetent men to perform important duties. No doubt these complaints are often the mere clamour of disappointed place-hunters, but they are also frequently well founded. Every different kind of government has its own difficulties in this matter, and none is free from the operation of some of the various influences that may tend to misdirect the stream of patronage. Under our own form of government (and the same may be said of free governments in general), those entrusted with patronage are under a temptation to use it corruptly, because they may thus purchase support which may help to prolong their own power. This abuse was formerly carried to a great excess in this country, and the Ministers of the day usually trusted to an unscrupulous use of the patronage vested in their hands as one of the principal means of maintaining themselves in office. So lately as in the reign of George the Third, not only were places and pensions bartered without shame for political support, but the dismissal of officers in the Army or Navy for votes given in the House of Commons was occasionally resorted to, and there were even instances of the removal of public servants from situations now regarded as permanent, for the avowed purpose of punishing their friends and relations for having pursued in Parliament a line of conduct obnoxious to the Minister.

A striking improvement has taken place in the practice of Governments, and in the tone of public feeling upon this subject.   No Minister would now dare to incur the responsibility of abusing the patronage of the Crown and its power of dismissing its servants, by such acts as were committed with impunity less than a century ago.   In the last seventy or eighty years, public opinion has gradually brought the exercise of these powers of the Crown under the control of certain rules, which, though for the most part enforced by no written law, are yet practically binding upon the Government, and have put an end to many abuses.

Formerly, the appointment and promotion of naval and military officers was made, almost openly, a matter of mere favour.   No rules existed prescribing certain periods of service in the lower ranks in the Army and Navy, before the higher ones could be attained, and nothing was more common than to see men rise through political influence to the command of regiments and ships of the line, with scarcely any service or knowledge of their profession to recommend them.   There are now very strict rules, as to the time that officers must serve in different ranks before they can be promoted; and it is universally recognized as the duty of those entrusted with the powers of the Crown, to be guided in the distribution of promotion and professional employment in the Army and Navy by the rules of the Service and the merits of officers. I am far from asserting that favour has not still its influence in these matters, nor, human nature being such as it is, can we expect that this will ever cease to be the case. But it is certain that the exercise of patronage in the Army and Navy is now watched with so jealous an eye, that those by whom it is administered are compelled to be exceedingly careful how they employ it, and that thus gross abuses at least (such as were formerly of everyday occurrence) are now become rare, and the errors that are committed are chiefly errors of judgment. A Ministry, even if inclined to act corruptly, would no longer dare to abuse the military and naval patronage of the Crown for that purpose, since it is certain that far more would be lost than gained by the attempt.

The change which has taken place is not confined to the Army and Navy. The civil patronage of the Crown has been greatly reduced by the many economical reforms effected since the Peace of 1815, and especially since the Reform of Parliament in 1832; and some of the abuses which were formerly not uncommon, have been rendered impossible by the system now firmly established as to the tenure by which all civil offices are held, except what are called political offices,—that is to say, those which are usually conferred on Members of either House of Parliament. As a general rule, the Civil Servants who do not sit in Parliament hold their offices technically and legally during the pleasure of the Crown, but are in practice considered as having a right to remain in undisturbed possession of them, so long as they continue to discharge their functions properly. This principle is so universally recognized, that the dismissal of a person holding a permanent office is now never heard of, except for misconduct.

In most of the Public Departments a regular order of promotion has also been established, so that by far the majority of the higher permanent offices in the Civil Service are filled up by the appointment of persons who have been gradually advanced to them from its lower ranks. The rule that these promotions should be strictly governed by a fair consideration of the respective claims of the several candidates, from seniority and merit, is recognized in principle; nor is it often departed

from in practice, through undue favour or partiality. The odium which the Ministers who have
to decide upon these promotions know that they
would incur, both in their own offices and out of
doors, by being guilty of favouritism, acts as so
powerful a check upon abuse, that I believe it may
be said never to occur. Errors of judgment are
no doubt frequently committed, in performing the
very difficult duty of selecting public servants for
advancement; but the most common error, according to my observation, is that of giving undue
weight to seniority, and too little to ability and
merit, from fear of incurring the suspicion of partiality.

The strict control under which the exercise of
the patronage of the Crown has thus been brought,
and the reduction of its amount, have had an important, and, upon the whole, a highly beneficial
effect on the working of our system of Parliamentary Government, though it would be a mistake to suppose the advantage derived from these
changes to have been unmixed with some inconvenience. The gain has been, that the power of
corruption has been diminished, and that the distinct line drawn between permanent and political
offices, together with the complete establishment
of the practice of regarding the former as held

during good behaviour, has diminished the evils incidental to changes of Administration.   It is the very nature of Parliamentary Government, and indeed of all free Governments, to cause power to be from time to time transferred, from one man, or one set of men, to another; but by allowing these transfers to affect only a comparatively small number of high offices, and by retaining the great majority of the Public Servants permanently in their situations, the experience and traditional knowledge they possess of the business of the several departments of the State are rendered still available for the conduct of affairs.   By changing (when there is occasion for it) those to whom the supreme direction of the Government is entrusted, enough is done to secure its being carried on in conformity with the feelings and opinions of the Nation; while, by leaving the details of business in the same hands under successive Administrations, it is made to proceed with a regularity and consistency which would otherwise be wanting.*

The same arrangement also conduces to the Public being well served at a moderate cost.   A man can with prudence accept a far lower remuneration for his services, if they are permanently en-

* See some remarks on this subject in 'Macaulay's History of England,' vol. iii. p. 339.

U

gaged, than if his employment is precarious.   The
salaries now paid to our Civil Servants (excluding
of course the holders of political offices, upon whom
other motives are brought to bear) would command
a very inferior class of men, if, instead of knowing
that they are in no danger of losing their employment unless by misconduct, and that they may ultimately look forward to a retiring pension, they
were subject to be turned out of their situations at
any moment for no fault and without any compensation.   Men would hesitate before they abandoned
other pursuits to serve the State upon these conditions, unless they received very high remuneration for doing so, either in salary, or in the shape
of other and probably irregular emoluments.

The penalty of dismissal is also far greater in the
one case than in the other, and consequently the
security against misconduct afforded by apprehension of that punishment.   A Custom-house officer,
for instance, who risks the loss of a secure provision
for life, by taking a bribe to connive at some fraud
on the Revenue, is likely to be much less easily induced to do so, than one who hazards nothing but
a place which he only holds till the next turn of
the political wheel, and which he cannot expect to
keep for more than three or four years.   The general fidelity and trustworthiness of all the subor-

dinate public servants in this country, are no doubt in a great degree owing to this cause.

Another, and perhaps a still more valuable result of the permanent tenure by which the majority of public Servants in this Country hold their situations is, its tendency to mitigate the violence of party contests. When a change of Administration involves only a change in the holders of some fifty or sixty offices, usually entrusted to Members of the two Houses of Parliament, the prospect of such an event is obviously calculated to create much less excitement than when it leads, as in the United States, to the transfer of some thousands of offices of all classes, including the very lowest, from one Party to another. Of late years it has become the practice in the United States, when a President is installed in power, to remove all opponents of the Party to which he belongs from the offices they hold, down to a village postmastership, or the lowest clerkship in the Customs. Hence the pecuniary interests of a large part of the population are directly affected by Presidential elections, and it is not surprising that they should create the intense excitement evinced all over the Union when they are approaching. We are happily spared from having the bitterness of our Party struggles aggravated, as it would be, if the fall of one Minister and the

appointment of another were to be made the signal
for dismissing the vast number of persons employed
in the various branches of the Civil Service, and
filling up this multitude of places from the ranks
of the victorious Party.   There can be no doubt
that, were this to become the practice, it would
lead to a perpetual succession of fierce political contests, violently exciting the hopes and fears of all
classes of the population throughout the kingdom,
giving rise to the grossest corruption and to all
kinds of intrigues, and rousing the most baneful
passions.   Such a state of things would be almost
intolerable, and we pay a cheap price for avoiding
it in sacrificing something of the energy of the Government.

It is certain that something of the energy of the
Government is sacrificed by the curtailment of the
patronage of the Crown, and the virtual independence now given to the Civil Servants of the State,
because, however advantageous these changes may
be in other respects, they have doubtless diminished
the power of the Government to excite the zeal of
those it employs by the hope of reward, and to facilitate the success of its measures by selecting the
most efficient agents for their execution.   When
the manner in which the business is transacted in
the Government offices, and in those of private

merchants and manufacturers, is compared, it ought
to be borne in mind, that the latter are absolutely
free to choose whom they will employ, and to
change their servants at their pleasure; whereas
the head of a public department is compelled to
carry on its duties by the aid of men in the selection of whom he has generally had no voice, and
whom he cannot remove except for some flagrant
misconduct.

I have said that the force and energy of a Go-
verment are necessarily diminished by this restriction on its freedom of choice, but that this is a sacrifice wisely made; and the same remark applies
to those rules for the conduct of public business
which have been contemptuously called the system
of " red tape." Those who are entrusted with more
or less authority in the management of the vast
and complicated concerns of a great Nation, are
liable to be tempted to use their power rather for
their own selfish interests than for those of the
Public; for which reason it has been found necessary, in all countries, to lay down certain rules, and
to require certain forms to be adhered to in the
transaction of public business, for the purpose of
guarding against the abuses which would otherwise
be sure to arise. What is called the system of
" red tape " consists, in reality, only of the rules

of this kind which have been gradually established as experience has proved them to be necessary, and which, if carefully examined, would generally be found to be wise in themselves, though they are no doubt sometimes followed too slavishly.

In the organization of the public Departments of such a Nation as this, it is desirable not only to arm those who administer the Government with the means of conducting it with the greatest possible efficiency, but also to provide adequate checks against the tendency to corruption which is inherent in the nature of mankind. The advocates of what is called "Administrative Reform" seem to have overlooked the fact, that it is impossible to devise any system which shall be completely satisfactory in both respects. In order to give the utmost vigour and energy to the Government, those who direct it ought to have a large discretion as to the manner of conducting its business, and an unfettered freedom of action in appointing and dismissing those whom they employ. On the other hand, if the object is to guard against the possibility of jobs, and to prevent the patronage of the Crown from becoming an instrument of corruption, then rules must be laid down which will act more or less as restraints upon those to whom the powers of the Crown are for the time entrusted. By at-

tending exclusively to either of these objects, one
or other of the two opposite evils would be incurred, either that of destroying the vigour of the
Government, or else that of opening a door to dangerous abuses. Something must be sacrificed on
each side, in order to place the Public Service on
the footing which shall upon the whole be most
conducive to the welfare of the Nation. This is
what is aimed at by our existing system, and upon
the whole with considerable success. I have had
an opportunity of seeing a good deal of the interior
of several of our Public Offices; and I am convinced there is not one of them, the permanent
Members of which are not perfectly capable of
giving to the Minister who conducts it, as effective
assistance as he is entitled to expect. As a body,
the permanent Civil Servants of the State in this
country are remarkable for their intelligence, industry, and high sense of honour. There are certainly individuals of a different character to be
found in so numerous a body; but, taking them
altogether, I cannot doubt that they would show a
high average of fitness for their important duties.

I am far from thinking the constitution of our
Civil Service so good as not to be susceptible of
improvement; but the only attempt hitherto made
to amend it has been the adoption of a change

which, I am convinced, is one greatly for the worse. I allude to the practice which has been lately introduced of filling vacancies in the public departments, by what are called "competitive examinations." According to this new practice, the junior clerkships that become vacant in the Public Departments, instead of being filled up by the several Ministers to whom the patronage belongs, are made prizes for the successful competitors in examinations which are held from time to time in literature, mathematics, and certain other branches of knowledge. In some departments the competition is, I believe, an open one; that is to say, any young man having certain preliminary qualifications, may enter himself as a candidate for the prize. But the more general practice is for the Minister at the head of a department in which a vacancy has occurred, to name three candidates to compete for it.

With respect to this last mode of dealing with the patronage of the public offices, I must confess myself to be totally at a loss to comprehend upon what grounds it can have been adopted, since it appears to rest upon no principle whatever, and to be a futile attempt to make a compromise between two systems directly opposed to each other. If the principle of making admission into the Public

Service a prize to be competed for in literary examinations is a sound one, it ought to be distinctly
recognized and fully acted upon, and care ought
therefore to be taken to provide for having a real
and fair competition.   But under the system of
naming only three candidates, who are arbitrarily
chosen, to compete for each vacancy, there is nothing to ensure such a competition, or to prevent
the Minister from securing the success of a candidate in whom he is interested, by naming as his
opponents two young men whom he knows to be
his inferiors in acquirements.   Not only would it
be easy to do that, but it must be exceedingly difficult to avoid some practical unfairness, or at all
events giving plausible grounds for the suspicion
of unfairness, in naming candidates for this sort of
literary handicap.   Already, I believe, it has been
complained, that a highly qualified candidate has
sometimes failed because he has been pitted against
a still better one; while a greatly inferior man has
succeeded in gaining the prize, because, owing to
good luck or to favour, he has had to contend with
opponents even more deficient than himself.   On
the other hand, if it is desirable that the Ministers of the Crown should retain their patronage,
it ought to be a real patronage, and beneficial to
those on whom it is conferred.   But though it may

be convenient to a Minister to be able to oblige three persons instead of one, by naming three candidates for every vacancy at his disposal, a nomination to be one of three candidates for a single appointment, is a very doubtful advantage to the person receiving it. Two out of the three candidates must of necessity fail, however well qualified they may all be, and the disappointed ones will have lost the time and money expended in preparing for the contest, and will be left to seek some other profession or occupation in life under circumstances of great difficulty and disadvantage. For these reasons I hold that if we are to have competition at all, it ought to be free and unrestricted ; and that the field should be open to all comers possessing such preliminary qualifications as it may be necessary to require in order to secure having a proper description of candidates.

But I regard the principle of disposing of places in the Public Service by competitive examinations as being radically wrong. The first objection I have to the scheme is, that the examinations afford no test of the comparative fitness of the different candidates for employment in the Public Service. Brilliant talents and great acquirements are far less useful than moral qualities, in the holders of permanent offices. Industry, regularity, and fidelity, are the qualities which are most valuable in persons filling these situations, the great majority of which neither require, nor afford, a field for the exercise of more than average abilities. If therefore the scheme of competitive examinations were to prove successful in filling our Public Departments with men of first-rate talents, it may safely be predicted that they would not be content either with their occupation or with the advantages held out to them by the present scale of salaries in the Civil Service, since they would feel that in other pursuits their abilities would command far higher advantages, and find more scope for their exercise.

No doubt it would be possible to raise the general scale of salaries, so as to make the permanent Civil Service more attractive to men of the highest ability. But this would remove only one part of the difficulty, while it would occasion a formidable increase of the public expenditure, and, what is much worse, would open dangerous temptations to jobs, and to unfairness in making promotions in the various Departments; perhaps also in conducting the competitive examinations. While the present scale of payment enables the Public to command the services of men equal to the duties imposed upon them, it is hard to see on what grounds an increase of salaries could be justified.

The best paid of the permanent Civil Servants receive, it is true, emoluments which are small compared to those of successful lawyers, physicians, or merchants; but they have a compensation in the certainty, for the moderate amount of their remuneration. They are also relieved from any heavy responsibility, by the subordinate position they must always occupy; for they can only enjoy the permanent tenure of their offices upon the condition of remaining subordinate to the Ministers of the Crown, who are answerable to Parliament for the measures of the Government. The responsibility of the permanent Civil Servants is limited to the faithful execution of the instructions they receive from the Ministers, assuming of course that these instructions are consistent with the law. It is no arbitrary rule, which requires that all holders of permanent offices must be subordinate to some Minister responsible to Parliament, since it is obvious that, without it, the first principle of our system of Government—the control of all branches of the Administration by Parliament—would be abandoned. Hence, though it has been sometimes treated as an absurdity, that an experienced and able Under-Secretary, in any of our great Departments, should be made subordinate to even the least capable Minister who may

be raised to be its temporary head in the vicis-
situdes of party contests, this is in fact an inevitable consequence of the nature of our Government.   It is obvious that, if the able Under-Secretary were relieved from subordination to any
superior, either he must submit to the general rule
of retiring from office when he ceased to possess
the confidence of Parliament, or a system of irresponsible administration would be introduced into
the Department entrusted to him.   Accordingly,
when the talents and ambition of any of the permanent Servants of the Crown have led them to
aspire to the power and distinction of the higher
political offices, they have invariably given up the
humbler but safer situations they have previously
held.*   But a profession, the very nature of which
is to retain those who adhere to it in subordinate
situations, which holds out no great prizes, and the
distinguishing characteristic of which is, that it

* If I am not mistaken, both Mr. Huskisson and Mr. Herries
originally belonged to the permanent Civil Service, which they
quitted for political offices.   It is to be regretted that there are not
greater facilities for such transfers, and that able men cannot be
more frequently brought from permanent to political offices.   Such
removals have been rendered far more difficult than formerly by
confining the grant of pensions for political services within narrower
limits, and making it subject to more rigid conditions.   The existing
rules as to the grant of such pensions seem therefore to be founded
on a short-sighted economy.

offers only moderate though certain advantages, is, by this very circumstance, one into which it is inexpedient to bring the young men who stand in the first rank among their contemporaries for talents and acquirements.

Nor is it by any means certain that, by competitive examinations, we are likely to attain the object of raising the standard of the intellectual qualifications for their duties possessed by our Public Servants. I have already observed, that moral qualities, which cannot be tested at all by a competitive examination, are far more important to them than great intellectual endowments; it may be added, that, even with regard to the latter, such examinations are a most imperfect test. All that can be ascertained by examinations is, the comparative proficiency of the different candidates in certain kinds of knowledge, which can seldom be directly useful in carrying on the business of a public office. Great acquirements in literature or in science cannot assist a clerk in the War Office or Treasury, in checking a pay-list or examining an account; nor are they more serviceable in the performance of the ordinary duties of ninety-nine out of a hundred clerks in all the various departments of the State.

Competitive examinations must therefore, it is

to be presumed, have been adopted for the purpose
of ensuring the appointment of able clerks in our
public offices, on the assumption that the superior
proficiency of the successful candidates in the subjects in which they have been examined, justifies
the inference that they must possess also a superiority of mental power which will render them more
capable than their rivals of acquiring a knowledge
of the business of the Department into which they
are admitted, and of affording useful assistance in
conducting it.   But this inference will by no means
always, probably not even generally, prove correct.
The comparative proficiency of different young men
in certain studies, might possibly be some test of
their comparative abilities, if these studies had
been prosecuted under circumstances of equal advantage, and if equal labour had been devoted to
them by the competitors.   But as this cannot be
the case, competitive examinations can afford no
means of judging of anything beyond the positive
acquirements of the several candidates, or, in other
words, of the extent to which the memory has
been stored, and the expertness which has been
attained in such things as arithmetic and composition.   Now it is certain that judicious "cramming,"
as it is termed, may often enable a youth of inferior abilities to show a greater amount of such

expertness, and of acquired knowledge in a given range of subjects, than another, greatly his superior in all the most valuable qualities of the mind. Though only a short time has elapsed since these examinations were introduced, the practice of "cramming" is already so fully established, that putting young men through the process is become a regular profession. It is found that by carefully watching the examinations, so as to learn what are the habits of mind of the examiners, what are their views and opinions, and what kind of questions they are likely to ask, clever men have made themselves so skilful in preparing candidates for competition, that those to whom they have given a few months of this training, or "cramming," can be made morally certain of gaining the prize against competitors who have not had the same advantage, though they may be of superior ability to themselves, and have received a better general education. So completely is this fact recognized by those whose interest it affects, that I understand it is considered almost useless for a young man to go into a competitive examination without having been first in the hands of a professional "crammer," to whom as much as from £100 to £150 is sometimes paid for taking charge of a candidate for a few months before the examination. The grow-

ing up of this practice in so short a time seems
alone almost sufficient to condemn the whole system
of competitive examinations, since it is notorious
that the knowledge acquired by " cramming " is
often lost as quickly as it is gained.   At the end of
a very short time what has been learned by this
unnatural and unhealthy process is generally forgotten, and those who have undergone it not un-
commonly contract from it an utter distaste for
study, and even for serious reading, which lasts for
their lives.

Competitive examinations are therefore utterly
fallacious as a test even of that which they profess
to ascertain,—namely, the comparative ability and
the acquired knowledge of the candidates who
pass through them, if acquired knowledge is understood in its proper sense of that which has been
gained as a solid possession of the mind.   But this
is not all; it is a well-ascertained fact, that the
premature forcing of young minds has an injurious effect upon their vigour in after-life; and the
acquisition of a great amount of knowledge may
be dearly purchased, by weakening the powers of
judgment, of reflection, and of original thought.*
If, therefore, admissions into the Civil Service of

* See some interesting remarks on this subject in Sir B. Brodie's
' Psychological Inquiries,' page 28, and the eloquent passage he has

X

the State are in future to be given as a reward
to the successful candidates in competitive examinations, it is to be feared that, in the struggle to
obtain this much-coveted employment, young men
will be subjected to a system of education by which
they may acquire extraordinary proficiency in certain branches of knowledge, at the expense of
qualities much more conducive to their usefulness
in the real business of life. The adoption of this
scheme will therefore be calculated to render the
Public Servants, as a body, less, instead of better,
qualified than they now are for the work they have
to do, by filling the various Departments of the
State with men possessing knowledge for which
they would find little use in the performance of
their official duties, but often deficient in that common sense and power of thinking and acting for
themselves which would be invaluable, but which
the over-training of young men is apt to prevent
them from acquiring.

The mischief might not stop there ; the proposed change would probably tend to introduce
generally into the country a system of education
calculated to injure the minds of the whole class of
young men, from whom the candidates for the re-
quoted from Dr. Newman's Lectures (p. 245) on the evil effect of
compelling young men to "load their minds with a score of subjects
against an examination."

wards offered for competition would be drawn.   No more serious evil than this could be inflicted on the Nation ; and there is the more reason to apprehend that it may follow from this mode of selecting the persons on whom public appointments are to be conferred, in consequence of what experience has shown to be the effects of a similar system in France. In that country, employment in the service of the State is made, to a great extent, the prize of success in examinations known by the name of *Concours ;* and I have been informed on very high authority, that in the struggle to obtain these prizes, the different schools have gradually gone on increasing the amount of labour exacted from their pupils, until it has become most excessive.   The consequence is said to be, that diseases of the brain have become formidably common, and that the young men who have been thus overtasked in their early years, are in after-life usually found inferior, in the more useful qualities of the mind, to those who have received a more natural education.*

* It has been said by a very high French authority (whom I do not however think myself at liberty to quote by name), that the École Polytechnique turns out only " des bêtes savantes;" and this seems to be the real meaning of the opinion respecting this School which the Commissioners for inquiring into Foreign Military Education quote as having been expressed by General Paixhans. Speaking of the too great amount of abstract knowledge required from the pupils, the General says, " Leur cerveau fatigué d'études mathéma-

The experience of our own Universities of late years is said to be to the same effect. Many young men of the highest promise are found to break down their powers, either of body or of mind, and to render themselves physically or morally unfit for the real work of life, by the too intense labour they undergo in the struggle to obtain the highest places in the list of University honours. The cases however are comparatively rare, in which the voluntary exertions of young men competing for honours only, are carried to an injurious excess. University examinations usually act as a stimulus to industry with no more power than is desirable, in order to overcome the temptations of idleness and amusement. It is to be feared that examinations open to all candidates, and offering employment in the public service as the prize of success, will operate very differently. Most parents are so anxious to obtain this sort of employment for their sons, that the places of education which prove most successful in training candidates to compete for it will soon be generally preferred. The managers of places of education will be unable to resist

tiques compliquées, leurs vues incessamment dirigées vers l'abstraction, ne redescendent pas facilement à terre, à la terre des études et des travaux pratiques, lesquels sont en définitive ceux qui sont nécessaires au jour de la lutte en campagne, dans une armée assiégeante, ou dans une place assiégée."—*Report on Military Education*, p. 28.

this impulse, and will be led to vie with each other in striving [to force the largest possible amount of knowledge into the minds of their pupils. The consequence may be, that the rising generation in this country will, in a few years, be subjected to a system of over-driving like that which is said to prevail and to be so pernicious in France.

Nor can this be prevented by an endeavour on the part of the examiners to limit the extent to which the examinations should be carried. In a school, the stimulus of competition may be used, and at the same time the discretion of the master may guard against excessive labour being imposed on the scholars, as he has a control both over their conduct and over the examination.* But if there is to be competition at all, among candidates who are not under such control, the examination must necessarily be carried up to a point at which some of the candidates will be less fully instructed than others. If it should only test the possession of an amount of knowledge which all can acquire completely, there will be no means of distinguishing between the first and the last; while, if the exa-

* This was done by Dr. Arnold, who, while he attached much value to competition as a stimulus to exertion, expressed also a strong opinion as to the necessity of preventing the boys under him being overworked, and took great care to prevent it. See his Life, vol. i. p. 126.

mination is carried far enough to show the comparative inferiority of some of the competitors, it is impossible to limit the amount of labour their instructors will impose upon them in order that they may excel their rivals.

For these reasons, I should anticipate that the Public Servants obtained by competitive examinations will, in general, be less efficient than those appointed by the Government under the old system ; and if the information I have received be true, there are already greater symptoms than I should have expected so early, that this anticipation will prove correct. But in addition to this reason for disapproving the change, it is also, as I think, to be condemned on the ground that the object for which it was introduced is altogether a wrong one. The main object for which it was recommended by those who first urged its adoption was that of depriving the Government of patronage, which it was said habitually to abuse. That there may have been abuse in the disposal of the patronage of the Government I am not prepared to deny, though I am convinced the extent of the evil has been much exaggerated. But there is no power belonging to Governments which has not also been sometimes abused ; and if we are to withdraw every power that is susceptible of being so, we may have a Govern-

ment which can do no harm, but it will certainly
be one totally incapable of performing its proper
functions. And among the powers that are required to enable it to discharge these functions
with efficiency, there are few more necessary than
that of reward. A Government may enforce obedience to its command by punishment, but reward
is the great instrument by which it can call forth
zealous and able service. The Sovereigns and Ministers whose government has been most successful,
have almost invariably been remarkable for their
judicious exercise of the power of reward. But
among the rewards which a Government can be-
stow on those who have deserved well at its hands,
the conferring upon their sons or near relations
those appointments which are given to young men
as the beginning of a career in the Public Service,
is perhaps of all others that which is the least liable
to abuse, the least costly to the public, and at the
same time the most effectual. I therefore disapprove and regret the great diminution, not to say
the abolition, of the patronage of this kind formerly
possessed by the Government, by the introduction
of competitive examinations; and the more so because, in the war which has very properly been
made against the gross abuses of former times, the
means of reward possessed by the Government of

this Country had already, in the last forty years, been perhaps too much curtailed.

It may be answered, that it is wrong to reward any services, however meritorious, by conferring appointments on the incompetent sons or relations of those by whom such services have been rendered. No doubt it would be highly improper to saddle the Country with incompetent young men in situations of trust, from any motive whatever; but this might be guarded against without depriving the Government of patronage, its possession of which, if rightly used, is of great advantage to the Nation. None of the objections to competitive examinations for the admission of candidates into the service of the State, apply to the establishment of a rule, that no young man shall be allowed to obtain public employment without having undergone a strict examination by an independent and impartial authority, to ascertain his fitness for it. If the qualification to be required from candidates for the Public Service is judiciously fixed, and the examiners do their duty, examinations of this sort will effectually exclude incompetent persons from our public offices, without depriving the Government of its patronage, or incurring the other inconveniences to be apprehended from competitive examinations.

It has indeed been asserted that examinations in which the principle of competition is not adopted, invariably degenerate into a mere form. To reject a young man who submits himself to examination that it may be ascertained whether he is fit for an appointment conferred upon him, and thus to mar his prospects in life, is said to be so painful a duty that the examiners cannot be trusted to perform it, though they may safely be so as to placing fairly in the order of merit the candidates brought before them as competitors. I am not aware of there being any grounds for this assertion. The appointment of clerks upon probation only for the first year, as was formerly the practice in most of the Public Departments, did not indeed prove to afford much security against incompetent men becoming established in the service, since the power of rejection was seldom used; but it is a very different matter to dismiss a young man who has actually been admitted into the service, and to decline admitting him. And when the power of rejection was confided to the same Minister who had made the original appointment, it was not likely to be very severely used. But if the authority to conduct examinations for testing the competence of all candidates for the Public Service is entrusted to men well selected, and placed in an independent position, I see no reason to doubt that the duty will be properly performed.   Indeed, it is so, I believe, at present by the Civil Service Commissioners, by whom young men are now submitted to a test-examination before they are allowed to become candidates in a competitive examination for admission into the Public Service.

I have discussed the scheme of making admission into the Civil Service of the State the prize of successful competition in public examinations, somewhat fully, but not, I hope, more so than is proportioned to its importance in relation to the main subject of this Essay.   Indeed, the working of our Parliamentary Government is so much affected by the rules which regulate the exercise of the Patronage of the Crown, and the constitution of the Civil Service, that before closing this Chapter I shall venture to make some further observations with regard to them, and to offer some suggestions for improving the present organization of our Public Departments.

I have endeavoured to show, that security against improper appointments might be obtained without having recourse to competitive examinations; but it is not sufficient merely to provide that young men shall be debarred from admission into the service of the State, who are unfit even for the easy duties which are in the first instance imposed upon them. It is far more important, for the efficiency of the Public Departments, to ensure that promotion in them shall be given only to those who have shown themselves fit for it, by the manner in which they have performed their duties, and by the pains they have taken to acquire a knowledge of their business. With this view, the system of promotion which already exists in some offices should be made general, and at the same time more perfectly enforced. According to this system, the clerks in an office are divided into several classes, and each vacancy in one of the higher classes is filled, as it occurs, by the selection of any one of the class immediately below who may, in the judgment of the Head of the Department, have the best claim to promotion. It was intended that merit, rather than seniority, should be considered in forming this judgment; but the propriety of not excluding from consideration the comparative length of service of the different candidates having been admitted, it is to be feared that this system of promotion has a constant tendency to degenerate into one of mere seniority, or at all events into one in which the senior is passed over only for decided incompetence, and not on account of marked inferiority to a junior, in ability or industry. The too great regard shown to seniority in some offices, has probably furnished most of the grounds that really exist for the assertion so strongly made, that a large proportion of incompetent men are to be found filling important situations in our Public Departments.   Young men entering these Departments at seventeen or eighteen, cannot reasonably be expected always to prove diligent, and anxious to improve themselves, from a mere sense of duty.   Like men of the same age in every other profession, they have many temptations to idleness, and require some strong stimulus to exertion.   In an office, therefore, in which advancement is equally sure to all who abstain from gross misconduct, we have no right to look for the same diligence and ability as may be expected in one where these qualities find their sure reward in early promotion. None who are acquainted with the interior of our Public Departments, will have any difficulty in recognizing the superior efficiency of those in which merit has been allowed to have its proper weight over seniority in promotions.

Such being the case, it is most desirable that promotion should be given in every Department upon this principle; and, to enforce its being so, I would suggest that the rule should be distinctly laid down, as being applicable to all the Public Offices, by an Order in Council; and further, that whenever a promotion was made, the reasons for it should be recorded. The Minister at the head of the Department ought to be responsible for the promotions made in it, as for all other official acts; but he should be required to found his decision on a Report (which should be placed on record) from the Under Secretary, or the person holding by any other title, the highest permanent situation in the office, who has both the strongest interest in making a right choice among the candidates for promotion, and the best means of judging of their respective qualifications. No Minister would venture, without good reasons, to overrule the recommendations offered to him in such a Report. In order still further to ensure, so far as this can be done by any regulations, the right performance of the all-important duty of selecting candidates for promotion in the Public Departments, it ought further, I would suggest, to be prescribed by Order in Council, that a Register should be kept in each of these Departments, of the conduct of the different persons composing its establishment. A Register is already kept in most of them of attendance; but it would be of great advantage that the manner in which the several clerks perform their duties should be recorded, as well as the fact of their punctual attendance. And this might be accomplished, at least

to some extent, by having a Register in which, whenever a clerk received the praise of his superiors for
peculiar diligence or ability, shown in the performance of any business entrusted to him, or when,
on the other hand, he incurred reproof by negli-
gence or inattention, the commendation or the censure should be entered.   Whenever a vacancy occurred which had to be filled by promotion, this
Register would be referred to, and its establishment would be useful, not only on such occasions,
but also as a valuable addition to the means of enforcing discipline and giving a stimulus to exertion,
in the ordinary course of the business of the Department.

Such comparatively slight alterations as these
might be expected to improve the working of the
system of promotion in our Public Departments;
but there is another obstacle to the complete efficiency of these Departments, which they would do
nothing towards removing.   I allude to the want
of greater facilities for bringing men of talent and
of mature age into the Public Service.   With all
its advantages, a regular system of promotion in
the Government offices has the inconvenience of
rendering it exceedingly difficult for the Ministers
of the Crown to avail themselves of the great abilities and peculiar fitness for business, sometimes

displayed by men who have not been brought up in official employment. It would be absurd to propose to such men to become junior clerks, with the duties and emoluments proper to youths of eighteen, and there are, under the existing arrangements, very few appointments of a higher order that can be conferred upon them without disappointing the just expectations of those who have made the Public Service their profession. What seems to be wanted is, that there should be a few more offices placed upon the same footing as the permanent Under-Secretaryships of State and the corresponding situations in other Departments, which are very properly regarded as not falling within the regular course of promotion. The members of the Department where the vacancy occurs are not ineligible for these appointments, but are not regarded as having any preferable claim to them; and in general they are given to men not previously in the Public Service. This ought to continue to be the practice, not only because a wider field of selection is thus given to the Government in filling up situations of great importance, but also because other pursuits in life are more likely than the training of a public office, to produce men well fitted for these employments.

A moderate addition to the number of offices

disposable in this manner, would greatly facilitate the efficient management of public affairs; and if the Ministers, who keep their places only while they retain the confidence of Parliament, are to be held responsible for the manner in which the Public Service is conducted, it is only just that they should be enabled to obtain the best assistance in carrying it on. No increase of offices of this sort ought, however, to take place at the price of diminishing the prospects of reward now held out to those who have made the Public Service their profession. On the contrary, it seems to me that these prospects require to be improved. I see no reason to doubt the sufficiency of the general scale of salaries in our Public Departments; but I consider that, under the strong pressure of the desire for economy which formerly prevailed in the House of Commons, the abolition of the agencies, and other appointments of little labour which were often held with clerkships, has been carried too far, and has unduly restricted the means which the Government possessed, of rewarding peculiar merit in its permanent Servants. This is a fault which I should be glad to see corrected, at the same time that provision was made for enabling the Government to confer a few more offices, of some value, on men who have not risen to them in the regular order of promotion.

Perhaps both these objects might be accomplished, while the organization of the Government, as an instrument for the gradual amendment of our laws, might also be improved by giving some extension to the Privy Council, and employing it more systematically than is now the practice, in the preparation of business for Parliament. It has not been unusual for the Ministers of the Crown to entrust to Committees composed of some of their own body, and of persons holding office, but not in the Cabinet, the task of preparing for their consideration measures they desire to bring before Parliament. The Reform Bills of 1831 were prepared, as is well known, by Committees of this kind, as were most of the important bills introduced and passed by Lord Melbourne's Administration. Much good work has been done by such Committees; but those who have served upon them must be aware, that it is difficult to make them as extensively useful as might be desirable. The business of most of our Public Departments is so heavy, that few of those who hold offices in the Government can spare from their proper departmental duties, the time necessary for giving effective assistance in considering subjects of difficulty with a view to legislation, especially when it is necessary for that purpose to collect and digest information not readily accessible. The proceedings also of Committees of official men, as hitherto constituted, have hardly been of a sufficiently formal character, to furnish a convenient basis for legislation.

The consequence is, that of late years the employment of Commissions, specially named on each occasion as it occurs, has to a great extent superseded the use of Official Committees in preparing measures for the consideration of the Cabinet, and ultimately of Parliament. Much advantage has no doubt been derived from the employment of Commissions, and for some purposes it will probably always be necessary for the Ministers of the Crown to avail themselves of their assistance; but I cannot help thinking that they have been a good deal abused, and that they do not constitute the best machinery for effecting all the purposes to which they have been applied. They have perhaps been most abused in order to shelter the Government from the responsibility that properly belongs to it. When public attention has been strongly called to some existing evil, and an urgent demand for the application of a remedy to it has arisen, it has been no uncommon expedient on the part of an Administration which feels itself to be wanting either in the capacity, or in the power, necessary for dealing with a difficult subject, to refer it to

a Commission. This, at all events, answers the
purpose of staving off the evil day for the Government, of being compelled to submit any measure
to Parliament with the risk of defeat which it involves; and by the time the Commission has reported, public attention may have been diverted to
some new subject, thus enabling the Administration
to evade altogether the duty of attempting to correct an acknowledged defect in our polity. Or if
the subject should prove to be one on which something must at last be done, the Government shelters
itself from responsibility behind the Commission,
yet often without adopting its views in a complete
and consistent form. Nor are Commissions always
very effective instruments for accomplishing their
intended objects. They are generally, though not
always, composed of unpaid members, who have
other occupations and who naturally devote to the
business in which they are acting as volunteers, only
the time they can spare from their more regular
avocations, so that it is extremely difficult to command the steady and continuous services of men fit
for the duty imposed upon them.

Committees of the Privy Council might, I think,
undertake with advantage much of the work which
has thus been done by less formal Committees of
men in office and by Commissions, provided a

limited number of men of experience and ability were appointed Privy Councillors, with salaries assigned to them, in consideration of their assisting in the performance of this duty. Men who had distinguished themselves by long and useful service, either in Parliament or in high permanent office, would find a fitting reward, and an honourable retirement from more laborious duties, in being appointed paid Privy Councillors. The Privy Council already possesses the power of summoning witnesses and calling for information, and with the addition of these paid members, it would afford the means of constituting Committees well able to conduct important public inquiries, and to prepare Bills for the consideration of the Government. Every such Committee ought, I think, to be presided over by a Cabinet Minister, and there are a sufficient number of Cabinet Officers with no departmental duties, or very light ones, to remove all difficulty in making this arrangement. The responsibility of the Government for what was done by these Committees would thus be provided for, and might, I think, be further secured by requiring that their reports, before being acted upon, should be approved by the Crown on the advice of its Ministers. The usefulness of the Privy Council might thus be greatly extended, and it might be enabled to discharge functions analogous to those which are, I believe, performed with advantage by the Conseil d'État in France.

Improvements of the kind I have described, with others it would not be difficult to suggest, might, I believe, add greatly to the efficiency of the Government; but in making any such changes I am persuaded that a departure from the principles on which the Civil Service is now conducted, ought to be most carefully avoided. This remark applies more especially to the tenure by which the Civil Servants of the State generally hold their offices.

The safe working of Parliamentary Government depends in no small degree upon strictly adhering to the practice upon this subject which I have described above, as having been for a long time firmly established in this Country. Much evil would arise from departing from it in either direction; on the one hand, by more directly limiting the authority of the Ministers of the Crown to dismiss any of its subordinate servants; on the other, by allowing a more frequent or capricious exercise of this authority. I have already pointed out the bad consequences to be apprehended from the last; those of deviating from the existing practice on the other side would be but little less serious. An absolute legal power on the part of the Crown to dismiss

any of its Servants, on the advice of its responsible*
Ministers, is indispensable, in order to give to the
latter, that authority over those by whose agency
and assistance they carry on the public business,
without which they could not justly be held ac-
countable by Parliament, for the manner in which
affairs are conducted.   If the tenure of offices now
regarded as permanent were to be altered, and they
were in future to be held by law as well as by practice during good behaviour, it would be necessary
that the law should also strictly define the misconduct for which they might be taken away.   But
it would be impossible to limit the power of dismissal to cases in which such misconduct could be
proved before a court of law without incurring the
risk of having the Executive Government paralyzed
by the passive resistance of persons holding these
situations, and by the obstructions they would be
able to throw in the way of Ministers they wished
to oppose.   Law would be too clumsy an instrument
for regulating the conduct of the Ministers of the

* When the responsible Ministers of the Crown are themselves
dismissed, the Sovereign must necessarily act in the first instance
without advice ; but it is now, I believe, a settled point, that those
who accept the offices thus vacated, render themselves responsible
for the dismissal of their predecessors, so that this forms no exception to the general rule, that there can be no exercise of the Crown's
authority for which it must not find some Minister willing to make
himself responsible.

Crown and the permanent Civil Servants of the State in their relations to each other. This is now far more effectually and far more safely accomplished by the power of public opinion.

So great is the authority of public opinion, that no Minister now ever thinks of dismissing a public Servant from those offices which are regarded as permanent, unless for gross misconduct; but at the same time he has the power (and public opinion would support him in using it) of dismissing such a servant for misconduct, which it might be impossible for any law to define beforehand, and of which there might be no legal evidence, though there was a moral certainty. An attempt to embarrass the Government by passive resistance, and by those difficulties which might so easily be thrown in its way by its permanent Servants, if they were independent, would be precisely the kind of misconduct which would be most dangerous, and of which either a legal definition beforehand, or the proof by legal evidence, would be most difficult. The knowledge that there is no legal restriction on the power of dismissal, to prevent a Minister from dealing with such a case as it would deserve, has probably been the principal reason why such cases do not arise; and, by preventing the possibility of a struggle between a Government and its Servants, has kept up the good feeling which has hitherto existed between them. All who have had experience of the manner in which the business of our great Public Departments is transacted, would, I am sure, concur with me in bearing witness, that it is a point of honour among the permanent Members of these Departments, not to allow any party feelings to interfere with the zealous and faithful discharge of their official duties; to give their assistance, within the sphere of those duties, as cordially and honestly to a Ministry from which they differ in political opinions, as to one composed of their own friends; and to abstain carefully from taking part in active opposition to their official superiors for the time being, however much they may be opposed to them in feeling.

This respect, on the part both of Ministers and of their subordinates, for rights and duties not defined, or capable of being so, by any positive law, can only be enforced by public opinion, jealously watching and marking with reprobation every departure on either side from those rules of conduct which have now been observed for many years with so much advantage. Few greater misfortunes could happen to the Country, than that they should fall into disuse; I think it therefore right to remark, that some symptoms of danger to their permanence

may perhaps be observed.   What is most to be
feared is, that the habit which has grown up of regarding situations in the Public Service as having
almost the character of freeholds, may lead their
possessors to consider themselves too safe from dismissal, and may thus encourage them to depart
from that understanding which has hitherto existed, that persons employed by a Government are
not at liberty to oppose it, and, above all, not to
use the Press as the means of doing so.   No Administration could long submit to an internal opposition from its own Servants ; but would be driven
to put down any attempt of the kind, by exerting
the legal power of dismissing all who should directly or indirectly take part in it, from offices held
technically during the pleasure of the Crown.   It
would indeed be the duty of a Minister to use this
power, rather than suffer his measures to be obstructed, and perhaps defeated, by the very persons
upon whose agency he is obliged to depend for
carrying them into execution.

But a few dismissals of public Servants on such
grounds, would go far to shake the whole system
of regarding the tenure of non-political offices as
one during good behaviour, and to substitute for
it the practice which now prevails in the United
States.   Secret opposition to the Government is

not a charge which could easily be proved against
a permanent Civil Servant, even though there might
be such a moral certainty of its truth as would
justify the punishment of the offender by dismissal.
But the more grounds there might really be for in-
flicting such a punishment, the more surely it would
be denounced as an injustice by the political friends
of the sufferer; so that, if power were subsequently
to come into their hands, they might be expected
to retaliate by a similar measure directed against
some friend of their opponents, perhaps on much
lighter grounds.   For it is a truth which ought
never to be lost sight of, that rules of conduct restraining the violence of political parties, which
rest only upon opinion, are peculiarly liable to be
broken down by departures from them, which, in
the first instance, may be of rare occurrence, and of
apparently trifling importance, but which gradually
increase in frequency and in gravity.   A first in-
fringement (perhaps not without some plausible
reason) of a wholesome conventional rule, by one
party against its opponents, becomes a precedent
and an excuse for their also breaking it, when they
in turn have the power of doing so, probably with
somewhat less ground for it.   Thus one departure
from the rule is followed by another and another,
with less and less justification, until the autho-

rity of the rule is altogether destroyed. This is
the process by which the decay of free institutions
has been too often brought about, through the
gradual deterioration of political morality in party
contests.   Great therefore is the responsibility of
those, who set the first examples of even trifling
departures from any wholesome rule of political
conduct, which men have been accustomed to respect.

These considerations lead me to regard with great
alarm some few examples, which have of late years
occurred, of persons who hold permanent offices
under the Government meddling in political contests by being concerned in party newspapers, or
writing in the newspapers on the disputed political
questions of the day. Whether this is done in order
to support or to oppose the Administration for the
time being, is not very material ; in either case,
such conduct is a departure from that strict neutrality in party contests, which it has hitherto been
considered the duty of the permanent Civil Servants to observe, and which is the only condition
on which they can hope that their present secure
tenure of office will be allowed to continue.   On
the appointment of a new Government after some
great party struggle, could the Ministers who succeeded to power be blamed, if they regarded as

political offices, and therefore liable to change,
those places which they might find in the hands of
men who had, through the newspapers, been taking
an active part in the contest?

I must not, however, pursue this question further; and, before I close this Chapter, I will only
add, that the conclusions to be drawn from a consideration of the whole subject to which it relates,
may, I think, be thus summed up. The practice
of our Government, in all that relates to patronage,
has been greatly improved in the last century; the
system which has by degrees grown up, with respect to the appointment of the Servants of the
State, is upon the whole a good one; and, though
still susceptible of further improvements, it is to
the influence of a sound public opinion, rather than
to any new laws or regulations with regard to patronage, that we ought to look for preventing it
from being made the instrument of corruption. If
this object were sought, by depriving the Ministers
of the Crown of all powers susceptible of being
abused, the Government must be reduced to a
state of utter helplessness, since it cannot possess
vital force and energy without having power to
reward those who serve it well, and to employ
those it thinks most capable of doing so; while
the means placed at its disposal for these purposes

may, by their very nature, be perverted to the ends of corruption. No law can effectually guard against this abuse; for laws can only take cognizance of men's acts, not of the motives which guide them in the exercise of a discretionary power. But opinion can judge of matters which are beyond the reach of positive law; and the corrupt use by a Government of the patronage with which it is entrusted, will be effectually restrained by public opinion, if only public opinion itself is sound, and the Nation shows itself to be capable of appreciating what is honourable and right in the conduct of its rulers, and prompt to reprobate what is wrong. If the feelings of the People themselves were thoroughly right and earnest upon these questions of patronage, those who wield authority over them would, even from selfish motives, be careful to abstain from abuses which would then only bring them into disgrace. This is but another proof of that great truth, which cannot be too constantly borne in mind, that the success of all free Constitutions depends far less on their particular form, than on the spirit and public virtue of the people to be governed by them. When a strong sense of public duty, respect for the constituted authorities and for the law, and a high standard of political right and wrong generally prevail in a Nation, even very defective institutions will produce the fruits of good government; while, with a People of an opposite character, the best Constitution which the wit of man could devise would fail to prevent the worst abuses, and to guard against the ultimate establishment of tyranny in the hands of a mob, of an oligarchy, or of a single despot.

CHAPTER IX.

PARLIAMENTARY GOVERNMENT IN THE BRITISH COLONIES.

ALTHOUGH it formed no part of my original design to inquire how far the system of Government I have been considering is adapted to the British Colonies, yet as the question is both highly interesting in itself, and also one upon which some light may perhaps be thrown by the reasoning contained in the foregoing pages, a few remarks upon it will not, I trust, appear misplaced at the end of this Essay. It will be my object in the following Chapter to support, by some additional reasons, an opinion I have elsewhere* expressed, against the hasty extension to all the British Colonies possessing representative institutions, of what

* See 'Colonial Policy of Lord John Russell's Administration,' vol. i. pp. 33–37.

is generally known in them by the name of "Responsible," but ought rather to be called "Parliamentary" or "Party" Government.

Referring to the account I have given* of the evils that generally belong to Parliamentary Government, and detract from its advantages, I have to observe that, owing to the conditions under which it has to work in Colonies at an early stage of their progress, the worst of these evils are likely to be felt there more seriously than they are in a great Nation. And first, with regard to corruption. In such Colonies the Legislatures, being drawn from a small population, can consist of but a small number of Members; and when Assemblies, composed of such limited numbers, are invested with all the power given to them by a complete control over the Executive Government, the high relative value of individual votes affords a strong temptation to the exercise of corrupt influence for the purpose of gaining them. We may therefore expect that a strong tendency to jobbing and corruption will be shown by the Colonial Legislatures. This apprehension is strengthened by our experience of Municipal Corporations in this country. The Town Councils of English Boroughs are not very unlike these Assemblies, either in the

* See Chapter III.

number of their members, or in the general character of the business with which they have to deal; and it is notorious how apt they are to allow their conduct to be warped by private interests, to the injury of the public.* Yet, there are checks upon the misuse of their power by English Corporations, from which Colonial Assemblies are free. The former are subject to the immediate control of Parliament, and of Courts of Law perfectly independent, and above being affected by local passions; and, what is still more important, they are amenable to the opinion of a Public, of which the community they represent forms but a small fraction, and over which they can exercise little or no influence. In all these respects, the circumstances in which Colonial Assemblies are placed are very different, and much more likely to encourage abuses.

Again, from the state of society, and from the nature of their occupations, there are but few of the inhabitants of the Colonies, even in proportion to their numbers, who are well qualified for the Public Service, and can also afford to devote their time to it without making it their profession.

---

* Some remarkable examples of the gross abuses that take place were brought to light by the inquiry into the state of the police in corporate towns.

Serious difficulty cannot fail to arise from this cause in providing for the effective performance of the business of the higher offices of Colonial Governments, when they are held by the uncertain tenure of the support of a Parliamentary majority; and, what is worse, those who so hold these offices will be exposed to a strong temptation to avail themselves of their power while it lasts, to grasp at irregular gains, in order to make up for what they might otherwise lose by relinquishing their private occupations for precarious employment in the Public Service. The temptation to do so will be rendered more powerful by the low salaries usually attached to these offices, and by the facilities for jobs of various kinds afforded by the circumstances of an advancing Colony.

Of all the evils, however, incidental to Parliamentary Government, its tendency to give a pernicious influence to party spirit is probably that which will be most aggravated by the circumstances of a comparatively small society. Factious animosities are usually bitter in proportion as the field in which they are displayed is contracted, partly perhaps because hostile partisans are there brought more immediately into contact with each other. Accordingly, party spirit is generally found to be very acrimonious in Colonies, even when they do not enjoy Representative institutions; it can therefore be no matter of surprise if it should run to great excesses, when they are brought under a system of government of which Party is the basis, and which recognizes party contests as the legitimate means for determining by whom office and power shall be enjoyed.

The tendency of this kind of government to inflame party animosities, and to give undue influence to party considerations in the administration of public affairs, is likely to be the more felt in the smaller Colonies, because matters directly affecting the interest of individuals occupy so large a share of the attention of their Governments and Legislatures. These Legislatures have seldom occasion to consider those high questions of national policy, affecting the relations of the State with foreign Powers and with its dependencies, which take up so much of the time of the Imperial Parliament. They are principally occupied with questions as to local improvements and works of utility; as to the mode of dealing with the public lands; as to taxation; and as to the amount of the Civil Establishment, and the rate at which salaries should be fixed. These questions are also considered and decided much more with reference to their bearing on the personal interests of individuals, than the corresponding questions in a larger society. Questions of commercial policy and of taxation, with which Parliament has to deal, do indeed deeply affect the interests of individuals, and so also do those as to the amount of establishments to be maintained, and the rate at which public servants are to be paid. And it is also true that it is their effect upon private interests which has often caused such questions to be discussed in this Country with so much eagerness. But still they are here considered as affecting the interests of numerous classes, rather than those of individuals. It happens comparatively seldom, that Members of the House of Commons know anything of the effect the votes they give upon such questions will have on the interests of particular persons, and they are still more rarely influenced by the consideration that a certain vote will benefit or will injure Mr. A. or Mr. B., for whom they may entertain feelings of regard or animosity. But in a small Colonial Assembly there is hardly any question to be decided, with respect to which the Members do not know how it will affect the interests, not only of classes of the community, but of particular men whom they are daily meeting, and who are regarded by some of their number as friends and by others as enemies.

So also with regard to the measures of the Executive Government. In deciding on the measures of the Government, and on the various administrative questions that come before them, the Ministers of the Crown in this country can rarely be exposed to the temptation of allowing themselves to be influenced by a consideration of the manner in which the interests of particular persons will be affected by their determination. In a small Colonial society, on the contrary, the Members of the local Government must often be aware that its acts will have a material influence on the interests of persons well known to them, and who are regarded by them as friends they wish to serve, or as political enemies they are not sorry to injure. Even, therefore, though they may conduct themselves with perfect impartiality, and although they should never yield to the temptation of showing favour to their supporters, or the reverse to their opponents, (which, when party struggles run high, it is not easy to suppose will always be the case,) it must be difficult for them to gain credit for acting with this high regard to principle.

These circumstances help to explain the extreme bitterness of party strife in the Colonies, even before "Responsible Government" was introduced, and why it is that discussions in their Assemblies have

ever been apt to be carried on in that tone of viru-
lent personality, which must strike all who are in
the habit of reading the accounts of their debates.
Where this spirit prevails, and where sometimes
one faction, sometimes another, is invested with
the whole power of the Government, it is obvious
that little fairness towards opponents is to be expected in the use made of that power, by those in
whose hands it is placed for the time. The patronage of the Government is more especially likely to
be abused under such circumstances, and there is
much danger that it may be so in the manner most
pernicious to society, by conferring judicial appointments on unscrupulous partisans, thus throwing discredit on the administration of justice, which
it is so important to keep not only pure, but above
suspicion.

This system of government has only been established for a comparatively short time in any of
our Colonies, yet already these evil tendencies are
showing themselves in a very marked manner;
and general reasoning warrants the apprehension
that, by degrees, they will become more manifest,
and will bear their natural fruit, unless some means
of preventing their development can be discovered.
But these means have still to be found. An able
Governor, it is true, by a judicious use of the in-

fluence of his office, rather than of its authority, may do something to mitigate evils as they arise, and to check corruption and party violence, but his power in this respect is very limited. Nor ought it to be overlooked, that a Governor appointed by the Crown, and bound to obey the instructions he receives by its authority, while he is at the same time required to carry on his administration by means of Ministers who are responsible to the local Legislature for every act of the Government, is placed in a difficult and anomalous position. It is to be feared that the difficulty of reconciling this system of Government with the relation of a Colony to the Mother-Country has not yet been felt as strongly as it is likely to be hereafter; and that, unless great judgment and forbearance are shown on both sides, it will be impossible to maintain that authority on the part of the latter, without which its connection with its dependencies would be reduced to a barren and onerous responsibility.

From what I have said, it will be seen that the circumstances of the Colonies, and the relation in which they stand to the Parent State, are calculated to increase the difficulties of Parliamentary Government, and to aggravate some of the worst faults which I have described in the preceding pages as inherent in its nature, and as constituting no small drawback from its advantages even among ourselves. On the other hand, these same circumstances, and the connection of the Colonies with the Mother-Country, rendered their adoption of Parliamentary Government unnecessary for some of the purposes it answers in this Country, and afforded facilities for securing to these young societies all the substantial advantages of good government, and of political freedom, under such Representative Constitutions as many of them formerly possessed.

These Constitutions bore a strong resemblance in their working to that of England before the Revolution of 1688. I have already shown that at that period, when the Sovereign not only reigned but governed (to adopt the distinction drawn by a French statesman), the system of government in England was altogether unlike what it has now become, under a Constitution nominally the same; and I have observed that it was well suited to the state of society at that time. I have now further to point out, that it had some important advantages over the system by which it has been superseded, when it was administered by wise Sovereigns. Party spirit was not excited by it, as it is by Parliamentary Government; and the power possessed by the Crown, of distributing rewards and public employment without reference to any consideration but the merits of those on whom they were conferred, called forth great zeal and ability in the service of the State, and conduced to a vigorous administration of the affairs of the Nation with comparatively little taint of corruption. At the same time, the necessity of applying to Parliament when supplies beyond the ordinary revenue were required, acted as a check upon the improper exercise of the large powers entrusted to the King; and, while it enforced economy in the public expenditure, it also gave weight to the remonstrances of the Representatives of the People when they were called for by any abuses. With Kings who were fit for their high office, and had judgment enough to understand the necessity of keeping on good terms with their Parliament, this was a sufficient security against misgovernment.

If we were to form our judgment only from the best reigns, it would be difficult to resist the conclusion that, at all events so long as the affairs of the Country had not grown to be highly complicated by its advance in wealth and population, this system of Government worked better than our own would have done. But there was this great, not to say fatal, drawback from its advantages, that its success depended entirely upon the personal character of the wearer of the Crown; and that, while it was impossible that the reins of Government should not sometimes fall into bad hands, the Law and the Constitution provided no means by which the great power attached to the kingly office could be taken from an unworthy holder. The only effectual remedy the Nation possessed against an abuse of the Royal authority was by armed resistance to it,—a remedy much too violent and dangerous to be used, except in extreme cases.

The institutions of the British Colonies, possessing Representative Legislatures, having been originally modelled on our own, the powers entrusted by them to the Governors were until lately almost the same as those exercised by the English Kings prior to the Revolution of 1688; and their possession of these powers, when they used them wisely, was productive of the same benefit to those over whom they ruled. But there was this most important difference between a Colonial Governor and an English Sovereign of the Houses of Plantagenet or Tudor, that the former was responsible to a distant and generally an impartial authority, to which the Colonists could always appeal to relieve them from a Governor who abused his power. The Crown could recall any Governor who failed in the discharge of his duties; and if it refused to do so on a well-grounded complaint from the inhabitants of a Colony, they were entitled to lay their grievance before Parliament, to which the Ministers on whose advice the Crown had acted were bound to answer for what had been done.* Thus the chief objection to the system of Government which formerly prevailed in this Country did not apply to its operation in the Colonies, while there was no apparent obstacle to its producing in them the same advantages it had done here.

Unfortunately, however, when public attention began to be directed to Colonial affairs, this form of government, which was in itself admirably adapted for promoting the welfare of young societies, had become discredited by the manner in which it had been administered, and by abuses of different kinds which had been suffered to grow up. During the long war of the French Revolution, the spirit of reckless extravagance in which the

* It will be seen from the above statement that the responsibility of Colonial Governors under the former system of Government was a substantial one. It was therefore a mistake to give to Parliamentary or Party Government in the Colonies, the name of "Responsible Government," in order to distinguish it from that which it superseded. Under the old system, the responsibility of those who exercised power was quite as real as under the new one; indeed it was much more so, since those to whom authority is now committed are under no effective responsibility, except to their own partisans.

government of this Country was carried on (the natural consequence of providing for a large part of the national expenditure by loans), extended to the Colonies, and led to the practice of defraying many charges of their internal government by grants of the Imperial Parliament. This practice, beside other objections to it, had the bad effect of depriving the Legislatures of these Colonies of their due weight. When the Governors had the easy resource of drawing upon the British Treasury, for expenses they could not induce the Colonial Assemblies to provide for, they were not obliged to show the deference to these Bodies that would otherwise have been necessary, and were thus encouraged to pay too little attention in their administration to the wishes and opinions of those over whom they ruled. To the same cause must also be attributed the bad system which arose, of the Ministers of the Crown abusing their Colonial patronage, for the purpose of strengthening their own Parliamentary interest. In proportion as the pecuniary assistance of Parliament diminished the need for the willing co-operation of the local Legislatures in the government of the Colonies, the Ministers of the day naturally grew less solicitous to obtain this co-operation by a good administration, and at the same time became too anxious to use their Colonial patronage to maintain their ascendency in the Imperial Parliament. There can be no doubt that, in the times I am speaking of, unfit men were often appointed to governments, and to other important offices in the Colonies, to the great injury of their inhabitants; and it is probable that the true explanation of this fact is to be found in the circumstance I have mentioned.

The practice of providing for Colonial expenses from the British Treasury, and the consequent abuse of Colonial patronage, which had been encouraged by the great war of the Revolution, did not cease with its termination; and it was not until after the passing of the Reform Act of 1832, and mainly owing to that measure, that a change of system was gradually accomplished. There was, however, another cause which contributed to the mal-administration of the Colonies, and which Parliamentary Reform did nothing to remove: I refer to the commercial policy to which this Country so long adhered. While it continued to be a received opinion in the Country, and a fixed principle of our legislation, that the chief advantage the Parent State had to look for from her Colonies was the monopoly of their trade, and while they were held to have a right in return to peculiar favour for their produce in the British market, questions were continually arising on which there was a conflict of interests, or of supposed interests, between the Nation and her Dependencies. So long as this state of things lasted, Governors appointed by the Crown were necessarily liable to be brought into antagonism with the societies placed under their authority, and to be suspected of not always exercising their power with a single view to the welfare of the governed. It was not until the new commercial policy of this Country, (begun by the Repeal of the Corn Laws in 1846, and completed by that of the former Navigation Laws in 1849,) had been sanctioned by Parliament, and had at length, after a severe struggle, been acquiesced in by the Colonies, that the administration of their affairs by Governors appointed from home ceased to be exposed to a disturbing influence from this cause.

Abuses of a different kind had also arisen in some Colonies. In Jamaica, for instance, a large part of the duties which, according to the British Constitution, properly belong to the Executive Government, had been transferred to Committees of the Assembly. This was particularly the case with regard to financial business. The Governor, as representing the Crown, had lost the right which belongs to the Sovereign in this Country of originating all grants of money by recommending them to the Representative branch of the Legislature. He had also lost the control of the sums granted by the Assembly, and the duty of superintending their application to the Public Service. These functions had been assumed by the Assembly, or by the members of that body under another name, who were thus invested with great power without a corresponding responsibility. The consequence was, that gross abuses and extravagance in the public expenditure had prevailed, as might have been expected.

Owing to these and other causes, (among which must be reckoned the slight attention which Parliament, during the long war, and for some years afterwards, was in the habit of giving to the affairs of the Colonies,) the Representative Constitutions, which some of them possessed, had failed to work in a satisfactory manner, and there were good grounds for general complaints of mal-administration, when the demand for "responsible government" arose, and was granted in Canada. The circumstances of that Colony were such as, perhaps, to render this, upon the whole, as good a plan as could have been adopted for meeting the difficulties which had arisen, and providing for the administration of its affairs, when the union of the two Provinces of Upper and Lower Canada had brought a large population under the authority of the same Legislature. But even in Canada the experiment has been far from proving in all respects successful, and in the other Colonies which, following its example, have established a similar form of government, its effects have afforded still stronger grounds for believing that Representative Constitutions of a different character would have worked better.

This remark applies especially to the Australian Colonies, which have availed themselves of the power of altering their Constitutions, conferred upon them by Parliament in 1850, in order to establish " responsible government." In New South Wales and Victoria this form of Government has superseded a previously existing Representative Constitution, which was granted to these Colonies, then undivided, by an Act passed in 1842. The Constitution given at that time to New South Wales differed in some important points from the ancient form of Colonial Constitutions, but it substantially agreed with them, in respect to the nature and extent of the powers with which it invested the Governor. Though it was hardly in operation long enough to give it a very fair trial, this Constitution may be considered to have had very tolerable success. While it continued in force, party spirit occasionally ran high, and controversies sometimes arose and were carried on with no little acrimony between the Governor and the Legislature, that Body was also guilty of several very obvious mistakes, but in general its measures were well directed to meet the wants of the community. The finances were, during this period, judiciously managed, the laws were vigorously and impartially administered, and the Colony made rapid advances in wealth and prosperity.

The new form of government which has been substituted for that which produced these results, has not hitherto appeared to work equally well. Changes of administration have followed each other with almost ludicrous rapidity, and those who have been successively called upon to fill the chief places in these ephemeral Governments, have been able to accomplish little for the public good. They have failed in doing so, partly because those who have been brought into office have often been men of little education or experience, but more from the circumstances in which they have been placed. If men of the highest capacity had under this system been called to power, their short tenure of it, and their want of adequate authority while in office, from their never being able to command more than a precarious majority, must have prevented the affairs of the Colony from being managed by them on any settled and consistent plan. All the advantages of following a steady and well-considered course of action are lost, when power is perpetually shifted from the hands of one set of men to those of another, having perhaps quite opposite views. In this respect the new system has proved very inferior to the old one, under which the Governors were themselves responsible for the policy they pursued, and were assisted in their administration by men who held the chief offices under them during good behaviour, instead of at the uncertain pleasure of a Parliamentary majority, and were answerable only for executing faithfully the directions they received. Under the new arrangement, the government of these Colonies has been conducted with little steadiness or energy, and their Legislatures, instead of applying themselves diligently to the public business, and then allowing their Members to return to their private concerns (from which in a young society they cannot be long detained without injury to the community), have been spending valuable time to little purpose, in party struggles, and in debates arising from the frequent changes of administration.

From the accounts that have been published of recent political transactions in these Colonies, such appear to have been the effects of the last changes in their form of government. It is right however to add, that those changes were not confined to bringing the Executive Government under the immediate control of the Legislatures, by adopting the principle of "responsible government," but included an alteration in the Constitution of the Legislatures. By the Acts of Parliament of 1842 and 1850, the Legislatures of New South Wales, and the other Australian Colonies, were made to consist of a single Chamber, of which one-third of the Members were nominated by the Crown. This arrangement has been altered, and Legislatures have been created, consisting of two Chambers, and not admitting any nominated Members to sit with the Representatives of the People. The wisdom of this alteration, at the time it was made, may be questioned, since the former Constitution of these Legislatures was peculiarly adapted to diminish the difficulties inseparable from the first establishment of Parliamentary Government in Colonies which still have but a small population. With a Legislature of a single Chamber, the want of a sufficient number of fit persons to compose it was less felt, than when the Members are divided into two bodies; and if the Crown's power of nominating one-third of the former Legislative Councils had been allowed to continue, on the establishment of Parliamentary Government, it would have been practically exercised by the Administration of the day. The Ministers would thus have been enabled to exercise that authority in the Legislature which I have shown to be the very foundation of this system of government, and the want of which has been so much felt since it was adopted in the Australian Colonies. The difficulties would also have been averted that arise from Parties being so divided, that none is strong enough to govern, while each has sufficient power, when combined with the allies it finds in Opposition, to render government by its rivals impossible.*

These are considerations it would have been well to have weighed carefully, before the Australian Colonies resolved so hastily to use the power of altering the Constitutions which Parliament had conferred upon them, and to adopt alterations recommended to them, as the result seems to prove, with very little political wisdom. But though the changes that have been made have already in a

* The nomination of one-third of the Legislative Council on the advice of an Administration supported by a majority of that Body, would probably have had an effect not very different from that produced by the election of the Aldermen in the reformed English Town Councils by the Council itself, to which I have already referred in a former Chapter.

few short years produced, as I believe, a very injurious effect upon the welfare and the moral condition of these rising Colonies, we may still hope that the practical good sense, and the capacity for self-government, which distinguish the English race, will enable the inhabitants of Australia ultimately to find some means of correcting the evils arising from the political institutions they have adopted.

But if the premature adoption of what is so improperly termed " Responsible Government " has been a mistake in Australia, it has been one of a far more serious character in New Zealand, and has there produced most disastrous results. In the last-named Colony there existed, when the change took place, a large native population, which, having been defeated in war, had submitted to British authority, and had lived under it in perfect contentment during the few years which had intervened since the re-establishment of peace. This population, the Maories (as they are called), found themselves placed by the change under a government in which they had themselves no influence, and in which all real authority was transferred from the impartial hands of the Governor appointed by the Crown, to the English Colonists.* All effective power was

* It may perhaps be objected that this is not a correct statement, since the Governor was made independent of his responsible ad-

exercised by the Colonists, through the Legislatures and the Executive Officers, whom they directly or indirectly appointed; while the Maories had no share in choosing either the Members of the General and Provincial Legislatures, or those to whom Executive authority was committed.

The native race was thus reduced to a position very like that of the Roman Catholic population of Ireland, under the rule of the Protestant minority, before the Union. In New Zealand, as might have been expected from what had before happened in Ireland, the ruling class governed with an exclusive view to their own interest, and without regard for the welfare or the feelings of the race shut out from political power. So governed, the Maories speedily became discontented. The impartiality and fairness of the previous Government had gained their confidence and their affection; for four or five years perfect tranquillity had been preserved,

visers in the administration of native affairs. It is true that an arrangement was made with this professed object, but it proved a mere delusion, and only increased the evil. No sufficient funds were placed at the disposal of the Governor to provide for the expense of the various measures required for the benefit of the natives. And even if this blunder had been avoided, as all the measures of the Government necessarily affected the interests of both races, the attempt to provide a distinct administration for the natives could have no other effect but that of creating confusion, and weakening the Government.

during which they had been daily advancing in wealth and civilization, while they had contributed largely to the revenue of the Colony, and their industry had greatly promoted the extension of its trade. But under the new order of things they soon found just cause for discontent, and discontent naturally drove a warlike race of half-reclaimed savages into acts of violence, which the Government was compelled to resist and to punish. Thus, a war was kindled, in which the resources of the civilized power can hardly fail to be successful, but in which the Maories have not yet been subjugated, while they have been able to inflict upon the superior race, some portion at least of the sufferings they have themselves had to endure. A large portion of the Maori race has already perished in the war, or from the hardships it has brought upon them, and it is to be feared that the remainder will be reduced to a state of misery and degradation. But no inconsiderable number of the settlers and of the British force employed in this miserable and inglorious warfare have also been killed, flourishing settlements have been laid waste, much property destroyed, and a very large amount of money expended.

These deplorable results of establishing "Responsible Government," under circumstances in which

it has the effect of putting a race, little advanced
in civilization, under the unchecked dominion of
Europeans forming a minority of the whole population, ought to serve as a warning against the
repetition of a similar mistake.

THE END.

JOHN EDWARD TAYLOR, PRINTER,
LITTLE QUEEN'S STREET, LINCOLN'S INN FIELDS.

ALBEMARLE STREET, LONDON,
November, 1863.

MR. MURRAY'S

GENERAL LIST OF WORKS.

ALBERT (PRINCE). THE PRINCIPAL SPEECHES AND ADDRESSES of H.R.H. THE PRINCE CONSORT ; with an Introduction giving some Outlines of his Character. Portrait. 8vo. 10s. 6d.

ABBOTT'S (REV. J.) Philip Musgrave ; or, Memoirs of a Church of England Missionary in the North American Colonies. Post 8vo. 2s.

ABERCROMBIE'S (JOHN) Enquiries concerning the Intellectual Powers and the Investigation of Truth. *16th Edition.* Fcap. 8vo. 6s. 6d.

———————————— Philosophy of the Moral Feelings. *12th Edition.* Fcap. 8vo. 4s.

ACLAND'S (REV. CHARLES) Popular Account of the Manners and Customs of India. Post 8vo. 2s.

ÆSOP'S FABLES. A New Translation. With Historical Preface. By Rev. THOMAS JAMES. With 100 Woodcuts, by TENNIEL and WOLF. *50th Thousand.* Post 8vo. 2s. 6d.

AGRICULTURAL (THE) JOURNAL. Of the Royal Agricultural Society of England. 8vo. *Published half-yearly.*

AIDS TO FAITH : a Series of Essays. By various Writers. Edited by WILLIAM THOMSON, D.D., Lord Archbishop of York. 8vo. 9s.

CONTENTS.

Rev. H. L. MANSEL—*On Miracles.*	Rev. GEORGE RAWLINSON—*The Pentateuch.*
BISHOP FITZGERALD—*Christian Evidences.*	ARCHBISHOP THOMSON—*Doctrine of the Atonement.*
REV. DR. McCAUL—*On Prophecy.*	
Rev. F. C. COOK — *Ideology and Subscription.*	Rev. HAROLD BROWNE— *On Inspiration.*
Rev. DR. McCAUL—*Mosaic Record of Creation.*	BISHOP ELLICOTT—*Scripture and its Interpretation.*

AMBER-WITCH (THE). The most interesting Trial for Witch-craft ever known. Translated from the German by LADY DUFF GORDON. Post 8vo. 2s.

ARMY LIST (MONTHLY) *Published by Authority.* Fcap. 8vo. 1s. 6d.

ARTHUR'S (LITTLE) History of England. By LADY CALLCOTT. *120th Thousand.* With 20 Woodcuts. Fcap. 8vo. 2s. 6d.

ATKINSON'S (MRS.) Recollections of Tartar Steppes and their Inhabitants. With Illustrations. Post 8vo. 12s.

AUNT IDA'S Walks and Talks ; a Story Book for Children. By a LADY. Woodcuts. 16mo. 5s.

AUSTIN'S (JOHN) LECTURES ON JURISPRUDENCE ; or, the Philosophy of Positive Law. 3 Vols. 8vo. 39s.

———————————— (SARAH) Fragments from German Prose Writers. With Biographical Notes. Post 8vo. 10s.

B

ADMIRALTY PUBLICATIONS; Issued by direction of the Lords
Commissioners of the Admiralty:—

A MANUAL OF SCIENTIFIC ENQUIRY, for the Use of Travellers.
Edited by Sir JOHN F. HERSCHEL, and Rev. ROBERT MAIN. *Third
Edition.* Woodcuts. Post 8vo. 9s.

AIRY'S ASTRONOMICAL OBSERVATIONS MADE AT GREENWICH.
1836 to 1847. Royal 4to. 50s. each.

———— ASTRONOMICAL RESULTS. 1848 to 1858. 4to. 8s. each.

———— APPENDICES TO THE ASTRONOMICAL OBSERVA-
TIONS.

1836.—I. Bessel's Refraction Tables.
    II. Tables for converting Errors of R.A. and N.P.D. } 8s.
        into Errors of Longitude and Ecliptic P.D.
1837.—I. Logarithms of Sines and Cosines to every Ten }
        Seconds of Time. } 8s.
    II. Table for converting Sidereal into Mean Solar Time.
1842.—Catalogue of 1439 Stars. 8s.
1845.—Longitude of Valentia. 8s.
1847.—Twelve Years' Catalogue of Stars. 14s.
1851.—Maskelyne's Ledger of Stars. 6s.
1852.—I. Description of the Transit Circle. 5s.
    II. Regulations of the Royal Observatory. 2s.
1853.—Bessel's Refraction Tables. 3s.
1854.—I. Description of the Zenith Tube. 3s.
    II. Six Years' Catalogue of Stars. 10s.
1856.—Description of the Galvanic Apparatus at Greenwich Ob-
    servatory. 8s.

———— MAGNETICAL AND METEOROLOGICAL OBSERVA-
TIONS. 1840 to 1847. Royal 4to. 50s. each.

———— ASTRONOMICAL, MAGNETICAL, AND METEOROLO-
GICAL OBSERVATIONS, 1848 to 1860. Royal 4to. 50s. each.

———— ASTRONOMICAL RESULTS. 1859. 4to.

———— MAGNETICAL AND METEOROLOGICAL RESULTS.
1848 to 1859. 4to. 8s. each.

———— REDUCTION OF THE OBSERVATIONS OF PLANETS.
1750 to 1830. Royal 4to. 50s.

———————————— LUNAR OBSERVATIONS. 1750
to 1830. 2 Vols. Royal 4to. 50s. each.

———————————— 1831 to 1851. 4to. 20s.

BERNOULLI'S SEXCENTENARY TABLE. *London*, 1779. 4to.

BESSEL'S AUXILIARY TABLES FOR HIS METHOD OF CLEAR-
ING LUNAR DISTANCES. 8vo.

————FUNDAMENTA ASTRONOMIÆ: *Regiomontii*, 1818. Folio. 60s.

BIRD'S METHOD OF CONSTRUCTING MURAL QUADRANTS.
London, 1768. 4to. 2s. 6d.

———— METHOD OF DIVIDING ASTRONOMICAL INSTRU-
MENTS. *London*, 1767. 4to. 2s. 6d.

COOK, KING, AND BAYLY'S ASTRONOMICAL OBSERVATIONS.
London, 1782. 4to. 21s.

EIFFE'S ACCOUNT OF IMPROVEMENTS IN CHRONOMETERS.
4to. 2s.

ENCKE'S BERLINER JAHRBUCH, for 1830. *Berlin*, 1828. 8vo. 9s.

GROOMBRIDGE'S CATALOGUE OF CIRCUMPOLAR STARS.
4to. 10s.

HANSEN'S TABLES DE LA LUNE. 4to. 20s.

HARRISON'S PRINCIPLES OF HIS TIME-KEEPER. PLATES.
1797. 4to. 5s.

HUTTON'S TABLES OF THE PRODUCTS AND POWERS OF
NUMBERS. 1781. Folio. 7s. 6d.

ADMIRALTY PUBLICATIONS—*continued.*

LAX'S TABLES FOR FINDING THE LATITUDE AND LONGI-
TUDE. 1821. 8vo. 10s.

LUNAR OBSERVATIONS at GREENWICH. 1783 to 1819. Compared
with the Tables, 1821. 4to. 7s. 6d.

MASKELYNE'S ACCOUNT OF THE GOING OF HARRISON'S
WATCH. 1767. 4to. 2s. 6d.

MAYER'S DISTANCES of the MOON'S CENTRE from the
PLANETS. 1822, 3s.; 1823, 4s. 6d. 1824 to 1835, 8vo. 4s. each.

———— THEORIA LUNÆ JUXTA SYSTEMA NEWTONIANUM.
4to. 2s. 6d.

———— TABULÆ MOTUUM SOLIS ET LUNÆ. 1770. 4to. 5s.

———— ASTRONOMICAL OBSERVATIONS MADE AT GOT-
TINGEN, from 1756 to 1761. 1826. Folio. 7s. 6d.

NAUTICAL ALMANACS, from 1767 to 1866. 8vo. 2s. 6d. each.

———— SELECTIONS FROM THE ADDITIONS
up to 1812. 8vo. 5s. 1834-54. 8vo. 5s.

———— SUPPLEMENTS, 1828 to 1833, 1837 and 1838.
8vo. 2s. each.

———— TABLE requisite to be used with the N.A.
1781. 8vo. 5s.

POND'S ASTRONOMICAL OBSERVATIONS. 1811 to 1835. 4to. 21s.
each.

RAMSDEN'S ENGINE for DIVIDING MATHEMATICAL INSTRUMENTS.
4to. 5s.

———— ENGINE for DIVIDING STRAIGHT LINES. 4to. 5s.

SABINE'S PENDULUM EXPERIMENTS to DETERMINE THE FIGURE
OF THE EARTH. 1825. 4to. 40s.

SHEPHERD'S TABLES for CORRECTING LUNAR DISTANCES. 1772.
Royal 4to. 21s.

———— TABLES, GENERAL, of the MOON'S DISTANCE
from the SUN, and 10 STARS. 1787. Folio. 5s. 6d.

TAYLOR'S SEXAGESIMAL TABLE. 1780. 4to. 15s.

———— TABLES OF LOGARITHMS. 4to. 3l.

TIARK'S ASTRONOMICAL OBSERVATIONS for the LONGITUDE
of MADEIRA. 1822. 4to. 5s.

———— CHRONOMETRICAL OBSERVATIONS for DIFFERENCES
of LONGITUDE between DOVER, PORTSMOUTH, and FALMOUTH. 1823.
4to. 5s.

VENUS and JUPITER: OBSERVATIONS of, compared with the TABLES.
London, 1822. 4to. 2s.

WALES' AND BAYLY'S ASTRONOMICAL OBSERVATIONS.
1777. 4to. 21s.

WALES' REDUCTION OF ASTRONOMICAL OBSERVATIONS
MADE IN THE SOUTHERN HEMISPHERE. 1764—1771. 1788. 4to.
10s. 6d.

BABBAGE'S (CHARLES) Economy of Machinery and Manufactures.
Fourth Edition. Fcap. 8vo. 6s.

———— Ninth Bridgewater Treatise. 8vo. 9s. 6d.

———— Reflections on the Decline of Science in England,
and on some of its Causes. 4to. 7s. 6d.

BAIKIE'S (W. B.) Narrative of an Exploring Voyage up the Rivers
Quorra and Tshadda in 1854. Map. 8vo. 16s.

BANKES' (GEORGE) STORY OF CORFE CASTLE, with documents relating
to the Time of the Civil Wars, &c. Woodcuts. Post 8vo. 10s. 6d.

BARBAULD'S (Mrs.) Hymns in Prose for Children. With 112
Original Designs by Barnes, Wimperis, Coleman, and Kennedy.
Engraved by Cooper. Small 4to.

BARROW'S (Sir John) Autobiographical Memoir, including
Reflections, Observations, and Reminiscences at Home and Abroad.
From Early Life to Advanced Age. Portrait. 8vo. 16s.

———— Voyages of Discovery and Research within the
Arctic Regions, from 1818 to the present time. 8vo. 15s.

———————— Life and Voyages of Sir Francis Drake. With numerous Original Letters. Post 8vo. 2s.

BATES' (H. W.) Naturalist on the River Amazons during
eleven years of Adventure and Travel. Second Edition. Illustrations.
2 Vols. Post 8vo.

BEES AND FLOWERS. Two Essays. By Rev. Thomas James.
Reprinted from the "Quarterly Review." Fcap. 8vo. 1s. each.

BELL'S (Sir Charles) Mechanism and Vital Endowments of the
Hand as evincing Design. Sixth Edition. Woodcuts. Post 8vo. 6s.

BENEDICT'S (Jules) Sketch of the Life and Works of Felix
Mendelssohn-Bartholdy. Second Edition. 8vo. 2s. 6d.

BERTHA'S Journal during a Visit to her Uncle in England.
Containing a Variety of Interesting and Instructive Information. Seventh
Edition. Woodcuts. 12mo.

BIRCH'S (Samuel) History of Ancient Pottery and Porcelain :
Egyptian, Assyrian, Greek, Roman, and Etruscan. With 200 Illustrations. 2 Vols. Medium 8vo. 42s.

BLUNT'S (Rev. J. J.) Principles for the proper understanding of
the Mosaic Writings, stated and applied, together with an Incidental
Argument for the truth of the Resurrection of our Lord. Being the
Hulsean Lectures for 1832. Post 8vo. 6s. 6d.

———————— Undesigned Coincidences in the Writings of the Old
and New Testament, an Argument of their Veracity : containing
the Books of Moses, Historical and Prophetical Scriptures, and the
Gospels and Acts. 8th Edition. Post 8vo. 6s.

———————— History of the Church in the First Three Centuries.
Third Edition. Post 8vo. 7s. 6d.

———————— Parish Priest; His Duties, Acquirements and Obligations. Fourth Edition. Post 8vo. 7s. 6d.

———————— Lectures on the Right Use of the Early Fathers.
Second Edition. 8vo. 15s.

———————— Plain Sermons Preached to a Country Congregation.
Second Edition. 3 Vols. Post 8vo. 7s. 6d. each.

———————— Literary Essays, reprinted from the Quarterly Review.
8vo. 12s.

BLACKSTONE'S COMMENTARIES on the Laws of England.
Adapted to the present state of the law. By R. Malcolm Kerr, LL.D.
Third Edition. 4 Vols. 8vo. 63s.

———————————————————— For Students. Being
those Portions which relate to the British Constitution and the
Rights of Persons. Post 8vo. 9s.

BLAKISTON'S (Capt.) Narrative of the Expedition sent to explore the Upper Waters of the Yang-Tsze. Illustrations. 8vo. 18s.

BLOMFIELD'S (Bishop) Memoir, with Selections from his Correspondence. By his Son. 2nd Edition. Portrait, 2 Vols. post 8vo. 18s.

BOOK OF COMMON PRAYER. Illustrated with Coloured Borders, Initial Letters, and Woodcuts. A new edition. 8vo.

BORROW'S (George) Bible in Spain; or the Journeys, Adventures, and Imprisonments of an Englishman in an Attempt to circulate the Scriptures in the Peninsula. 3 Vols. Post 8vo. 27s.; or Popular Edition, 16mo, 3s. 6d.

———— Zincali, or the Gipsies of Spain; their Manners, Customs, Religion, and Language. 2 Vols. Post 8vo. 18s.; or Popular Edition, 16mo, 3s. 6d.

———— Lavengro; The Scholar—The Gipsy—and the Priest. Portrait. 3 Vols. Post 8vo. 30s.

———— Romany Rye; a Sequel to Lavengro. Second Edition. 2 Vols. Post 8vo. 21s.

———— Wild Wales: its People, Language, and Scenery. 3 Vols. Post 8vo. 30s.

BOSWELL'S (James) Life of Samuel Johnson, LL.D. Including the Tour to the Hebrides. Edited by Mr. Croker. Portraits. Royal 8vo. 10s.

BRACE'S (C. L.) History of the Races of the Old World. Designed as a Manual of Ethnology. Post 8vo. 9s.

BRAY'S (Mrs.) Life of Thomas Stothard, R.A. With Personal Reminiscences. Illustrated with Portrait and 60 Woodcuts of his chief works. 4to.

BREWSTER'S (Sir David) Martyrs of Science, or the Lives of Galileo, Tycho Brahe, and Kepler. Fourth Edition. Fcap. 8vo. 4s. 6d.

———— More Worlds than One. The Creed of the Philosopher and the Hope of the Christian. Eighth Edition. Post 8vo. 6s.

———— Stereoscope: its History, Theory, Construction, and Application to the Arts and to Education. Woodcuts. 12mo. 5s. 6d.

———— Kaleidoscope: its History, Theory, and Construction, with its application to the Fine and Useful Arts. Second Edition. Woodcuts. Post 8vo. 5s. 6d.

BRINE'S (Capt.) Narrative of the Rise and Progress of the Taeping Rebellion in China. Plans. Post 8vo. 10s. 6d.

BRITISH ASSOCIATION REPORTS. 8vo. York and Oxford, 1831-32, 13s. 6d. Cambridge, 1833, 12s. Edinburgh, 1834, 15s. Dublin, 1835, 13s. 6d. Bristol, 1836, 12s. Liverpool, 1837, 16s. 6d. Newcastle, 1838, 15s. Birmingham, 1839, 13s. 6d. Glasgow, 1840, 15s. Plymouth, 1841, 13s. 6d. Manchester, 1842, 10s. 6d. Cork, 1843, 12s. York, 1844, 20s. Cambridge, 1845, 12s. Southampton, 1846, 15s. Oxford, 1847, 18s. Swansea, 1848, 9s. Birmingham, 1849, 10s. Edinburgh, 1850, 15s. Ipswich, 1851, 16s. 6d. Belfast, 1852, 15s. Hull, 1853, 10s. 6d. Liverpool, 1854, 18s. Glasgow, 1855, 15s.; Cheltenham, 1856, 18s.; Dublin, 1857, 15s.; Leeds, 1858, 20s. Aberdeen, 1859, 15s. Oxford, 1860. Manchester, 1861. 15s.

BRITISH CLASSICS. A New Series of Standard English
   Authors, printed from the most correct text, and edited with elucida-
   tory notes. Published occasionally in demy 8vo. Volumes, varying in
   price.

Already Published.

GOLDSMITH'S WORKS. Edited by PETER CUNNINGHAM, F.S.A.
   Vignettes. 4 Vols. 30s.

GIBBON'S DECLINE AND FALL OF THE ROMAN EMPIRE.
   Edited by WILLIAM SMITH, LL.D. Portrait and Maps. 8 Vols. 60s.

JOHNSON'S LIVES OF THE ENGLISH POETS. Edited by PETER
   CUNNINGHAM, F.S.A. 3 Vols. 22s. 6d.

BYRON'S POETICAL WORKS. Edited, with Notes. 6 vols. 45s.

In Preparation.

WORKS OF POPE. With Life, Introductions, and Notes, by REV. WHIT-
   WELL ELWIN. Portrait.

HUME'S HISTORY OF ENGLAND. Edited, with Notes.

LIFE AND WORKS OF SWIFT. Edited by JOHN FORSTER.

BROUGHTON'S (LORD) Journey through Albania and other
   Provinces of Turkey in Europe and Asia, to Constantinople, 1809—10.
   Third Edition. Illustrations. 2 Vols. 8vo. 30s.

———————— Visits to Italy. 3rd Edition. 2 vols. Post 8vo. 18s.

BUBBLES FROM THE BRUNNEN OF NASSAU. By an Old
   MAN. *Sixth Edition.* 16mo. 5s.

BUNYAN (JOHN) and Oliver Cromwell. Select Biographies. By
   ROBERT SOUTHEY. Post 8vo. 2s.

BUONAPARTE'S (NAPOLEON) Confidential Correspondence with his
   Brother Joseph, sometime King of Spain. *Second Edition.* 2 vols. 8vo.
   26s.

BURGHERSH'S (LORD) Memoir of the Operations of the Allied
   Armies under Prince Schwarzenberg and Marshal Blucher during the
   latter end of 1813—14. 8vo. 21s.

———————— Early Campaigns of the Duke of Wellington in
   Portugal and Spain. 8vo. 8s. 6d.

BURGON'S (Rev. J. W.) Memoir of Patrick Fraser Tytler.
   Second Edition. Post 8vo. 9s.

———————— Letters from Rome, written to Friends at Home.
   Illustrations. Post 8vo. 12s.

BURN'S (LIEUT.-COL.) French and English Dictionary of Naval
   and Military Technical Terms. *Fourth Edition.* Crown 8vo. 15s.

BURNS' (ROBERT) Life. By JOHN GIBSON LOCKHART. Fifth
   Edition. Fcap. 8vo. 3s.

BURR'S (G. D.) Instructions in Practical Surveying, Topogra-
   phical Plan Drawing, and on sketching ground without Instruments.
   Third Edition. Woodcuts. Post 8vo. 7s. 6d.

BUTTMAN'S LEXILOGUS; a Critical Examination of the
   Meaning of numerous Greek Words, chiefly in Homer and Hesiod.
   Translated by Rev. J. R. FISHLAKE. *Fifth Edition.* 8vo. 12s.

BUXTON'S (SIR FOWELL) Memoirs. With Selections from his
   Correspondence. By his Son. Portrait. *Fifth Edition.* 8vo. 16s.
   Abridged Edition, Portrait. Fcap. 8vo. 2s. 6d.

BYRON'S (Lord) Life, Letters, and Journals. By Thomas Moore. Plates. 6 Vols. Fcap. 8vo. 18s.

———— Life, Letters, and Journals. By Thomas Moore. Portraits. Royal 8vo. 9s.

———— Poetical Works. Portrait. 6 Vols. 8vo. 45s.

———— Poetical Works. Plates. 10 Vols. Fcap. 8vo. 30s.

———— Poetical Works. 8 Vols. 24mo. 20s.

———— Poetical Works. Plates. Royal 8vo. 9s.

———— Poetical Works. Portrait. Crown 8vo. 6s.

———— Childe Harold. With 80 Engravings. Small 4to. 21s.

———— Childe Harold. With 30 Vignettes. 12mo. 6s.

Childe Harold. 16mo. 2s. 6d.

Childe Harold. Vignettes. 16mo. 1s.

———— Childe Harold. Portrait. 16mo. 6d.

———— Tales and Poems. 24mo. 2s. 6d.

———— Miscellaneous. 2 Vols. 24mo. 5s.

———— Dramas and Plays. 2 Vols. 24mo. 5s.

———— Don Juan and Beppo. 2 Vols. 24mo. 5s.

———— Beauties. Selected from his Poetry and Prose. Portrait. Fcap. 8vo. 3s. 6d.

CARNARVON'S (Lord) Portugal, Gallicia, and the Basque Provinces. From Notes made during a Journey to those Countries. *Third Edition.* Post 8vo. 3s. 6d.

———————— Recollections of the Druses of Lebanon. With Notes on their Religion. *Third Edition.* Post 8vo. 5s. 6d.

CAMPBELL'S (Lord) Lives of the Lord Chancellors and Keepers of the Great Seal of England. From the Earliest Times to the Death of Lord Eldon in 1838. *Fourth Edition.* 10 Vols. Crown 8vo. 6s. each.

———————— Lives of the Chief Justices of England. From the Norman Conquest to the Death of Lord Tenterden. *Second Edition.* 3 Vols. 8vo. 42s.

———————— Shakspeare's Legal Acquirements Considered. 8vo. 5s. 6d.

———————— Life of Lord Chancellor Bacon. Fcap. 8vo. 2s. 6d.

———————— (George) Modern India. A Sketch of the System of Civil Government. With some Account of the Natives and Native Institutions. *Second Edition.* 8vo. 16s.

———————— India as it may be. An Outline of a proposed Government and Policy. 8vo. 12s.

———————— (Thos.) Short Lives of the British Poets. With an Essay on English Poetry. Post 8vo. 3s. 6d.

ALVIN'S (John) Life. With Extracts from his Correspondence. By Thomas H. Dyer. Portrait. 8vo. 15s.

CALLCOTT'S (Lady) Little Arthur's History of England. 130th *Thousand.* With 20 Woodcuts. Fcap. 8vo. 2s. 6d.

CASTLEREAGH (The) DESPATCHES, from the commencement of the official career of the late Viscount Castlereagh to the close of his life. Edited by the MARQUIS OF LONDONDERRY. 12 Vols. 8vo. 14s. each.

CATHCART'S (Sir George) Commentaries on the War in Russia and Germany, 1812-13. Plans. 8vo. 14s.

———— Military Operations in Kaffraria, which led to the Termination of the Kaffir War. *Second Edition*. 8vo. 12s.

CAVALCASELLE (G. B.). Notices of the Lives and Works of the Early Flemish Painters. Woodcuts. Post 8vo. 12s.

CHAMBERS' (G. F.) Handbook of Descriptive and Practical Astronomy. Illustrations. Post 8vo. 12s.

CHANTREY (Sir Francis). Winged Words on Chantrey's Woodcocks. Edited by JAS. P. MUIRHEAD. Etchings. Square 8vo. 10s. 6d.

CHARMED ROE (The); or, The Story of the Little Brother and Sister. By OTTO SPECKTER. Plates. 16mo. 5s.

CHURTON'S (Archdeacon) Gongora. An Historical Essay on the Age of Philip III. and IV. of Spain. With Translations. Portrait. 2 Vols. Small 8vo. 15s.

CLAUSEWITZ'S (Carl Von) Campaign of 1812, in Russia. Translated from the German by LORD ELLESMERE. Map. 8vo. 10s. 6d.

CLIVE'S (Lord) Life. By REV. G. R. GLEIG, M.A. Post 8vo. 3s. 6d.

COBBOLD'S (Rev. R. H.) Pictures of the Chinese drawn by a Native Artist, described by a Foreign Resident. With 24 Plates. Crown 8vo. 9s.

COLCHESTER (The) PAPERS. The Diary and Correspondence of Charles Abbott, Lord Colchester, Speaker of the House of Commons, 1802-1817. Edited by HIS SON. Portrait. 3 Vols. 8vo. 42s.

COLERIDGE'S (Samuel Taylor) Table-Talk. *Fourth Edition.* Portrait. Fcap. 8vo. 6s.

———— (Henry Nelson) Introductions to the Greek Classic Poets. *Third Edition.* Fcap. 8vo. 5s. 6d.

———— (Sir John) on Public School Education, with especial reference to Eton. *Third Edition.* Fcap. 8vo. 2s.

COLONIAL LIBRARY. [See Home and Colonial Library.]

COOK'S (Rev. F. C.) Sermons Preached at Lincoln's Inn Chapel, and on Special Occasions. 8vo.

COOKERY (Modern Domestic). Founded on Principles of Economy and Practical Knowledge, and adapted for Private Families. By a Lady. *New Edition.* Woodcuts. Fcap. 8vo. 5s.

CORNWALLIS (The) Papers and Correspondence during the American War,—Administrations in India,—Union with Ireland, and Peace of Amiens. Edited by CHARLES ROSS. *Second Edition.* 3 Vols. 8vo. 63s.

COWPER'S (Mary Countess) Diary while Lady of the Bedchamber to Caroline Princess of Wales. Portrait. 8vo.

CRABBE'S (Rev. George) Life, Letters, and Journals. By his SON. Portrait. Fcap. 8vo. 3s.

———— Poetical Works. With his Life. Plates. 8 Vols. Fcap. 8vo. 24s.

———— Life and Poetical Works. Plates. Royal 8vo. 7s.

CROKER'S (J. W.) Progressive Geography for Children. *Fifth Edition.* 18mo. 1s. 6d.

———— Stories for Children, Selected from the History of England. *Fifteenth Edition.* Woodcuts. 16mo. 2s. 6d.

———— Boswell's Life of Johnson. Including the Tour to the Hebrides. Portraits. Royal 8vo. 10s.

———— LORD HERVEY's Memoirs of the Reign of George the Second, from his Accession to the death of Queen Caroline. Edited with Notes. *Second Edition.* Portrait. 2 Vols. 8vo. 21s.

———— Essays on the Early Period of the French Revolution. 8vo. 15s.

———— Historical Essay on the Guillotine. Fcap. 8vo. 1s.

CROMWELL (OLIVER) and John Bunyan. By ROBERT SOUTHEY. Post 8vo. 2s.

CROWE'S (J. A.) Notices of the Early Flemish Painters; their Lives and Works. Woodcuts. Post 8vo. 12s.

———— AND CAVALCASELLE'S History of Painting in Italy, from 2nd to 16th Century. Derived from Historical Researches as well as inspection of the Works of Art in that Country. Illustrations. 2 Vols. 8vo.

CUNNINGHAM'S (ALLAN) Poems and Songs. Now first collected and arranged, with Biographical Notice. 24mo. 2s. 6d.

———— (CAPT. J. D.) History of the Sikhs. From the Origin of the Nation to the Battle of the Sutlej. *Second Edition.* Maps. 8vo. 15s.

CURETON (REV. W.) Remains of a very Ancient Recension of the Four Gospels in Syriac, hitherto unknown in Europe. Discovered, Edited, and Translated. 4to. 24s.

CURTIUS' (PROFESSOR) Student's Greek Grammar, for the use of Colleges and the Upper Forms. Translated under the Author's revision. Edited by DR. WM. SMITH. Post 8vo. 7s. 6d.

———— Smaller Greek Grammar for the use of the Middle and Lower Forms, abridged from the above. 12mo. 3s. 6d.

CURZON'S (HON. ROBERT) Visits to the Monasteries of the Levant. *Fourth Edition.* Woodcuts. Post 8vo. 15s.

———— ARMENIA AND ERZEROUM. A Year on the Frontiers of Russia, Turkey, and Persia. *Third Edition.* Woodcuts. Post 8vo. 7s. 6d.

CUST'S (GENERAL) Annals of the Wars of the 18th & 19th Centuries. 9 Vols. Fcap. 8vo. 5s. each.

DARWIN'S (CHARLES) Journal of Researches into the Natural History of the Countries visited during a Voyage round the World. Post 8vo. 9s.

———— Origin of Species by Means of Natural Selection; or, the Preservation of Favoured Races in the Struggle for Life. Post 8vo. 14s.

———— Fertilization of Orchids through Insect Agency, and as to the good of Intercrossing. Woodcuts. Post 8vo. 9s.

DAVIS'S (NATHAN) Visit to the Ruined Cities of Numidia and Carthaginia. Illustrations. 8vo. 16s.

DAVY'S (SIR HUMPHRY) Consolations in Travel; or, Last Days of a Philosopher. *Fifth Edition.* Woodcuts. Fcap. 8vo. 6s.

———— Salmonia; or, Days of Fly Fishing. *Fourth Edition.* Woodcuts. Fcap. 8vo. 6s.

DELEPIERRE'S (Octave) History of Flemish Literature and its celebrated Authors. From the Twelfth Century to the present Day. 8vo. 9s.

DENNIS' (George) Cities and Cemeteries of Etruria. Plates. 2 Vols. 8vo. 42s.

DIXON'S (Hepworth) Story of the Life of Lord Bacon. Portrait. Fcap. 8vo. 7s. 6d.

DOG-BREAKING; the Most Expeditious, Certain, and Easy Method, whether great excellence or only mediocrity he required. By Lieut.-Col. Hutchinson. Third Edition. Woodcuts. Post 8vo. 9s.

DOMESTIC MODERN COOKERY. Founded on Principles of Economy and Practical Knowledge, and adapted for Private Families. New Edition. Woodcuts. Fcap. 8vo. 5s.

DOUGLAS'S (General Sir Howard) Life and Adventures; From Notes, Conversations, and Correspondence. By S. W. Fullom. Portrait. 8vo. 15s.

———— On the Theory and Practice of Gunnery. 5th Edition. Plates. 8vo. 21s.

———— Military Bridges, and the Passages of Rivers in Military Operations. Third Edition. Plates. 8vo. 21s.

———— Naval Warfare with Steam. Second Edition. 8vo. 8s. 6d.

———— Modern Systems of Fortification, with special reference to the Naval, Littoral, and Internal Defence of England. Plans. 8vo. 12s.

DRAKE'S (Sir Francis) Life, Voyages, and Exploits, by Sea and Land. By John Barrow. Third Edition. Post 8vo. 2s.

DRINKWATER'S (John) History of the Siege of Gibraltar, 1779-1783. With a Description and Account of that Garrison from the Earliest Periods. Post 8vo. 2s.

DU CHAILLU'S (Paul B.) EQUATORIAL AFRICA, with Accounts of the Gorilla, the Nest-building Ape, Chimpanzee, Crocodile, &c. Illustrations. 8vo. 21s.

DUDLEY'S (Earl of) Letters to the late Bishop of Llandaff. Second Edition. Portrait. 8vo. 10s. 6d.

DUFFERIN'S (Lord) Letters from High Latitudes, being some Account of a Yacht Voyage to Iceland, &c., in 1856. Fourth Edition. Woodcuts. Post 8vo. 9s.

DYER'S (Thomas H.) Life and Letters of John Calvin. Compiled from authentic Sources. Portrait. 8vo. 15s.

———— History of Modern Europe, from the taking of Constantinople by the Turks to the close of the War in the Crimea. Vols. 1 & 2. 8vo. 30s.

EASTLAKE'S (Sir Charles) Italian Schools of Painting. From the German of Kugler. Edited, with Notes. Third Edition. Illustrated from the Old Masters. 2 Vols. Post 8vo. 30s.

EASTWICK'S (E. B.) Handbook for Bombay and Madras, with Directions for Travellers, Officers, &c. Map. 2 Vols. Post 8vo. 24s.

EDWARDS' (W. H.) Voyage up the River Amazon, including a Visit to Para. Post 8vo. 2s.

ELDON'S (LORD) Public and Private Life, with Selections from his Correspondence and Diaries. By HORACE TWISS. *Third Edition.* Portrait. 2 Vols. Post 8vo. 21s.

ELLIS (REV. W.) Visits to Madagascar, including a Journey to the Capital, with notices of Natural History, and Present Civilisation of the People. *Fifth Thousand.* Map and Woodcuts. 8vo. 16s.

———— (MRS.) Education of Character, with Hints on Moral Training. Post 8vo. 7s. 6d.

ELLESMERE'S (LORD) Two Sieges of Vienna by the Turks. Translated from the German. Post 8vo. 2s.

———————— Second Campaign of Radetzky in Piedmont. The Defence of Temeswar and the Camp of the Ban. From the German. Post 8vo. 6s. 6d.

———————— Campaign of 1812 in Russia, from the German of General Carl Von Clausewitz. Map. 8vo. 10s. 6d.

———————— Poems. Crown 4to. 24s.

———————— Essays on History, Biography, Geography, and Engineering. 8vo. 12s.

ELPHINSTONE'S (HON. MOUNTSTUART) History of India—the Hindoo and Mahomedan Periods. *Fourth Edition.* Map. 8vo. 18s.

ENGEL'S (CARL) Music of the Most Ancient Nations; particularly of the Assyrians, Egyptians, and Hebrews; with Special Reference to the Discoveries in Western Asia and in Egypt. Illustrated. 8vo.

ENGLAND (HISTORY OF) from the Peace of Utrecht to the Peace of Versailles, 1713—83. By LORD MAHON. *Library Edition,* 7 Vols. 8vo. 93s.; or *Popular Edition,* 7 Vols. Post 8vo. 35s.

———————— From the First Invasion by the Romans, down to the 14th year of Queen Victoria's Reign. By MRS. MARKHAM. *118th Edition.* Woodcuts. 12mo. 6s.

ENGLISHWOMAN IN AMERICA. Post 8vo. 10s. 6d.

ERSKINE'S (ADMIRAL) Journal of a Cruise among the Islands of the Western Pacific, including the Fejees, and others inhabited by the Polynesian Negro Races. Plates. 8vo. 16s.

ESKIMAUX and English Vocabulary, for Travellers in the Arctic Regions. 16mo. 3s. 6d.

ESSAYS FROM "THE TIMES." Being a Selection from the LITERARY PAPERS which have appeared in that Journal. *Seventh Thousand.* 2 vols. Fcap. 8vo. 8s.

EXETER'S (BISHOP OF) Letters to the late Charles Butler, on the Theological parts of his Book of the Roman Catholic Church; with Remarks on certain Works of Dr. Milner and Dr. Lingard, and on some parts of the Evidence of Dr. Doyle. *Second Edition.* 8vo. 16s.

FALKNER'S (FRED.) Muck Manual for the Use of Farmers. A Treatise on the Nature and Value of Manures. *Second Edition.* Fcap. 8vo. 5s.

FAMILY RECEIPT-BOOK. A Collection of a Thousand Valuable and Useful Receipts. Fcap. 8vo. 5s. 6d.

FANCOURT'S (COL.) History of Yucatan, from its Discovery to the Close of the 17th Century. With Map. 8vo. 10s. 6d.

FARRAR'S (REV. A. S.) Sermons on Science in Theology. 8vo. 9s.

——————— Critical History of Free Thought in reference to the Christian Religion. Being the Bampton Lectures, 1862. 8vo. 16s.

——————— (F. W.) Origin of Language, based on Modern Researches. Fcap. 8vo. 5s.

FEATHERSTONHAUGH'S (G. W.) Tour through the Slave States of North America, from the River Potomac to Texas and the Frontiers of Mexico. Plates. 2 Vols. 8vo. 26s.

FELLOWS' (SIR CHARLES) Travels and Researches in Asia Minor, more particularly in the Province of Lycia. New Edition. Plates. Post 8vo. 9s.

FERGUSSON'S (JAMES) Palaces of Nineveh and Persepolis Restored: an Essay on Ancient Assyrian and Persian Architecture. Woodcuts. 8vo. 16s.

——————— Rock-Cut Temples of India, described with 75 Photographs taken on the Spot. By Major Gill. Medium 8vo. ?

——————— Handbook of Architecture. Being a Concise and Popular Account of the Different Styles prevailing in all Ages and Countries in the World. With 850 Illustrations. 8vo. 26s.

——————— History of the Modern Styles of Architecture, completing the above work. With 312 Illustrations. 8vo. 31s. 6d.

FERRIER'S (T. P.) Caravan Journeys in Persia, Afghanistan, Herat, Turkistan, and Beloochistan, with Descriptions of Meshed, Balk, and Candahar, &c. Second Edition. Map. 8vo. 21s.

——————— History of the Afghans. Map. 8vo. 21s.

FISHER'S (REV. GEORGE) Elements of Geometry, for the Use of Schools. Fifth Edition. 18mo. 1s. 6d.

——————— First Principles of Algebra, for the Use of Schools. Fifth Edition. 18mo. 1s. 6d.

FLOWER GARDEN (THE). An Essay. By REV. THOS. JAMES. Reprinted from the "Quarterly Review." Fcap. 8vo. 1s.

FORBES' (C. S.) Iceland; its Volcanoes, Geysers, and Glaciers. Illustrations. Post 8vo. 14s.

FORD'S (RICHARD) Handbook for Spain, Andalusia, Ronda, Valencia, Catalonia, Granada, Gallicia, Arragon, Navarre, &c. Third Edition. 2 Vols. Post 8vo. 30s.

——————— Gatherings from Spain. Post 8vo. 3s. 6d.

FORSTER'S (JOHN) Arrest of the Five Members by Charles the First. A Chapter of English History re-written. Post 8vo. 12s.

——————— Debates on the Grand Remonstrance, 1641. With an Introductory Essay on English freedom under the Plantagenet and Tudor Sovereigns. Second Edition. Post 8vo. 12s.

——————— Oliver Cromwell, Daniel De Foe, Sir Richard Steele, Charles Churchill, Samuel Foote. Biographical Essays. Third Edition. Post 8vo. 12s.

FORSYTH'S (WILLIAM) New Life of Cicero. Post. 8vo.

FORTUNE'S (ROBERT) Narrative of Two Visits to the Tea Countries of China, between the years 1843-52, with full Descriptions of the Tea Plant. *Third Edition.* Woodcuts. 2 Vols. Post 8vo. 18s.

———— Chinese,— Inland,— on the Coast,— and at Sea. 1853-56. Woodcuts. 8vo. 16s.

———— Yedo and Peking. Being a Journey to the Capitals of Japan and China. With Notices of the Agriculture and Trade of those Countries, Illustrations. 8vo. 15s.

FRANCE (HISTORY OF). From the Conquest by the Gauls to the Death of Louis Philippe. By Mrs. MARKHAM. *56th Thousand.* Woodcuts. 12mo. 6s.

FRENCH (THE) in Algiers; The Soldier of the Foreign Legion— and the Prisoners of Abd-el-Kadir. Translated by Lady DUFF GORDON. Post 8vo. 2s.

GALTON'S (FRANCIS) Art of Travel ; or, Hints on the Shifts and Contrivances available in Wild Countries. *Third Edition.* Woodcuts. Post 8vo. 7s. 6d.

GEOGRAPHICAL (THE) Journal. Published by the Royal Geographical Society of London. 8vo.

GERMANY (HISTORY OF). From the Invasion by Marius, to the present time. By Mrs. MARKHAM. *Fifteenth Thousand.* Woodcuts. 12mo. 6s.

GIBBON'S (EDWARD) History of the Decline and Fall of the Roman Empire. *A New Edition.* Preceded by his Autobiography. Edited, with Notes, by Dr. WM. SMITH. Maps. 8 Vols. 8vo. 60s.

———— (The Student's Gibbon) ; Being an Epitome of the above work, incorporating the Researches of Recent Commentators. By Dr. WM. SMITH. *Ninth Thousand.* Woodcuts. Post 8vo. 7s. 6d.

GIFFARD'S (EDWARD) Deeds of Naval Daring; or, Anecdotes of the British Navy. New Edition. Fcap. 8vo. 3s. 6d.

GOLDSMITH'S (OLIVER) Works. A New Edition. Printed from the last editions revised by the Author. Edited by PETER CUNNINGHAM. Vignettes. 4 Vols. 8vo. 30s. (Murray's British Classics.)

GLADSTONE'S (RIGHT HON. W. E.) Financial Statements of 1853, 60, and 63; also his Speeches on Tax-Bills, 1861, and on Charities, 1863. 8vo.

GLEIG'S (REV. G. R.) Campaigns of the British Army at Washington and New Orleans. Post 8vo. 2s.

———— Story of the Battle of Waterloo. Post 8vo. 3s. 6d.

———— Narrative of Sale's Brigade in Affghanistan. Post 8vo. 2s.

———— Life of Robert Lord Clive. Post 8vo. 3s. 6d.

———— Life and Letters of Sir Thomas Munro. Post 8vo 3s. 6d.

GORDON'S (SIR ALEX. DUFF) Sketches of German Life, and Scenes from the War of Liberation. From the German. Post 8vo. 3s. 6d.

———— (LADY DUFF) Amber-Witch : A Trial for Witchcraft. From the German. Post 8vo. 2s.

———— French in Algiers. 1. The Soldier of the Foreign Legion. 2. The Prisoners of Abd-el-Kadir. From the French. Post 8vo. 2s.

GOUGER'S (HENRY) Personal Narrative of Two Years' Imprisonment in Burmah. *Second Edition.* Woodcuts. Post 8vo. 12s.

GRENVILLE (The) PAPERS. Being the Public and Private
Correspondence of George Greaville, including his PRIVATE DIARY.
Edited by W. J. SMITH. 4 Vols. 8vo. 16s. each.

GREY'S (SIR GEORGE) Polynesian Mythology, and Ancient
Traditional History of the New Zealand Race. Woodcuts. Post
8vo. 10s. 6d.

GROTE'S (GEORGE) History of Greece. From the Earliest Times
to the close of the generation contemporary with the death of Alexander
the Great. *Fourth Edition.* Maps. 8 vols. 8vo. 112s.

———— (MRS.) Memoir of Ary Scheffer. Post 8vo. 8s. 6d.

———— Collected Papers. 8vo. 10s. 6d.

HALLAM'S (HENRY) Constitutional History of England, from the
Accession of Henry the Seventh to the Death of George the Second.
Seventh Edition. 3 Vols. 8vo. 30s.

———— History of Europe during the Middle Ages.
Tenth Edition. 3 Vols. 8vo. 30s.

———— Literary History of Europe, during the 15th, 16th and
17th Centuries. *Fourth Edition.* 3 Vols. 8vo. 36s.

———— Literary Essays and Characters. Selected from the
last work. Fcap. 8vo. 2s.

———— Historical Works. History of England,—Middle Ages
of Europe,—Literary History of Europe. 10 Vols. Post 8vo. 6s. each.

———— (ARTHUR) Remains; in Verse and Prose. With Preface, Memoir, and Portrait. Fcap. 8vo. 7s. 6d.

HAMILTON'S (JAMES) Wanderings in North Africa. Post 8vo. 12s.

HART'S ARMY LIST. (*Quarterly and Annually.*) 8vo. 10s. 6d.
and 21s.

HANNAH'S (Rev. Dr.) Bampton Lectures for 1863; the Divine
and Human Elements in Holy Scripture. 8vo.

HAY'S (J. H. DRUMMOND) Western Barbary, its wild Tribes and
savage Animals. Post 8vo. 2s.

HEAD'S (SIR FRANCIS) Horse and his Rider. Woodcuts. Post 8vo. 5s.

———— Rapid Journeys across the Pampas. Post 8vo. 2s.

———— Descriptive Essays. 2 Vols. Post 8vo. 18s.

———— Bubbles from the Brunnen of Nassau. 16mo. 5s.

———— Emigrant. Fcap. 8vo. 2s. 6d.

———— Stokers and Pokers; or, N.-Western Railway. Post
8vo. 2s.

———— Defenceless State of Great Britain. Post 8vo. 12s.

———— Faggot of French Sticks. 2 Vols. Post 8vo. 12s.

———— Fortnight in Ireland. Map. 8vo. 12s.

———— (SIR EDMUND) Shall and Will; or, Future Auxiliary
Verbs. Fcap. 8vo. 4s.

HAND-BOOK—TRAVEL-TALK. English, German, French, and Italian. 18mo. 3s. 6d.

———— NORTH GERMANY, HOLLAND, BELGIUM, and the Rhine to Switzerland. Map. Post 8vo. 10s.

———— KNAPSACK GUIDE TO BELGIUM AND THE RHINE. Post 8vo. (In the Press.)

———— SOUTH GERMANY, Bavaria, Austria, Styria, Salzberg, the Austrian and Bavarian Alps, the Tyrol, Hungary, and the Danube, from Ulm to the Black Sea. Map. Post 8vo. 10s.

———— KNAPSACK GUIDE TO THE TYROL. Post 8vo. (In the Press.)

———— PAINTING. German, Flemish, and Dutch Schools. Edited by DR. WAAGEN. Woodcuts. 2 Vols. Post 8vo. 24s.

———— LIVES OF THE EARLY FLEMISH PAINTERS, with Notices of their Works. By CROWE and CAVALCASELLE. Illustrations. Post 8vo. 12s.

———— SWITZERLAND, Alps of Savoy, and Piedmont. Maps. Post 8vo. 9s.

———— KNAPSACK GUIDE TO SWITZERLAND. Post 8vo. (In the Press.)

———— FRANCE, Normandy, Brittany, the French Alps, the Rivers Loire, Seine, Rhone, and Garonne, Dauphiné, Provence, and the Pyrenees. Maps. Post 8vo. 10s.

———— KNAPSACK GUIDE TO FRANCE. Post 8vo. (In the Press.)

———— PARIS AND ITS ENVIRONS. Map. Post 8vo. (Nearly Ready.)

———— SPAIN, Andalusia, Ronda, Granada, Valencia, Catalonia, Gallicia, Arragon, and Navarre. Maps. 2 Vols. Post 8vo. 30s.

———— PORTUGAL, LISBON, &c. Map. Post 8vo.

———— NORTH ITALY, Piedmont, Liguria, Venetia, Lombardy, Parma, Modena, and Romagna. Map. Post 8vo. 12s.

———— CENTRAL ITALY, Lucca, Tuscany, Florence, The Marches, Umbria, and the Patrimony of St. Peter's. Map. Post 8vo. 10s.

———— ROME AND ITS ENVIRONS. Map. Post 8vo. 9s.

———— SOUTH ITALY, Two Sicilies, Naples, Pompeii, Herculaneum, and Vesuvius. Map. Post 8vo. 10s.

———— KNAPSACK GUIDE TO ITALY AND ROME. 1 Vol. Post 8vo. (In Preparation.)

———— SICILY, Palermo, Messina, Catania, Syracuse, Etna, and the Ruins of the Greek Temples. Map. Post 8vo. (In the Press.)

———— PAINTING. The Italian Schools. From the German of KUGLER. Edited by Sir CHARLES EASTLAKE, R.A. Woodcuts. 2 Vols. Post 8vo. 30s.

———— LIVES OF THE EARLY ITALIAN PAINTERS, AND PROGRESS OF PAINTING IN ITALY, from CIMABUE to BASSANO. By Mrs. JAMESON. Woodcuts. Post 8vo. 12s.

———— DICTIONARY OF ITALIAN PAINTERS. By A LADY. Edited by RALPH WORNUM. With a Chart. Post 8vo. 6s. 6d.

HAND-BOOK—GREECE, the Ionian Islands, Albania, Thessaly, and Macedonia. Maps. Post 8vo. 15s.

———— TURKEY, Malta, Asia Minor, Constantinople, Armenia, Mesopotamia, &c. Maps. Post 8vo. (*In the Press.*)

———— EGYPT, Thebes, the Nile, Alexandria, Cairo, the Pyramids, Mount Sinai, &c. Map. Post 8vo. 15s.

———— SYRIA & PALESTINE, Peninsula of Sinai, Edom, and Syrian Desert. Maps. 2 Vols. Post 8vo. 24s.

———— BOMBAY AND MADRAS. Map. 2 Vols. Post 8vo. 24s.

———— DENMARK, Norway and Sweden. Maps. Post 8vo. 15s.

———— RUSSIA, The Baltic and Finland. Maps. Post 8vo. 12s.

———— MODERN LONDON. A Complete Guide to all the Sights and Objects of Interest in the Metropolis. Map. 16mo. 3s. 6d.

———— WESTMINSTER ABBEY. Woodcuts. 16mo. 1s.

———— KENT AND SUSSEX, Canterbury, Dover, Ramsgate, Sheerness, Rochester, Chatham, Woolwich, Brighton, Chichester, Worthing, Hastings, Lewes, Arundel, &c. Map. Post 8vo. 10s.

———— SURREY, HANTS, Kingston, Croydon, Reigate, Guildford, Winchester, Southampton, Portsmouth, and Isle of Wight. Maps. Post 8vo. 7s. 6d.

———— BERKS, BUCKS, AND OXON, Windsor, Eton, Reading, Aylesbury, Uxbridge, Wycombe, Henley, the City and University of Oxford, and the Descent of the Thames to Maidenhead and Windsor. Map. Post 8vo. 7s. 6d.

———— WILTS, DORSET, AND SOMERSET, Salisbury, Chippenham, Weymouth, Sherborne, Wells, Bath, Bristol, Taunton, &c. Map. Post 8vo. 7s. 6d.

———— DEVON AND CORNWALL, Exeter, Ilfracombe, Linton, Sidmouth, Dawlish, Teignmouth, Plymouth, Devonport, Torquay, Launceston, Truro, Penzance, Falmouth, &c. Maps. Post 8vo. 7s. 6d.

———— NORTH AND SOUTH WALES, Bangor, Carnarvon, Beaumaris, Snowdon, Conway, Menai Straits, Carmarthen, Pembroke, Tenby, Swansea, The Wye, &c. Maps. 2 Vols. Post 8vo. 12s.

———— CATHEDRALS OF ENGLAND—Southern Division, Winchester, Salisbury, Exeter, Wells, Chichester, Rochester, Canterbury. With 110 Illustrations. Vols. Crown 8vo. 24s.

———— CATHEDRALS OF ENGLAND—Eastern Division, Oxford, Peterborough, Norwich, Ely, and Lincoln. With 90 Illustrations. Crown 8vo. 18s.

———— CATHEDRALS OF ENGLAND—Western Division, Bristol, Gloucester, Hereford, Worcester, and Lichfield. Illustrations. Crown 8vo.

———— FAMILIAR QUOTATIONS. From English Authors. *Third Edition.* Fcap. 8vo. 5s.

HEBER'S (BISHOP) Journey through India. *Twelfth Edition.*
2 Vols. Post 8vo. 7*s.*

———— Poetical Works. *Sixth Edition.* Portrait. Fcap. 8vo. 6*s.*

———— Sermons Preached in England. *Second Edition.* 8vo.

———— Hymns for Church Service. 16mo. 2*s.*

HEIRESS (THE) in Her Minority; or, The Progress of Character.
By the Author of "BERTHA'S JOURNAL." 2 Vols. 12mo. 18*s.*

HERODOTUS. A New English Version. Edited, with Notes
and Essays, historical, ethnographical, and geographical. By Rev. G.
RAWLINSON, assisted by SIR HENRY RAWLINSON and SIR J. G. WIL-
KINSON. *Second Edition.* Maps and Woodcuts. 4 Vols. 8vo. 48*s.*

HERVEY'S (LORD) Memoirs of the Reign of George the Second,
from his Accession to the Death of Queen Caroline. Edited, with Notes,
by MR. CROKER. *Second Edition.* Portrait. 2 Vols. 8vo. 21*s.*

HESSEY (REV. DR.). Sunday—Its Origin, History, and Present
Obligations. Being the Bampton Lectures for 1860. *Second Edition.*
8vo. 16*s.*

HICKMAN'S (WM.) Treatise on the Law and Practice of Naval
Courts-Martial. 8vo. 10*s.* 6*d.*

HILLARD'S (G. S.) Six Months in Italy. 2 Vols. Post 8vo. 16*s.*

HOLLWAY'S (J. G.) Month in Norway. Fcap. 8vo. 2*s.*

HONEY BEE (THE). An Essay. By REV. THOMAS JAMES.
Reprinted from the "Quarterly Review." Fcap. 8vo. 1*s.*

HOOK'S (DEAN) Church Dictionary. *Eighth Edition.* 8vo. 16*s.*

———— (THEODORE) Life. By J. G. LOCKHART. Reprinted from the
"Quarterly Review." Fcap. 8vo. 1*s.*

HOOKER'S (Dr. J. D.) Himalayan Journals; or, Notes of an Oriental
Naturalist in Bengal, the Sikkim and Nepal Himalayas, the Khasia
Mountains, &c. *Second Edition.* Woodcuts. 2 Vols. Post 8vo. 18*s.*

HOPE'S (A. J. BERESFORD) English Cathedral of the Nineteenth
Century. With Illustrations. 8vo. 12*s.*

HORACE (Works of). Edited by DEAN MILMAN. With 300
Woodcuts. Crown 8vo. 21*s.*

———— (Life of). By DEAN MILMAN. Woodcuts, and coloured
Borders. 8vo. 9*s.*

HUME'S (DAVID) History of England, from the Invasion of Julius
Cæsar to the Revolution of 1688. Abridged for Students. Correcting
his errors, and continued to 1858. *Twenty-fifth Thousand.* Woodcuts.
Post 8vo. 7*s.* 6*d.*

HUTCHINSON (COL.) on the most expeditious, certain, and
easy Method of Dog-Breaking. *Third Edition.* Woodcuts. Post 8vo. 9*s.*

HUTTON'S (H. E.) Principia Græca; an Introduction to the Study
of Greek. Comprehending Grammar, Delectus, and Exercise-book,
with Vocabularies. *Third Edition.* 12mo. 3*s.* 6*d.*

c

18 LIST OF WORKS

HOME AND COLONIAL LIBRARY. A Series of Works

adapted for all circles and classes of Readers, having been selected for their acknowledged interest and ability of the Authors. Post 8vo. Published at 2s. and 3s. 6d. each, and arranged under two distinctive heads as follows:—

CLASS A.

HISTORY, BIOGRAPHY, AND HISTORIC TALES.

1. SIEGE OF GIBRALTAR. By JOHN DRINKWATER. 2s.
2. THE AMBER-WITCH. By LADY DUFF GORDON. 2s.
3. CROMWELL AND BUNYAN. By ROBERT SOUTHEY. 2s.
4. LIFE OF SIR FRANCIS DRAKE. By JOHN BARROW.
5. CAMPAIGNS AT WASHINGTON. By REV. G. R. GLEIG. 2s.
6. THE FRENCH IN ALGIERS. By LADY DUFF GORDON. 2s.
7. THE FALL OF THE JESUITS. 2s.
8. LIVONIAN TALES. 2s.
9. LIFE OF CONDE. By LORD MAHON. 3s. 6d.
10. SALE'S BRIGADE. By REV. G. R. GLEIG. 2s.
11. THE SIEGES OF VIENNA. By LORD ELLESMERE. 2s.
12. THE WAYSIDE CROSS. By CAPT. MILMAN. 2s.
13. SKETCHES OF GERMAN LIFE. By SIR A. GORDON. 3s. 6d.
14. THE BATTLE OF WATERLOO. By REV. G. R. GLEIG. 3s. 6d.
15. AUTOBIOGRAPHY OF STEFFENS. 2s.
16. THE BRITISH POETS. By THOMAS CAMPBELL. 3s. 6d.
17. HISTORICAL ESSAYS. By LORD MAHON. 3s. 6d.
18. LIFE OF LORD CLIVE. By REV. G. R. GLEIG. 3s. 6d.
19. NORTH-WESTERN RAILWAY. By SIR F. B. HEAD. 2s.
20. LIFE OF MUNRO. By REV. G. R. GLEIG. 3s. 6d.

CLASS B.

VOYAGES, TRAVELS, AND ADVENTURES.

1. BIBLE IN SPAIN. By GEORGE BORROW. 3s. 6d.
2. GIPSIES OF SPAIN. By GEORGE BORROW. 3s. 6d.
3 & 4. JOURNALS IN INDIA. By BISHOP HEBER. 2 Vols. 7s.
5. TRAVELS IN THE HOLY LAND. By IRBY and MANGLES. 2s.
6. MOROCCO AND THE MOORS. By J. DRUMMOND HAY. 2s.
7. LETTERS FROM THE BALTIC. By a LADY. 2s.
8. NEW SOUTH WALES. By MRS. MEREDITH. 2s.
9. THE WEST INDIES. By M. G. LEWIS. 2s.
10. SKETCHES OF PERSIA. By SIR JOHN MALCOLM. 3s. 6d.
11. MEMOIRS OF FATHER RIPA. 2s.
12 & 13. TYPEE AND OMOO. By HERMANN MELVILLE. 2 Vols. 7s.
14. MISSIONARY LIFE IN CANADA. By REV. J. ABBOTT. 2s.
15. LETTERS FROM MADRAS. By a LADY. 2s.
16. HIGHLAND SPORTS. By CHARLES ST. JOHN. 3s. 6d.
17. PAMPAS JOURNEYS. By SIR F. B. HEAD. 2s.
18. GATHERINGS FROM SPAIN. By RICHARD FORD. 3s. 6d.
19. THE RIVER AMAZON. By W. H. EDWARDS. 2s.
20. MANNERS & CUSTOMS OF INDIA. By REV. C. ACLAND. 2s.
21. ADVENTURES IN MEXICO. By G. F. RUXTON. 3s. 6d.
22. PORTUGAL AND GALLICIA. By LORD CARNARVON. 3s. 6d.
23. BUSH LIFE IN AUSTRALIA. By REV. H. W. HAYGARTH. 2s.
24. THE LIBYAN DESERT. By BAYLE ST. JOHN. 2s.
25. SIERRA LEONE. By a LADY. 3s. 6d.

*** Each work may be had separately.

IRBY AND MANGLES' Travels in Egypt, Nubia, Syria, and the Holy Land. Post 8vo. 2s.

JAMES' (Rev. Thomas) Fables of Æsop. A New Translation, with Historical Preface. With 100 Woodcuts by Tenniel and Wolf. *Thirty-eighth Thousand.* Post 8vo. 2s. 6d.

JAMESON'S (Mrs.) Lives of the Early Italian Painters, from Cimabue to Bassano, and the Progress of Painting in Italy. *New Edition.* With Woodcuts. Post 8vo. 12s.

JESSE'S (Edward) Scenes and Occupations of Country Life. *Third Edition.* Woodcuts. Fcap. 8vo. 6s.

———— Gleanings in Natural History. *Eighth Edition.* Fcap. 8vo. 6s.

JOHNSON'S (Dr. Samuel) Life. By James Boswell. Including the Tour to the Hebrides. Edited by the late Mr. Croker. Portraits. Royal 8vo. 10s.

———— Lives of the most eminent English Poets. Edited by Peter Cunningham. 3 vols. 8vo. 22s. 6d. (Murray's British Classics.)

JOURNAL OF A NATURALIST. Woodcuts. Post 8vo. 9s 6d.

JOWETT (Rev. B.) on St. Paul's Epistles to the Thessalonians, Galatians, and Romans. *Second Edition.* 2 Vols. 8vo. 30s.

KEN'S (Bishop) Life. By A Layman. *Second Edition.* Portrait. 2 Vols. 8vo. 18s.

———— Exposition of the Apostles' Creed. Extracted from his "Practice of Divine Love." Fcap. 1s. 6d.

———— Approach to the Holy Altar. Extracted from his "Manual of Prayer" and "Practice of Divine Love." Fcap. 8vo. 1s. 6d.

KING'S (Rev. S. W.) Italian Valleys of the Alps; a Tour through all the Romantic and less-frequented "Vals" of Northern Piedmont. Illustrations. Crown 8vo. 18s.

———— (Rev. C. W.) Antique Gems; their Origin, Use, and Value, as Interpreters of Ancient History, and as illustrative of Ancient Art. Illustrations. 8vo. 42s.

KING EDWARD VITH's Latin Grammar; or, an Introduction to the Latin Tongue, for the Use of Schools. *Sixteenth Edition.* 12mo. 3s. 6d.

———————————— First Latin Book; or, the Accidence, Syntax, and Prosody, with an English Translation for the Use of Junior Classes. *Fourth Edition.* 12mo. 2s. 6d.

KIRK'S (J. Foster) History of Charles the Bold, Duke of Burgundy. Portrait. 2 Vols. 8vo.

KUGLER'S Italian Schools of Painting: Edited, with Notes, by
SIR CHARLES EASTLAKE. *Third Edition.* Woodcuts. 2 Vols. Post
8vo. 30s.

——————— German, Dutch, and Flemish Schools of Painting.
Edited, with Notes, by DR. WAAGEN. *Second Edition.* Woodcuts. 2
Vols. Post 8vo. 24s.

LABARTE'S (M. JULES) Handbook of the Arts of the Middle Ages
and Renaissance. With 200 Woodcuts. 8vo. 18s.

LATIN GRAMMAR (KING EDWARD VITH'S). For the Use of
Schools. *Sixteenth Edition.* 12mo. 3s. 6d.

——————— First Book (KING EDWARD VITH'S); or, the Accidence,
Syntax, and Prosody, with English Translation for Junior Classes.
Fourth Edition. 12mo. 2s. 6d.

LAYARD'S (A. H.) Nineveh and its Remains. Being a Narrative of Researches and Discoveries amidst the Ruins of Assyria.
With an Account of the Chaldean Christians of Kurdistan; the Yezedis,
or Devil-worshippers; and an Enquiry into the Manners and Arts of
the Ancient Assyrians. *Sixth Edition.* Plates and Woodcuts. 2 Vols.
8vo. 36s.

——————————————— Nineveh and Babylon; being the Result
of a Second Expedition to Assyria. *Fourteenth Thousand.* Plates.
8vo. 21s. Or *Fine Paper,* 2 Vols. 8vo. 30s.

——————— Popular Account of Nineveh. 15th *Edition.* With
Woodcuts. Post 8vo. 5s.

LEAKE'S (COL.) Topography of Athens, with Remarks on its
Antiquities. *Second Edition.* Plates. 2 Vols. 8vo. 30s.

——————— Travels in Northern Greece. Maps. 4 Vols. 8vo. 60s.

——————— Disputed Questions of Ancient Geography. Map.
8vo. 6s. 6d.

——————— Numismata Hellenica, and Supplement. Completing
a descriptive Catalogue of Twelve Thousand Greek Coins, with
Notes Geographical and Historical. With Map and Appendix. 4to.
63s.

——————— Peloponnesiaca. 8vo. 15s.

——————— Degradation of Science in England. 8vo. 3s. 6d.

LESLIE'S (C. R.) Handbook for Young Painters. With Illustrations. Post 8vo. 10s. 6d.

——————————— Autobiographical Recollections, with Selections
from his Correspondence. Edited by TOM TAYLOR. Portrait. 2 Vols.
Post 8vo. 18s.

——————————— Life of Sir Joshua Reynolds. With an Account
of his Works, and a Sketch of his Cotemporaries. By TOM TAYLOR.
2 Vols. 8vo. (*In the Press.*)

LETTERS FROM THE BALTIC. By a LADY. Post 8vo. 2s.

——————————— MADRAS. By a LADY. Post 8vo. 2s.

——————————— SIERRA LEONE. By a LADY. Post 8vo. 3s. 6d.

LEWIS' (Sir G. C.) Essay on the Government of Dependencies. 8vo. 12s.

———— Glossary of Provincial Words used in Herefordshire and some of the adjoining Counties. 12mo. 4s. 6d.

———— (Lady Theresa) Friends and Contemporaries of the Lord Chancellor Clarendon, illustrative of Portraits in his Gallery. With a Descriptive Account of the Pictures, and Origin of the Collection. Portraits. 3 Vols. 8vo. 42s.

———— (M. G.) Journal of a Residence among the Negroes in the West Indies. Post 8vo. 2s.

LIDDELL'S (Dean) History of Rome. From the Earliest Times to the Establishment of the Empire. With the History of Literature and Art. 2 Vols. 8vo. 28s.

———— Student's History of Rome. Abridged from the above Work. 25th Thousand. With Woodcuts. Post 8vo. 7s. 6d.

LINDSAY'S (Lord) Lives of the Lindsays; or, a Memoir of the Houses of Crawford and Balcarres. With Extracts from Official Papers and Personal Narratives. Second Edition. 3 Vols. 8vo. 24s.

————Report of the Claim of James, Earl of Crawford and Balcarres, to the Original Dukedom of Montrose, created in 1488. Folio. 15s.

———— Scepticism; a Retrogressive Movement in Theology and Philosophy. 8vo. 9s.

LISPINGS from LOW LATITUDES; or, the Journal of the Hon. Impulsia Gushington. Edited by Lord Dufferin. With 24 Plates, 4to. 21s.

LITTLE ARTHUR'S HISTORY OF ENGLAND. By Lady Callcott. 120th Thousand. With 20 Woodcuts. Fcap. 8vo. 2s. 6d.

LIVINGSTONE'S (Rev. Dr.) Popular Account of his Missionary Travels in South Africa. Illustrations. Post 8vo. 6s.

LIVONIAN TALES. By the Author of "Letters from the Baltic." Post 8vo. 2s.

LOCKHART'S (J. G.) Ancient Spanish Ballads. Historical and Romantic. Translated, with Notes. Illustrated Edition. 4to. 21s. Or, Popular Edition, Post 8vo. 2s. 6d.

———— Life of Robert Burns. Fifth Edition. Fcap. 8vo. 3s.

LONDON'S (Bishop of) Dangers and Safeguards of Modern Theology. Containing Suggestions to the Theological Student under present difficulties. Second Edition. 8vo. 9s.

LOUDON'S (Mrs.) Instructions in Gardening for Ladies. With Directions and Calendar of Operations for Every Month. Eighth Edition. Woodcuts. Fcap. 8vo. 5s.

———— Modern Botany; a Popular Introduction to the Natural System of Plants. Second Edition. Woodcuts. Fcap. 8vo. 6s.

LOWE'S (Sir Hudson) Letters and Journals, during the Captivity of Napoleon at St. Helena. By William Forsyth. Portrait. 3 Vols. 8vo. 45s.

LUCAS' (SAMUEL) Secularia; or, Surveys on the Main Stream of History. 8vo. 12s.

LUCKNOW: A Lady's Diary of the Siege. *Fourth Thousand.* Fcap. 8vo. 4s. 6d.

LYELL'S (SIR CHARLES) Principles of Geology; or, the Modern Changes of the Earth and its Inhabitants considered as illustrative of Geology. *Ninth Edition.* Woodcuts. 8vo. 18s.

———— Visits to the United States, 1841-46. *Second Edition.* Plates. 4 Vols. Post 8vo. 24s.

———— Geological Evidences of the Antiquity of Man. *Second Edition.* Illustrations. 8vo. 14s.

MAHON'S (LORD) History of England, from the Peace of Utrecht to the Peace of Versailles, 1713—83. *Library Edition,* 7 Vols. 8vo. 93s. *Popular Edition,* 7 Vols. Post 8vo. 35s.

———— "Forty-Five;" a Narrative of the Rebellion in Scotland. Post 8vo. 3s.

———— History of British India from its Origin till the Peace of 1783. Post 8vo. 3s. 6d.

———— Spain under Charles the Second; 1690 to 1700. *Second Edition.* Post 8vo. 6s. 6d.

———— Life of William Pitt, with Extracts from his MS. Papers. *Second Edition.* Portraits. 4 Vols. Post 8vo. 42s.

———— Condé, surnamed the Great. Post 8vo. 3s. 6d.

———— Belisarius. *Second Edition.* Post 8vo. 10s. 6d.

———— Historical and Critical Essays. Post 8vo. 3s. 6d.

———— Miscellanies. *Second Edition.* Post 8vo. 5s. 6d.

———— Story of Joan of Arc. Fcap. 8vo. 1s.

———— Addresses. Fcap. 8vo. 1s.

McCLINTOCK'S (CAPT. SIR F. L.) Narrative of the Discovery of the Fate of Sir John Franklin and his Companions in the Arctic Seas. *Twelfth Thousand.* Illustrations. 8vo. 16s.

McCULLOCH'S (J. R.) Collected Edition of RICARDO's Political Works. With Notes and Memoir. *Second Edition.* 8vo. 16s.

MAINE (H. SUMNER) on Ancient Law: its Connection with the Early History of Society, and its Relation to Modern Ideas. *Second Edition.* 8vo. 12s.

MALCOLM'S (SIR JOHN) Sketches of Persia. *Third Edition.* Post 8vo. 3s. 6d.

MANSEL (REV. H. L.) Limits of Religious Thought Examined. Being the Bampton Lectures for 1858. *Fourth Edition.* Post 8vo. 7s. 6d.

MANTELL'S (GIDEON A.) Thoughts on Animalcules; or, the Invisible World, as revealed by the Microscope. *Second Edition.* Plates. 16mo. 6s.

MANUAL OF SCIENTIFIC ENQUIRY, Prepared for the Use of Officers and Travellers. By various Writers. Edited by Sir J. F. HERSCHEL and Rev. R. MAIN. *Third Edition.* Maps. Post 8vo. 9s. (*Published by order of the Lords of the Admiralty.*)

MARKHAM'S (Mrs.) History of England. From the First Invasion by the Romans, down to the fourteenth year of Queen Victoria's Reign. 156th Edition. Woodcuts. 12mo. 6s.

———— History of France. From the Conquest by the Gauls, to the Death of Louis Philippe. Sixtieth Edition. Woodcuts. 12mo. 6s.

———— History of Germany. From the Invasion by Marius, to the present time. Fifteenth Edition. Woodcuts. 12mo. 6s.

———— History of Greece. From the Earliest Times to the Roman Conquest. By Dr. WM. SMITH. Woodcuts. 16mo. 3s. 6d.

———— History of Rome, from the Earliest Times to the Establishment of the Empire. By Dr. WM. SMITH. Woodcuts. 16mo. 3s. 6d.

———— (CLEMENTS, R.) Travels in Peru and India, for the purpose of collecting Cinchona Plants, and introducing Bark into India. Maps and Illustrations. 8vo. 16s.

MARKLAND'S (J. H.) Reverence due to Holy Places. *Third Edition.* Fcap. 8vo. 2s.

MARRYAT'S (JOSEPH) History of Modern and Mediæval Pottery and Porcelain. With a Description of the Manufacture. *Second Edition.* Plates and Woodcuts. 8vo. 31s. 6d.

———— (HORACE) Jutland, the Danish Isles, and Copenhagen. Illustrations. 2 Vols. Post 8vo. 24s.

———— Sweden and Isle of Gothland. Illustrations. 2 Vols. Post 8vo. 28s.

MATTHIÆ'S (AUGUSTUS) Greek Grammar for Schools. Abridged from the Larger Grammar. By Blomfield. *Ninth Edition.* Revised by EDWARDS. 12mo. 3s.

MAUREL'S (JULES) Essay on the Character, Actions, and Writings of the Duke of Wellington. *Second Edition.* Fcap. 8vo. 1s. 6d.

MAXIMS AND HINTS on Angling and Chess. By RICHARD PENN. Woodcuts. 12mo. 1s.

MAYNE'S (R. C.) Four Years in British Columbia and Vancouver Island. Its Forests, Rivers, Coasts, and Gold Fields, and Resources for Colonisation. Illustrations. 8vo. 16s.

MELVILLE'S (HERMANN) Typee and Omoo; or, Adventures amongst the Marquesas and South Sea Islands. 2 Vols Post 8vo. 7s.

MENDELSSOHN'S Life. By JULES BENEDICT. 8vo. 2s. 6d.

MEREDITH'S (MRS. CHARLES) Notes and Sketches of New South Wales. Post 8vo. 2s.

———— Tasmania, during a Residence of Nine Years. Illustrations. 2 Vols. Post 8vo. 18s.

MERRIFIELD (MRS.) on the Arts of Painting in Oil, Miniature, Mosaic, and Glass; Gilding, Dyeing, and the Preparation of Colours and Artificial Gems. 2 Vols. 8vo. 30s.

MESSIAH (THE): A Narrative of the Life, Travels, Death, Resurrection, and Ascension of our Blessed Lord. By A LAYMAN. Author of the "Life of Bishop Ken." Map. 8vo. 18s.

MILLS' (ARTHUR) India in 1858 ; A Summary of the Existing Administration—Political, Fiscal, and Judicial. *Second Edition.* Map. 8vo. 10s. 6d.

MILMAN'S (DEAN) History of Christianity, from the Birth of Christ to the Abolition of Paganism in the Roman Empire. *New Edition.* 3 Vols. 8vo. 36s.

——————————————— Latin Christianity ; including that of the Popes to the Pontificate of Nicholas V. *Second Edition.* 6 Vols. 8vo. 72s.

——————————————— the Jews, from the Earliest Period, brought down to Modern Times. 3 Vols. 8vo. 36s.

——————— Character and Conduct of the Apostles considered as an Evidence of Christianity. 8vo. 10s. 6d.

——————— Life and Works of Horace. With 300 Woodcuts. 2 Vols. Crown 8vo. 30s.

——————— Poetical Works. Plates. 3 Vols. Fcap. 8vo. 18s.

——————— Fall of Jerusalem. Fcap. 8vo. 1s.

——————— (CAPT. E. A.) Wayside Cross. A Tale of the Carlist War. Post 8vo. 2s.

MILNES' (R. MONCKTON, LORD HOUGHTON) Selections from Poetical Works. Fcap. 8vo.

MODERN DOMESTIC COOKERY. Founded on Principles of Economy and Practical Knowledge, and adapted for Private Families. *New Edition.* Woodcuts. Fcap. 8vo. 5s.

MONASTERY AND THE MOUNTAIN CHURCH. By Author of "Sunlight through the Mist." Woodcuts. 16mo. 4s.

MOORE'S (THOMAS) Life and Letters of Lord Byron. Plates. 6 Vols. Fcap. 8vo. 18s.

——————— Life and Letters of Lord Byron. Portraits. Royal 8vo. 9s.

MOTLEY'S (J. L.) History of the United Netherlands : from the Death of William the Silent to the Synod of Dort. Embracing the English-Dutch struggle against Spain; and a detailed Account of the Spanish Armada. Portraits. 2 Vols. 8vo. 30s.

MOUHOT'S (HENRI) Siam Cambojia, and Lao ; a Narrative of Travels and Discoveries. Illustrations. 8vo.

MOZLEY'S (REV. J. B.) Treatise on Predestination. 8vo. 14s.

——————— Primitive Doctrine of Baptismal Regeneration. 8vo. 7s.6d.

MUCK MANUAL (The) for Farmers. A Practical Treatise on the Chemical Properties of Manures. By FREDERICK FALKNER. *Second Edition.* Fcap. 8vo. 5s.

MUNDY'S (GEN.) Pen and Pencil Sketches during a Tour in India. *Third Edition.* Plates. Post 8vo. 7s. 6d.

——————— (ADMIRAL) Account of the Italian Revolution, with Notices of Garibaldi, Francis II., and Victor Emmanuel. Post 8vo. 12s.

MUNRO'S (GENERAL SIR THOMAS) Life and Letters. By the REV. G. R. GLEIG. Post 8vo. 3s. 6d.

MURCHISON'S (Sir Roderick) Russia in Europe and the Ural Mountains. With Coloured Maps, Plates, Sections, &c. 2 Vols. Royal 4to.

———————— Siluria ; or, a History of the Oldest Rocks containing Organic Remains. *Third Edition.* Map and Plates. 8vo. 42s.

MURRAY'S RAILWAY READING. For all classes of Readers.

[*The following are published :*]

WELLINGTON. By Lord Ellesmere. 6d.
NIMROD ON THE CHASE, 1s.
ESSAYS FROM "THE TIMES." 2 Vols. 8s.
MUSIC AND DRESS. 1s.
LAYARD'S ACCOUNT OF NINEVEH. 5s.
MILMAN'S FALL OF JERUSALEM. 1s.
MAHON'S "FORTY-FIVE." 3s.
LIFE OF THEODORE HOOK. 1s.
DEEDS OF NAVAL DARING. 2 Vols. 6s.
THE HONEY BEE. 1s.
JAMES' ÆSOP'S FABLES. 2s. 6d.
NIMROD ON THE TURF. 1s. 6d.
OLIPHANT'S NEPAUL. 2s. 6d.
ART OF DINING. 1s. 6d.
HALLAM'S LITERARY ESSAYS. 2s.

MAHON'S JOAN OF ARC. 1s.
HEAD'S EMIGRANT. 2s. 6d.
NIMROD ON THE ROAD. 1s.
WILKINSON'S ANCIENT EGYPTIANS. 12s.
GEORGE OF THE GUILLOTINE. 1s.
HOLLWAY'S NORWAY. 2s.
MAUREL'S WELLINGTON. 1s. 6d.
CAMPBELL'S LIFE OF BACON. 2s. 6d.
THE FLOWER GARDEN. 1s.
LOCKHART'S SPANISH BALLADS. 2s. 6d.
LUCAS ON HISTORY. 6d.
BEAUTIES OF BYRON. 3s.
TAYLOR'S NOTES FROM LIFE. 2s.
REJECTED ADDRESSES. 1s.
PENN'S HINTS ON ANGLING. 1s.

MUSIC AND DRESS. Reprinted from the "Quarterly Review." Fcap. 8vo. 1s.

NAPIER'S (Sir Wm.) English Battles and Sieges of the Peninsular War. *Third Edition.* Portrait. Post 8vo. 10s. 6d.

———————— Life and Letters. Edited by H. A. Bruce, M.P. Portraits. 2 Vols. Crown 8vo.

——— ———— Life of General Sir Charles Napier; chiefly derived from his Journals and Letters. *Second Edition.* Portraits. 4 Vols. Post 8vo. 48s.

NAUTICAL ALMANACK. Royal 8vo. 2s. 6d. (*Published by Authority.*)

NAVY LIST (Quarterly). (*Published by Authority.*) Post 8vo. 2s. 6d.

NELSON (Robert), Memoir of his Life and Times. By Rev. C. T. Secretan, M.A. Portrait. 8vo. 10s. 6d.

NEWBOLD'S (Lieut.) Straits of Malacca, Penang, and Singapore. 2 Vols. 8vo. 26s.

NEWDEGATE'S (C. N.) Customs' Tariffs of all Nations; collected and arranged up to the year 1855. 4to. 30s.

NICHOLLS' (Sir George) History of the English Poor-Laws. 2 Vols. 8vo. 28s.

———————— Irish and Scotch Poor-Laws. 2 Vols. 8vo. 26s.

———————— (Rev. H. G.) Historical Account of the Forest of Dean. Woodcuts, &c. Post 8vo. 10s. 6d.

—————— Personalities of the Forest of Dean, its successive Officials, Gentry, and Commonalty. Post 8vo. 3s. 6d.

NICOLAS' (Sir Harris) Historic Peerage of England. Exhibiting the Origin, Descent, and Present State of every Title of Peerage which has existed in this Country since the Conquest. By William Courthope. 8vo. 30s.

NIMROD On the Chace—The Turf—and The Road. Reprinted from the "Quarterly Review." Woodcuts. Fcap. 8vo. 3s. 6d.

O'CONNOR'S (R.) Field Sports of France ; or, Hunting, Shooting, and Fishing on the Continent. Woodcuts. 12mo. 7s. 6d.

OXENHAM'S (Rev. W.) English Notes for Latin Elegiacs ; designed for early Proficients in the Art of Latin Versification, with Prefatory Rules of Composition in Elegiac Metre. *Fourth Edition.* 12mo. 3s. 6d.

PAGET'S (John) Hungary and Transylvania. With Remarks on their Condition, Social, Political, and Economical. *Third Edition.* Woodcuts. 2 Vols. 8vo. 18s.

PARIS' (Dr.) Philosophy in Sport made Science in Earnest; or, the First Principles of Natural Philosophy inculcated by aid of the Toys and Sports of Youth. *Ninth Edition.* Woodcuts. Post 8vo. 7s. 6d.

PEEL'S (Sir Robert) Memoirs. Edited by Earl Stanhope and Mr. Cardwell. 2 Vols. Post 8vo. 7s. 6d. each.

PENN'S (Richard) Maxims and Hints for an Angler and Chess-player. *New Edition.* Woodcuts. Fcap. 8vo. 1s.

PENROSE'S (F. C.) Principles of Athenian Architecture, and the Optical Refinements exhibited in the Construction of the Ancient Buildings at Athens, from a Survey. With 40 Plates. Folio. 5l. 5s.

PERCY'S (John, M.D.) Metallurgy; or, the Art of Extracting Metals from their Ores and adapting them to various purposes of Manu-facture. *First Division* — Fuel, Fire-Clays, Copper, Zinc, and Brass. Illustrations. 8vo. 21s.

———— Iron and Steel, forming the *Second Division* of the above Work. Illustrations. 8vo.

PHILLIPP (Charles Spencer March) On Jurisprudence. 8vo. 12s.

PHILLIPS' (John) Memoirs of William Smith, the Geologist. Portrait. 8vo. 7s. 6d.

———— Geology of Yorkshire, The Coast, and Limestone District. Plates. 4to. Part I., 20s.—Part II., 30s.

———— Rivers, Mountains, and Sea Coast of Yorkshire. With Essays on the Climate, Scenery, and Ancient Inhabitants. *Second Edition,* Plates. 8vo. 15s.

PHILPOTT'S (Bishop) Letters to the late Charles Butler, on the Theological parts of his "Book of the Roman Catholic Church;" with Remarks on certain Works of Dr. Milner and Dr. Lingard, and on some parts of the Evidence of Dr. Doyle. *Second Edition.* 8vo. 16s.

POPE'S (Alexander) Life and Works. *A New Edition.* Con-taining nearly 500 unpublished Letters. Edited with a New Life, Introductions and Notes. By Rev. Whitwell Elwin. Portraits. 8vo. (*In the Press.*)

PORTER'S (Rev. J. L.) Five Years in Damascus. With Travels to Palmyra, Lebanon and other Scripture Sites. Map and Woodcuts. 2 Vols. Post 8vo. 21s.

———— Handbook for Syria and Palestine : including an Account of the Geography, History, Antiquities, and Inhabitants of these Countries, the Peninsula of Sinai, Edom, and the Syrian Desert. Maps. 2 Vols. Post 8vo. 24s.

PRAYER-BOOK (The Illustrated), with 1000 Illustrations of Borders, Initials, Vignettes, &c. Medium 8vo.

PRECEPTS FOR THE CONDUCT OF LIFE. Extracted from the Scriptures. *Second Edition.* Fcap. 8vo. 1s.

PRINSEP'S (JAS.) Essays on Indian Antiquities, Historic, Numismatic, and Palæographic, with Tables. Edited by EDWARD THOMAS. Illustrations. 2 Vols. 8vo. 52s. 6d.

PROGRESS OF RUSSIA IN THE EAST. An Historical Summary. Map. 8vo. 6s. 6d.

PUSS IN BOOTS. With 12 Illustrations. By OTTO SPECKTER. Coloured, 16mo. 2s. 6d.

QUARTERLY REVIEW (THE). 8vo. 6s.

RAWLINSON'S (REV. GEORGE) Herodotus. A New English Version. Edited with Notes and Essays. Assisted by SIR HENRY RAWLINSON and SIR J. G. WILKINSON. *Second Edition.* Maps and Woodcut. 4 Vols. 8vo. 48s.

———————— Historical Evidences of the truth of the Scripture Records stated anew, the Bampton Lectures for 1859. *Second Edition.* 8vo. 14s.

———————— History, Geography, and Antiquities of the Five Great Monarchies of the Ancient World. Illustrations. 8vo.
   Vol. I., Chaldæa and Assyria. 16s. Vols. II. and III., Babylon, Media, and Persia.

REJECTED ADDRESSES (THE). By JAMES AND HORACE SMITH. Fcap. 8vo. 1s., or *Fine Paper*, Portrait, fcap. 8vo. 5s.

REYNOLDS' (SIR JOSHUA) His Life and Times. From Materials collected by the late C. R. LESLIE, R.A. Edited by TOM TAYLOR. Portraits and Illustrations. 2 Vols. 8vo.

RICARDO'S (DAVID) Political Works. With a Notice of his Life and Writings. By J. R. M'CULLOCH. *New Edition.* 8vo. 16s.

RIPA'S (FATHER) Memoirs during Thirteen Years' Residence at the Court of Peking. From the Italian. Post 8vo. 2s.

ROBERTSON'S (CANON) History of the Christian Church, From the Apostolic Age to the Concordat of Worms, A.D. 1123. *Second Edition.* 3 Vols. 8vo. 38s.

———————— Life of Becket. Illustrations. Post 8vo. 9s.

ROBINSON'S (REV. DR.) Biblical Researches in the Holy Land. Being a Journal of Travels in 1838, and of Later Researches in 1852. Maps. 3 Vols. 8vo. 36s.

ROMILLY'S (SIR SAMUEL) Memoirs and Political Diary. By his SONS. *Third Edition.* Portrait. 2 Vols. Fcap. 8vo. 12s.

ROSS'S (SIR JAMES) Voyage of Discovery and Research in the Southern and Antarctic Regions, 1839-43. Plates. 2 Vols. 8vo. 36s.

ROWLAND'S (DAVID) Manual of the English Constitution; Its Rise, Growth, and Present State. Post 8vo. 10s. 6d.

———————— Laws of Nature the Foundation of Morals. Post 8vo

RUNDELL'S (MRS.) Domestic Cookery, adapted for Private Families. *New Edition.* Woodcuts. Fcap. 8vo. 5s.

RUSSELL'S (J. RUTHERFURD, M.D.) Art of Medicine—Its History and its Heroes. Portraits. 8vo. 14s.

RUSSIA; A Memoir of the Remarkable Events which attended the Accession of the Emperor Nicholas. By BARON M. KORFF. 8vo. 10s. 6d.

RUXTON'S (George F.) Travels in Mexico; with Adventures among the Wild Tribes and Animals of the Prairies and Rocky Mountains. Post 8vo. 3s. 6d.

SALE'S (Lady) Journal of the Disasters in Affghanistan. Post 8vo. 12s.

———— (Sir Robert) Brigade in Affghanistan. With an Account of the Defence of Jellalabad. By Rev. G. R. Gleig. Post 8vo. 2s.

SANDWITH'S (Humphry) Siege of Kars. Post 8vo. 3s. 6d.

SCOTT'S (G. Gilbert) Secular and Domestic Architecture, Present and Future. Second Edition. 8vo. 9s.

———— (Master of Baliol) Sermons Preached before the University of Oxford. Post 8vo. 8s. 6d.

SCROPE'S (G. P.) Geology and Extinct Volcanoes of Central France. Second Edition. Illustrations. Medium 8vo. 30s.

SELF-HELP. With Illustrations of Character and Conduct. By Samuel Smiles. 50th Thousand. Post 8vo. 6s.

SENIOR'S (N. W.) Suggestions on Popular Education. 8vo. 9s.

SHAFTESBURY (Lord Chancellor); Memoirs of his Early Life. With his Letters, &c. By W. D. Christie. Portrait. 8vo. 10s. 6d.

SHAW'S (T. B.) Student's Manual of English Literature. Edited, with Notes and Illustrations, by Dr. Wm. Smith. Post 8vo. 7s. 6d.

SIERRA LEONE; Described in Letters to Friends at Home. By A Lady. Post 8vo. 3s. 6d.

SIMMONS on Courts-Martial. 5th Edition. 8vo. 14s.

SMILES' (Samuel) Lives of British Engineers; from the Earliest Period to the Death of Robert Stephenson; with an account of their Principal Works, and a History of Inland Communication in Britain. Portraits and Illustrations. 3 Vols. 8vo. 63s.

———— Industrial Biography: Iron-Workers and Tool Makers. Post 8vo. 7s. 6d.

———— Story of George Stephenson's Life. Woodcuts. Post 8vo. 6s.

———— Self-Help. With Illustrations of Character and Conduct. Post 8vo. 6s.

———— Workmen's Earnings, Savings, and Strikes. Fcap. 8vo. 1s. 6d.

SOMERVILLE'S (Mary) Physical Geography. Fifth Edition. Portrait. Post 8vo. 9s.

———— Connexion of the Physical Sciences. Ninth Edition. Woodcuts. Post 8vo. 9s.

SOUTH'S (John F.) Household Surgery; or, Hints on Emergencies. Seventeenth Thousand. Woodcuts. Fcp. 8vo. 4s. 6d.

SMITH'S (DR. WM.) Dictionary of the Bible; its Antiquities, Biography, Geography, and Natural History. Illustrations. 3 Vols. 8vo. 105s.

———— Greek and Roman Antiquities. *2nd Edition.* Woodcuts. 8vo. 42s.

———————— Biography and Mythology. Woodcuts. 3 Vols. 8vo. 5l. 15s. 6d.

———————— Geography. Woodcuts. 2 Vols. 8vo. 30s.

—— Latin-English Dictionary. *9th Thousand.* 8vo. 21s.

—— Classical Dictionary. *10th Thousand.* Woodcuts. 8vo. 18s.

———— Smaller Classical Dictionary. *20th Thousand.* Woodcuts. Crown 8vo. 7s. 6d.

————————Dictionary of Antiquities. *20th Thousand.* Woodcuts. Crown 8vo. 7s. 6d.

———————— Latin-English Dictionary. *25th Thousand.* 12mo. 7s. 6d.

———— Latin-English Vocabulary; for those reading Phædrus, Cornelius Nepos, and Cæsar. *Second Edition.* 12mo. 3s. 6d.

—— Principia Latina—Part I. Containing a Grammar, Delectus, and Exercise Book, with Vocabularies. *3rd Edition.* 12mo. 3s. 6d.

———————— Part II. A Reading-book, containing Mythology, Geography, Roman Antiquities, and History. With Notes and Dictionary. *Second Edition.* 12mo. 3s. 6d.

———————— Part III. A Latin Poetry Book. Containing:—Hexameters and Pentameters; Eclogæ Ovidianæ; Latin Prosody. 12mo. 3s. 6d.

———————— Part IV. Latin Prose Composition. Containing Rules of Syntax, with copious Examples, Explanations of Synonyms, and a systematic course of Exercises on the Syntax. 12mo. 3s. 6d.

———————— Græca; a First Greek Course. A Grammar, Delectus, and Exercise-book, with Vocabularies. By H. E. HUTTON, M.A. *3rd Edition.* 12mo. 3s. 6d.

———— Student's Greek Grammar. By Professor CURTIUS. Post 8vo. 7s. 6d.

———————— Latin Grammar. Post 8vo. 7s. 6d.

———— Smaller Greek Grammar. Abridged from the above. 12mo. 3s. 6d.

———————— Latin Grammar. Abridged from the above. 12mo. 3s. 6d.

STANLEY'S (CANON) History of the Eastern Church. *Second Edition.* Plans. 8vo. 16s.

———————— Jewish Church. From ABRAHAM TO SAMUEL. *Second Edition.* Plans. 8vo. 16s.

———————— Sermons on Evangelical and Apostolical Teaching. *Second Edition.* Post 8vo. 7s. 6d.

———————— St. Paul's Epistles to the Corinthians. *Second Edition.* 8vo. 18s.

———————— Historical Memorials of Canterbury. *Third Edition.* Woodcuts. Post 8vo. 7s. 6d.

———————— Sinai and Palestine, in Connexion with their History. *Sixth Edition.* Map. 8vo. 16s.

———————— Bible in the Holy Land. Being Extracts from the above work. *Second Edition.* Woodcuts. Fcp. 8vo. 2s. 6d.

———————— ADDRESSES AND CHARGES OF BISHOP STANLEY. With Memoir. *Second Edition.* 8vo. 10s. 6d.

STANLEY'S (Canon) Sermons Preached during the Tour of H.R.H. the Prince of Wales in the East, with Notices of some of the Places Visited. 8vo. 9s.

SOUTHEY'S (Robert) Book of the Church. *Seventh Edition.* Post 8vo. 7s. 6d.

———— Lives of Bunyan and Cromwell. Post 8vo. 2s.

SPECKTER'S (Otto) Puss in Boots. With 12 Woodcuts. Square 12mo. 1s. 6d. plain, or 2s. 6d. coloured.

———— Charmed Roe; or, the Story of the Little Brother and Sister. Illustrated. 16mo.

ST. JOHN'S (Charles) Wild Sports and Natural History of the Highlands. Post 8vo. 3s. 6d.

———— (Bayle) Adventures in the Libyan Desert and the Oasis of Jupiter Ammon. Woodcuts. Post 8vo. 2s.

STANHOPE'S (Earl) Life of William Pitt. With Extracts from his M.S. Papers. *Second Edition.* Portraits. 2 Vols. Post 8vo. 42s.

———— Miscellanies. *Second Edition.* Post 8vo. 5s. 6d.

STEPHENSONS' (George and Robert) Lives. Forming the Third Volume of Smiles' "Lives of British Engineers." Portrait and Illustrations. 8vo. 21s.

STOTHARD'S (Thos.) Life. With Personal Reminiscences. By Mrs. Bray. With Portrait and 60 Woodcuts. 4to. 21s.

STREET'S (G. E.) Brick and Marble Architecture of Italy in the Middle Ages. Plates. 8vo. 21s.

STUDENT'S HUME. A History of England from the Invasion of Julius Cæsar to the Revolution of 1688. Based on the Work by David Hume. Continued to 1858. *Twenty-fifth Thousand.* Woodcuts. Post 8vo. 7s. 6d.
*** A Smaller History of England. 12mo. 3s. 6d.

———— HISTORY OF FRANCE; From the Earliest Times to the Establishment of the Second Empire, 1852. Edited by Dr. Wm. Smith. Woodcuts. Post 8vo. 7s. 6d.

———— HISTORY OF GREECE; from the Earliest Times to the Roman Conquest. With the History of Literature and Art. By Wm. Smith, LL.D. *25th Thousand.* Woodcuts. Crown 8vo. 7s. 6d. (Questions. 2s.)
*** A Smaller History of Greece. 12mo. 3s. 6d.

———— HISTORY OF ROME; from the Earliest Times to the Establishment of the Empire. With the History of Literature and Art. By H. G. Liddell, D.D. *25th Thousand.* Woodcuts. Crown 8vo. 7s. 6d.
*** A Smaller History of Rome. 12mo. 3s. 6d.

———— GIBBON; an Epitome of the History of the Decline and Fall of the Roman Empire. Incorporating the Researches of Recent Commentators. *9th Thousand.* Woodcuts. Post 8vo. 7s. 6d.

———— MANUAL OF ANCIENT GEOGRAPHY. By Rev. W. L. Bevan, M.A. Edited by Dr. Wm. Smith. Woodcuts. Post 8vo. 7s. 6d.

———— THE ENGLISH LANGUAGE. By George P. Marsh. Edited by Dr. Wm. Smith. Post 8vo. 7s. 6d.

———— ENGLISH LITERATURE. By T. B. Shaw. Edited by Dr. Wm. Smith. Post 8vo. 7s. 6d.

SWIFT'S (JONATHAN) Life, Letters, Journals, and Works. By JOHN FORSTER. 8vo. (*In Preparation.*)

SYME'S (PROFESSOR) Principles of Surgery. *5th Edition.* 8vo. 14s.

TAIT'S (BISHOP) Dangers and Safeguards of Modern Theology. 8vo. 9s.

TAYLOR'S (HENRY) Notes from Life. Fcap. 8vo. 2s.

THOMSON'S (ARCHBISHOP) Lincoln's Inn Sermons. 8vo. 10s. 6d.

———————— (DR.) New Zealand. Illustrations. 2 Vols. Post 8vo. 24s.

THREE-LEAVED MANUAL OF FAMILY PRAYER; arranged so as to save the trouble of turning the Pages backwards and forwards. Royal 8vo. 2s.

TOCQUEVILLE'S (M. DE) State of France before the Revolution, 1789, and on the Causes of that Event. Translated by HENRY REEVE, 8vo. 14s.

TRANSACTIONS OF THE ETHNOLOGICAL SOCIETY OF LONDON. New Series. Vols. I. and II. 8vo.

TREMENHEERE'S (H. S.) Political Experience of the Ancients, in its bearing on Modern Times. Fcap. 8vo. 2s. 6d.

TRISTRAM'S (H. B.) Great Sahara. Illustrations. Post 8vo. 15s.

TWISS' (HORACE) Public and Private Life of Lord Chancellor Eldon, with Selections from his Correspondence. Portrait. *Third Edition.* 2 Vols. Post 8vo. 21s.

TYNDALL'S (JOHN) Glaciers of the Alps. With an account of Three Years' Observations and Experiments on their General Phenomena. Woodcuts. Post 8vo. 14s.

TYTLER'S (PATRICK FRASER) Memoirs. By REV. J. W. BURGON, M.A. 8vo. 9s.

VAUGHAN'S (REV. DR.) Sermons preached in Harrow School. 8vo. 10s. 6d.

VENABLES' (REV. R. L.) Domestic Scenes in Russia. Post 8vo. 5s.

VOYAGE to the Mauritius. By Author of "PADDIANA." Post 8vo. 9s. 6d.

WAAGEN'S (DR.) Treasures of Art in Great Britain. Being an Account of the Chief Collections of Paintings, Sculpture, Manuscripts, Miniatures, &c. &c., in this Country. Obtained from Personal Inspection during Visits to England. 4 Vols. 8vo.

WALKS AND TALKS. A Story-book for Young Children. By AUNT IDA. With Woodcuts. 16mo. 5s.

WALSH'S (SIR JOHN) Practical Results of the Reform Bill of 1832. 8vo. 5s. 6d.

WATT'S (JAMES) Life. With Selections from his Private and Public Correspondence. By JAMES P. MUIRHEAD, M.A. *Second Edition.* Portrait. 8vo. 16s.

———————— Origin and Progress of his Mechanical Inventions. By J. P. MUIRHEAD. Plates. 3 Vols. 8vo. 45s.

WELLINGTON'S (The Duke of) Despatches during his various Campaigns. Compiled from Official and other Authentic Documents. By Col. Gurwood, C.B. 8 Vols. 8vo. 21s. each.

———————— Supplementary Despatches, and other Papers. Edited by his Son. Vols. I. to IX. 8vo. 20s. each.

———————— Selections from his Despatches and General Orders. By Colonel Gurwood. 8vo. 18s.

———————— Speeches in Parliament. 2 Vols. 8vo. 42s.

WILKINSON'S (Sir J. G.) Popular Account of the Private Life, Manners, and Customs of the Ancient Egyptians. *New Edition.* Revised and Condensed. With 500 Woodcuts. 2 Vols. Post 8vo. 12s.

———————— Dalmatia and Montenegro; with a Journey to Mostar in Hertzegovina, and Remarks on the Slavonic Nations. Plates and Woodcuts. 2 Vols. 8vo. 42s.

———————— Handbook for Egypt.—Thebes, the Nile, Alexandria, Cairo, the Pyramids, Mount Sinai, &c. Map. Post 8vo. 15s.

———————— On Colour, and on the Necessity for a General Diffusion of Taste among all Classes; with Remarks on laying out Dressed or Geometrical Gardens. With Coloured Illustrations and Woodcuts. 8vo. 18s.

———————— (G. B.) Working Man's Handbook to South Australia; with Advice to the Farmer, and Detailed Information for the several Classes of Labourers and Artisans. Map. 18mo. 1s. 6d.

WILSON'S (Bishop Daniel,) Life, with Extracts from his Letters and Journals. By Rev. Josiah Bateman. *Second Edition.* Illustrations. Post 8vo. 9s.

———————— (Genl. Sir Robert) Secret History of the French Invasion of Russia, and Retreat of the French Army, 1812. *Second Edition.* 8vo. 15s.

———————— Private Diary of Travels, Personal Services, and Public Events, during Missions and Employments in Spain, Sicily, Turkey, Russia, Poland, Germany, &c. 1812-14. 2 Vols. 8vo. 26s.

———————— Autobiographical Memoirs. Containing an Account of his Early Life down to the Peace of Tilsit. Portrait. 2 Vols. 8vo. 26s.

WOOD'S (Lieut.) Voyage up the Indus to the Source of the River Oxus, by Kabul and Badakhshan. Map. 8vo. 14s.

WORDSWORTH'S (Canon) Journal of a Tour in Athens and Attica. *Third Edition.* Plates. Post 8vo. 8s. 6d.

———————— Pictorial, Descriptive, and Historical Account of Greece, with a History of Greek Art, by G. Scharf, F.S.A. *New Edition.* With 600 Woodcuts. Royal 8vo. 28s.

WORNUM (Ralph). A Biographical Dictionary of Italian Painters : with a Table of the Contemporary Schools of Italy. By a Lady. Post 8vo. 6s. 6d.

YOUNG'S (Dr. Thos.) Life and Miscellaneous Works, edited by Dean Peacock and John Leitch. Portrait and Plates. 4 Vols. 8vo. 15s. each.

www.ingramcontent.com/pod-product-compliance
Lightning Source LLC
Chambersburg PA
CBHW032312280326
41932CB00009B/787